900 SHOWS A YEAR
A LOOK AT TEACHING
FROM A TEACHER'S SIDE
OF THE DESK

CONSULTING EDITOR
Jack L. Nelson
RUTGERS UNIVERSITY

900 Shows a Year

A LOOK AT TEACHING FROM A TEACHER'S SIDE OF THE DESK

Stuart B. Palonsky

University of Missouri—Columbia

RANDOM HOUSE   NEW YORK

For my parents

First Edition
98765432
Copyright © 1986 by Random House, Inc.

Library of Congress Cataloging in Publication Data

Palonsky, Stuart B.
  900 shows a year.

  Bibliography: p.
  Includes index.
  1. High school teaching—New York Metropolitan Area—
Case studies. 2. Public schools—New York Metropolitan
Area—Case studies. I. Title. II. Title: Nine hundred
shows a year.
LA339.N5P25 1985   371.1'02   85-14389
ISBN 0-394-34118-X

FOREWORD

What is teaching? Is it like being an actor, or a substitute parent, or jail warden, or intellectual, or servant, or friend? Many books have tried to explain what teachers do and what schools are. There are any number of books that seek to introduce prospective teachers to teaching, schools, and education. And among the many titles is astonishing variety. Still, it is a rare book that succeeds in describing the raw texture, atmosphere, and feeling— that sense of life, if you will—that is found in all schools.

In *900 Shows a Year* Stuart Palonsky offers his readers a vivid description of his experience teaching—the daily routine, boredom and anxieties, and moments of joy. Palonsky has a gift for capturing the ambitions, frustrations, and compromises that envelop school life. And further, he raises important questions about the teaching life.

Anyone who is a teacher, plans to become one, or wants to know more about education should read this book. All of us have spent considerable time in schools as students. We have all experienced much of what Palonsky describes, but have rarely drawn a coherent picture of our experiences. It is this author's richness of detail, talent for weaving the detail into larger contexts, and lively writing style that make this an eminently readable and insightful book.

Jack L. Nelson
Rutgers University

PREFACE

900 Shows a Year is a field study of public school teaching written from the perspective of a classroom teacher. The book details the events of one school year, from athletics to school politics, and recounts a full range of teaching and classroom experiences. The purpose of the book is to describe what it is like to be a teacher from the teachers' point of view, and explain why it is that teachers behave as they do.

Between 1982 and 1984, I worked as a high school teacher in a small suburban community in the New York metropolitan area. The community is referred to as Oldham, but that name, like all the others in this book, is a pseudonym designed to protect the privacy of the teachers, students, and school officials. The writing focuses on my first year in the school. It describes the way in which I was interviewed for the position, the processes by which I was groomed for the job, and the problems and pleasures I experienced in the classroom. While the book is critical, it is generally supportive of teachers, and it retains more than a fragile faith for the future of public education.

In a previous field study, I spent four months as a participant observer in a high school. I investigated the nature of student groups and student interactions by taking the role of a student, attending class and looking at the school through the students' eyes. This experience led to an appreciation of field research as a methodology for generating an insider's perspective of behavior in complex social institutions (Palonsky, 1975). Taking the role of one of the actors in a social situation enables the researcher to experience the world as the subjects experience it and to explain behavior from a shared, jointly constructed set of social understandings.

The unique perspective of the public school teacher had become a growing personal concern. Although I had been in the field of education for eighteen years, I had not been a full-time public school teacher other than for the first four years, and I had begun to feel that I had lost touch with what was going on in the working lives of teachers. My own experience in schools was no longer sufficient to understand the teachers' point of view, and the public school teachers with whom I had contact regularly reminded me of it. They would sometimes discount my views of public education, taunting me with, "You people from the university don't understand the real world of the classroom! When are you going to leave your ivory towers and get out in the trenches?"

Too many of the teachers I encountered in my graduate classes and those with whom I worked while supervising student teachers seemed numbed by their jobs. Often, they were not well read; they were not inclined to experiment with teaching methodology; and they were discouraging to the student teachers with whom they worked, often asking them: "Are you sure you want to go into teaching? Why don't you go into business or apply to law school? If I had it to do all over again. . . ."

The university at which I taught was a fairly selective state university. The education department was more selective, establishing minimum grade point and other admission criteria above those stipulated by the university. Many of the students who were planning to become teachers were among the brightest students in the school. The faculty believed that if there were more teachers such as those we were preparing, public schools would be dramatically improved; some even took to calling the students "change agents."

The university had been the recipient of a small scholarship fund earmarked for teacher education students. Each year the faculty selected three or four students who, during their undergraduate years, had demonstrated unusual promise for secondary school teaching. Each of the students received a cash award and a written commendation from the department. An informal follow-up study of the award recipients suggested some problems. All of those who had wanted to get teaching jobs had been successful, and many had joined well-respected New York area schools, but within two or three years more than 60 percent had voluntarily left the field. Any group of bright, talented people could be expected to have great job mobility and many doors open to them, and it is unreasonable to assume that it would not be difficult to retain the highest caliber of employee in many jobs. The majority of the university award recipients, however, indicated that they were not seduced into other fields or graduate schools as much as they were pushed out of teaching. They said that they had left teaching due to dissatisfactions with the job, rather than the lure of other careers.

They suggested that there was something about the nature of the job and the school environment that detracted from their teaching and demeaned their efforts. Some complained about the low pay. Others expressed outrage at the public relations outlook of administrators who were less concerned with instruction than with enhancing the image of the school. A few of the more ambitious students complained about the limited opportunity for career advancement, and all of them lamented the loneliness and isolation of the job and took exception to the public's notion that teaching was easy work.

My former students invited me to return to public school teaching to examine for myself the nature of the job and its problems. This writing is the result of that examination. The book is designed for use in courses in education at both the undergraduate and graduate levels. It should be of interest to those at the beginning level who are considering whether or not they should become teachers as well as by those practitioners enrolled in graduate courses in administration, supervision, and curriculum who are interested in school improvement.

The description of teaching and the behavior of teachers is found in Chapters One through Six; an analysis of teaching is in Chapter Seven. The

appendix contains a description of the research methodology and an explanation of how I constructed this study. Some readers might find it helpful to
read the appendix before beginning the data chapters.

I am grateful to the following people for reading and commenting on early
drafts of the manuscript: Anthony DiBattista, Jim Farrell, Rosemary Genova,
Mike Huff, Roberta Ellen Schick, Bob Silverman, and Rita Silverman. A
special word of thanks for the careful criticisms of Ken Carlson and Mike
Orfe and the encouragement of Jack Nelson and my editors at Random
House. I have tried to represent all the events and characters faithfully. If I
have failed, I am solely responsible.

Stuart B. Palonsky

CONTENTS

900 SHOWS A YEAR
A LOOK AT TEACHING
FROM A TEACHER'S SIDE
OF THE DESK

1

WELCOME TO OLDHAM HIGH

Oldham High School is a two-story building. It is simple and architecturally undistinguished. From the outside, it is easily recognized as a suburban public school. It has a gray brick façade, orange doors, a faculty parking lot filled with old cars, a flagpole, and a circular driveway. Students said they liked the building, but initially they had found it forbidding. Large chimneys suggested a factory, they said, and the black-framed, dark-tinted thermal glass made it difficult to see inside the school, giving it a somewhat ominous appearance.

An unlocked side door brought me into a nearly empty hallway of about 150 feet in length. There were only three people in the hall. Two women teachers were questioning a young, tearful student who had her back to a wall of orange-colored lockers.

"Did you or did you not smoke that cigarette?" asked one.

"You know the rules," said the other. "If you smoke, you're off the team, no more cheerleader!"

The teachers, I learned afterward, were the advisers to the cheerleading squad, and they earned about $1,000 extra pay for this job.

"Well, did you or didn't you?"

"Just tell the truth."

The girl did not respond. She was blond, blue-eyed, and pretty. Her cheerleading outfit—immaculate letter sweater, short skirt, and white sneakers—had no doubt inspired many athletes. She continued to sob but offered no denials or defense against the charge. She appeared to know that if she confessed to smoking, she would be summarily excluded from a privileged caste and become the high school equivalent of a social pariah. Rather than say anything, she cried. Her crying was an act of contrition which, with luck, could get her off with only a reprimand and a stern warning.

The cheerleader paid no attention to me, but the teachers looked me over and made a quick assessment. I might have been a parent, a school board member, a civil rights attorney looking for a client, or a member of the ethics committee of the National Association of High School Cheerleader Advisers, if such an organization existed. In fact, they had nothing to fear. I was not there to protect errant cheerleaders, I had a job interview with the principal. I was certified to teach social studies, a subject poorly regarded by students and school officials alike. I knew that it would be hard enough to interest the students in my subject five times a day, but watching the cheerleader advisers reminded me that teaching involved much more.

Oldham High had 1,200 students, most of whom seemed to be well cared for and well-dressed. At first glance, not only the cheerleader, but all the students looked to be blond, with very straight noses. One teacher, himself a white Protestant, described Oldham as a "preppy WASP enclave" in the heart of the ethnic Northeast. Another teacher claimed there were more alligators on the chests of the students than there were in the Florida Everglades. On that first day, the school looked pleasant. The floors were covered with a reddish-brown, industrial-grade carpet that complemented the orange lockers and the blue doors of the classrooms. The halls were painted an off-white, and they were clean. There were no art galleries or exhibits of sculpture or painting, no reproductions, no photographs, no artwork of any kind, but it was early in the year. Many classrooms had not been decorated; student artwork was not yet displayed; and there were no exhibits of student projects. After a few months, the school would reflect the talents and tastes of the students and teachers.

The bell rang loudly, and the halls were instantly filled with animated, fresh-looking kids just back from summer vacation, with new clothes and new stories to tell old friends. They seemed relaxed and happy, and their conversations were filled with quiet, restrained politenesses: "Excuse me." "Thank you." "Have a good day." "How's your horse?" "Going to dance class?" "Pretty dress." "Who do you have for English?" "Did you hear about Kim?" "Kristin and Scott broke up, can you believe it? They were practically married!" "Did you see the Porsche Tod was driving? Is that his or his father's?" "Give me a break." Not everyone in the school was wealthy, WASPy, and pampered, but it was a place where you would expect to find more Muffies and Buffies than toughies.

With some directions from the cheerleader advisers, I found my way to the main office. It was located off a central lobby area, and it housed an assistant principal, the director of athletics, the coordinator of student activities, a receptionist, two secretaries, and the principal. The receptionist was friendly and helpful. She shared an open space office with the principal's secretary and the assistant principal's secretary. Their office was neat and functional, equipped with the gray steel desks and filing cabinets common to public institutions. On one wall was a Picasso print next to a framed colonial street scene. On the opposite wall was a set of cubbyhole mailboxes for the teachers and a digital master time clock that could be set to the nearest hundredth of a second, but which was then, and always would be, 3 minutes faster than local time. My eyes scanned the room for a time clock for the teachers, and I was relieved not to find one.

The secretaries were separated from the main lobby area by a sliding transparent partition atop a waist-high wall. Because they could be seen readily by the students, the secretaries were not allowed to smoke cigarettes or drink coffee at their desks. The secretaries could smoke in a small workroom located at the rear of the office. The workroom contained a duplicating machine, coffeepot, sink, and a locked walk-in vault in which school supplies were stored. There was one yellowed sign tacked up amid the standard school notices:

> The objective of all dedicated employees should be to thoroughly analyze all situations, anticipate all problems prior to their occurrence, have answers for these problems, and move swiftly to solve these problems when called upon.
> However . . . when you are up to your eyeballs in alligators, it is difficult to remind yourself that your initial objective was to drain the swamp.

Three plastic alligators were nailed alongside. The receptionist noticed me reading the sign.

"It originally said 'up to your ass in alligators' but they made us change it; you never know who could come in here and be offended by it."

I smiled and told her that it looked a little anti-preppy to have dead alligators on the wall.

"Only a little," she said with a conspiratorial wink as she ushered me into the short, narrow passageway leading to the principal's office. Passing under a sign that read "Students check with secretary before going beyond this point," we walked by the small, windowless, and rather dark offices of the assistant principal, the athletic director, and the coordinator of athletics. The principal's office had two windows, but the view was obscured by pine trees growing close to the building. There was a large desk set in the far corner, two or three chairs, a black simulated leather couch, and a small bookcase containing several looseleaf binders and books on public school evaluation and supervision.

Cal Bullinger was just beginning his second year as principal, and he did not yet have tenure. He came from behind his desk, shook my hand cordially, and invited me to take one of the armchairs.

Cal was about 6'4", very thin, and in his late forties. A three-piece suit, starched white shirt, and close-cropped hair gave him the appearance of a business executive. His openness, blond hair, and bland accent easily betrayed his midwestern background. His father had been a gladiola farmer in Illinois, and Cal had attended public schools before entering college in Michigan. He was a music major in a conservative, church-affiliated school in the western part of the state, and later he was graduated from the University of Michigan with a master's degree in educational administration.

The Oldham teachers enjoyed repeating stories about Cal's administrative history in other schools. According to one story, while Cal observed a class discussion of Renaissance art, the teacher projected a slide of Michelangelo's "David" on the wall. In his observation report, Cal noted that the students had participated in the class and the teacher had met the targeted objectives, but he suggested that the slide of David may not have been appropriate for use in public schools. The teacher who told me the story shook his head in disbelief, wondering how his own teaching would be interpreted. Another teacher said that any nudity made Cal uncomfortable. "If Cal had his way," he said, "the football team would be made to shower with their uniforms on."

Cal's experience as principal at Oldham added to the teachers' repertoire of apocrypha. In the middle of a school day, one of the urinals in the boys' lavatory on the main floor sprang a leak, flooded the lobby, and shorted out the school's electricity. School was dismissed for the day. Cal was one of the first to arrive at the scene. Attempting to stem the flow of water, he put his finger in the broken pipe as water soaked his suit. Because of his Dutch ancestry, teachers teased Cal, asking him if he thought that he was the Dutch boy of legend who put his finger in the dike. "Yeah, I guess I thought I was Peter Stuyvesant," he said, blushing.

During the interview, Cal and I talked a bit about the Midwest, where I had done graduate work, and about sports. Cal told me he was a former basketball coach, but claimed that he was not especially enamored of high school athletics. He said that physical education teachers had things "too easy" because they did not have papers to take home or academic content to present. He suggested the reason why so many physical education teachers became school principals was that they had more time than other teachers to take graduate courses in administration. He said that he wanted to require all physical education teachers to coach at least two sports to keep them busy. Cal spoke well, but he was defensive about his academic ability, and apologized for not being an intellectual. "I'm not a scholar," he said, "just plain ol' Cal. Just a high school principal." He giggled self-consciously, shuffled his feet and rearranged his long legs.

We chatted amiably about my former teaching and school experiences. Cal asked me if I thought I could handle ninth graders after teaching at universities for the previous ten years. I explained that I had been teaching education courses and I looked forward to the content and rigor of ninth-grade social studies. We laughed; we got along. Our first impressions of each other were good. He would recommend me for the job. I thought I could work for him.

It was a very short interview; we had little of substance to discuss. He did not ask me what I had read or written, and we did not talk about the problems of teaching in general or the needs of this school in particular. It was the second week of school and any reasonably competent candidate would have looked good, but I wondered how he was judging my competence. As the principal, he could not be expected to assess every candidate's knowledge of subject or methodology; there are too many disparate fields taught in high school to expect that. Cal could not assess the extent to which I had the skill or knowledge necessary to be a good social studies teacher, but he could determine if I would fit in with the other teachers or present a threat to him or the community. I was wearing a tie, blue blazer, and tan slacks; my hair and beard were trimmed. But I worried that my black boots with pointy toes made me appear too ethnic or too urban.

After about fifteen minutes, we were joined by Troy Thayer, the supervisor of the social studies department. Troy had been the department chair at another high school in the district, and when that school withdrew to form its own district, state regulations permitted Troy to come to Oldham. Because Troy's supervisory certificate had been granted earlier than that of the person who held the position at Oldham, the state ruled the job belonged to Troy. The man Troy replaced was generally considered by the Oldham faculty to be of unusual talents and abilities, one of the outstanding leaders in education in that part of the state, they claimed. The teachers complained that Troy had forced a better man out of his job, and there was some residual resentment he had to endure. The former supervisor became a teacher in Troy's department, but within two years he left the district.

While he was with his former school, Troy had contacted me at the university to do some inservice[1] workshops for teachers in his district. Troy and I had spoken for a few minutes after my inservice presentation and I remembered having been impressed by him. I recalled Troy as being knowledgeable about teaching and sincere. Before Troy joined us, Cal expressed some personal dissatisfaction with him. "He's really a nice guy with a lot of grand ideas," Cal said, gesturing in the air as if he were conducting a concert, "but he's terribly disorganized and scattered. He starts a million things in the beginning of the year and never finishes any of them. Now, I don't want this to leave this office, but if you get the job, I'd like you to keep an eye on Troy."

The idea of spying on someone toward whom I was favorably predisposed did not appeal to me, and I was not sure if this was not just some clever new interview trick administrators used to test the applicant's loyalty or ethics. I was confused and uncomfortable, and I mumbled something that Cal interpreted as accedence. I did not correct him.

Troy Thayer was a tall, nice-looking man in his late thirties who, other than his 1960s-style sideburns, dressed in a manner that fit in well at Oldham High: sport jacket, blue button-down shirt, a red knit tie, tan cotton slacks, and topsiders. Troy greeted me cordially, but he appeared somewhat uneasy. This was not to be a typical interview for him. I had heard about the job informally through a friend and former student who was now a member of the Oldham social studies department. I had not filled out the standard application forms or supplied transcripts, but they needed a quick replacement for a teacher who resigned just days before school opened, leaving five classes and 130 students needing instruction.

If Troy had had the luxury of time, I am sure he would have asked me some of the questions from the standard interview sheet he later showed me. For example,

---

[1]Inservice typically refers to those two or three days during the school year designed to improve the quality of instruction by having teachers listen to "experts" from universities tell them about the latest educational fad or finding. The university people rarely have any understanding of the problems of the school or the concerns of the teachers. They come in not at the teachers' request, but at the invitation of the principal or supervisor. At best, inservice days provide teachers with a break in the teaching routine and a chance to catch up on paperwork as they listen to the speakers. At worst, they convince teachers that there is no help for their problems outside their own resources. I rarely enjoyed inservice as a presenter; I would like it less as part of the audience.

1. Is it true that there are really no "new ideas" in education?
2. Are you more comfortable teaching in the cognitive domain or the affective domain?
3. Should we work to reduce teacher talk in the classroom?
4. What kind of thinking do you promote?

Instead, we discussed the nature of the social studies program. The freshmen took something called the fundamentals of social studies, which was a multidisciplinary social science course designed to introduce students to social inquiry and selected concepts from history, psychology, sociology, economics, geography, political science, and anthropology. This approach was a leftover from the curriculum reforms of the 1960s, but it sounded interesting to me, even though I really did not know if I could teach high school freshmen. My previous experience in high school had been with juniors and seniors.

It was not entirely clear at the time of the interview what other courses were open. I had a general social studies teaching certificate that permitted me to teach all the courses offered by the department, including Western civilization, American history, sociology, political science, and psychology. My former liberal arts colleagues at the university were astounded that *anyone* would know all these fields well enough to teach them. I assured them that I was only certified by the state to teach, not necessarily qualified to do so. No other member of the social studies department wanted to teach the fundamentals course, so I would be the new "fundies" teacher, as the freshmen students were called. Troy indicated that although there were not enough books for all the students and the curriculum was a little vague, there was a great deal of latitude and limitless possibilities for instruction. Troy told me that A-level freshmen, a homogeneous grouping of the best and brightest, could handle very difficult reading material. He said that he had once used copies of the Allegory of the Cave to have students consider the nature of reality.

According to the parable, men, who have been bound and imprisoned for most of their lives, are able to see only the shadows of persons and objects projected on a wall from a fire behind them. They hear human voices, but see only the shadows and not the people who cast them. As the imprisoned men are betrayed by their senses, they conclude that the shadows are real and capable of speech and thought. The reading is often used to distinguish between the reality of the material world of appearances, as perceived through the senses, and the reality of the world of ideas, as perceived through the intellect. It seemed like an interesting way to engage students in a discussion of metaphysics, and I began to think that it might be fun to teach freshmen. I told Troy that I was surprised to hear that fourteen-year-olds could handle Plato.

"Plato?" Cal interrupted for the first time. "Plato wrote that? Gee, I'm glad to hear that the kids are reading Plato."

Troy did not comment, and he excused himself to teach a class after telling Cal that I had his support. As I thanked Troy, Cal hastily scribbled directions to the office of the superintendent of schools.

"I think you'll be fine for the job," Cal told me, "but there is one more thing."

"What's that?"

"Coaching. Paul said that you could coach wrestling."

Paul was the person who had recommended me for the job, and he had probably added the story about coaching to burnish my image and make me a more attractive candidate.

"I did coach wrestling," I told Cal, "but that was fourteen years ago. Is wrestling co-ed now because of Title IX?"

Cal laughed, but he would not let me off the hook.

"I have no reservations about recommending you to Dr. Szabo, the superintendent, but it would help if you could coach . . . I mean . . . would coach," he corrected himself. "I know you can coach."

I groaned. My wrestling experience was limited and decidedly mediocre, and I told Cal about it in the hope that the truth would set me free.

"Paul said that you were a state champ," he said.

"I cannot imagine what state that could be," I told Cal. "It must have been the state of prevarication."

If I had told Paul that I had been a state champ of any kind, it was probably a case of failed humor. I often joked that during my freshman year at college, I had been undefeated, untied, and unscored upon as an intercollegiate wrestler in dual meet competition. I usually paused for effect, and just as people would begin to question this unheard-of feat, I would hasten to add that I had wrestled only one match that season, won it by forfeit, and soon after quit the team. Perhaps I had forgotten to add this disclaimer when I had told the story to Paul.

I promised Cal that I would think about coaching. As I left the office, the receptionist told me Paul would like to see me before I left. I was anxious to tell him how my interviews were progressing, get some advice before my final interview with the superintendent, and perhaps try out a few flying drop-kicks on him, but Cal told me that I did not have time; Dr. Szabo was expecting me in ten minutes.

The superintendent's office was adjacent to the only other school in the district, another grade 9–12 high school. Oldham High was part of the Oldham-Webster Regional High School District, which received students from four separate kindergarten to grade 8 school districts, each with its own superintendent, board of education, and curricula. While the kindergarten to grade 12 district is the most common, there were thirty-two other high school districts in the state. Szabo would later tell me the district was very proud of the fact that although it ranked fourteenth in equalized valuation per pupil ($187,000), it ranked twenty-second in expenditures per pupil ($3,200) among the high school districts in the state.[2] In other words, it was a wealthy school district that was proudly parsimonious.

Ron Szabo's office was located in a small red building that also contained the offices of two assistant superintendents, the business manager, and a small secretarial and clerical staff. The building had been designed as a temporary structure, but it was becoming more permanent each year, as there were no immediate plans to replace it. Dr. Szabo had a corner office smaller than Cal Bullinger's office at the high school. There was inexpensive wood paneling on the walls, and the office furniture had begun to fray. Szabo, as they said in the district, had worked his way up through the ranks. He had been an English and social studies teacher, a guidance counselor, a director of guidance, a high school principal, and an assistant superintendent of schools before landing his current position. Along the way, he had earned master's degrees in school administration and guidance, and he had recently completed a doctorate in educational administration at the state university.

Ron Szabo was born in one of the state's small cities. His father was a municipal employee, and Szabo described his background as being lower middle class. The oldest of three children, he was the first person in his family to attend college. He chose the state university, which was less than ten miles from his home. He described himself as ambitious, easily bored after several years at one job, and anxious to move on and up in the field of education. Szabo's doctoral dissertation explored the reasons why teachers leave the classroom to become school administrators. He conducted a survey of teachers and administrators in the state, and concluded that many teachers leave the classroom because of job dissatisfaction; needs critical to their personal sense of

[2]In 1982, the school district was ranked fourteenth in equalized valuation per pupil among the thirty-three regional high school districts in the state ($187,462). Equalized valuation refers to the value of real property where state authority is used to ensure that the rate of assessment is consistent throughout the state. (It does not include the state's contribution to public schools.) The district cost per pupil was about 10 percent below the mean costs for regional high school districts, and the district ranked twenty-second out of thirty-three in per-pupil expenditures.

themselves as effective teachers were not able to be satisfied in the classroom. It was possible to make teachers feel better about their jobs and themselves, he wrote, if they were given greater opportunity to make decisions and assume the responsibilities typically reserved for administrators.

Szabo exuded a low-keyed charm and a pleasant manner. He was tall and trim, with silver gray hair, a self-confident handshake, and a warm smile. He conducted a relaxed interview, asking some general questions about social studies and team teaching and school discipline. I was no longer concerned about difficult questions. No one would ask me about books or articles in the fields of education, history, or social science; no one would challenge me to compare various schools of historiography, or ask whether I preferred to teach sociology as a "conflict theorist" or as a "structural-functionalist." No one would ask me to submit to a battery of personality tests to see if I was suited for the job. I was not asked to meet with the school psychologist, nor was this ordinarily required of job aspirants.

After a few minutes, we were joined by Dr. Krystyna Mokowski, the assistant superintendent for curriculum and instruction. Dr. Mokowski had direct responsibility for what was taught in the schools and for the quality of the instruction. The various principals had little control over these areas. At the building level, curriculum and instruction were the responsibility of the subject supervisors, who reported to Mokowski. She also played a direct role in the supervision of teachers. By state law, every teacher who was considered for tenure must have his or her teaching observed directly by someone from the superintendent's office. Szabo chose not to observe teachers and delegated this task to Mokowski. The Oldham-Webster district had a reputation as a place in which it was difficult to get tenure. In the upcoming academic year, four teachers would be denied tenure at Oldham High, including two in areas in which there were nationwide shortages: math and science. Dr. Mokowski had a strong hand in all these decisions.

Teachers said that her classroom observations caused great anxiety. The observations were typically unannounced, lasting one forty-two-minute period and followed by a one-period discussion. A written evaluation would follow in about a month, and it was usually careful, detailed, and voluminous. She admitted that her role was not to improve a teacher's style, technique, or ability to relate to students. She was not there to improve teaching or help the teacher, but to evaluate —coldly, critically, but fairly—in accordance with district policy and state law.

It was a difficult job. Dr. Mokowski had taught English for nine years in a high school in another part of the state, and had degrees in English and education from a small out-of-state college, but in addition to English, she had to pass judgment on teachers in other fields, including the foreign languages she did not speak, metal shop, physics, and physical education. Her doctorate was in educational administration, and for her dissertation she studied isolation and alienation among elementary school teachers.

Dr. Mokowski projected a no-nonsense demeanor. I immediately got the sense that she was a serious person with a demanding job to do. There was a humorless severity about her that invited irreverent teacher comments. In her mid-thirties, she was not married, and the men teachers, in particular, enjoyed ribald speculations about her relationship with Dr. Szabo. It was more a tribute to her power over the teachers than any apparent coquettishness. Dr. Mokowski was of average height, worked out in a gym to combat a weight problem, and typically dressed in dark business suits. She used little, if any, makeup, and wore her long, dark hair tightly wound in a large bun. She did much of the dirty work in the district. She was the person in the central office with whom the teachers were most likely to deal. It was she who evaluated them, criticized them, and supervised them. The teachers referred to her as the Polish Princess and the Dragon Lady.

While Dr. Mokowski and I talked about teaching, Dr. Szabo had been reading through my curriculum vitae.

"This is a very impressive résumé," he said.

I thanked him, wondering what it was that had impressed him. I had been a member of several search committees at the university, and I knew that it is often an obscure entry or reference that catches the eye. I had three degrees from reasonably good schools, 130 semester hours of course work in history and the social sciences, seventeen years of teaching in high school and universities, academic publications, and presentations at national meetings of professional and research groups. I was also certified bilingual by the United States Army, and I was a Vietnam era veteran.

"I see you coached wrestling," he said.

"That was fourteen years ago," I demurred. "The last wrestling match I saw was in [the film] *Garp,* and that was two years ago!"

Neither Szabo nor Mokowski responded in any way at first. After a brief and unpleasant pause, Dr. Szabo said he had neither seen the film nor read the book written by John Irving in which the main character, T. S. Garp, was killed by a member of a feminist cult while he conducted wrestling practice.

"Did you see that movie, Krys?"

Dr. Mokowski shook her head no.

"You really have good credentials, but it is going to be hard to sell you to the board. They think social studies teachers are a dime a dozen."

We laughed. He told me that because of my teaching experience and degrees, I would be the most expensive teacher he had ever recommended to the board (over $30,000), and while they might be willing to pay that much for a math or science teacher, he was looking for something extra to make me look good.

"What about the coaching? It would make it easier if you were willing to coach. It's one of the realities of public schools. You know that."

"What did you coach?" I asked Szabo.

"Oh, I used to be a football coach and I certainly wouldn't want to do it again, but I'd really like to have you in the district, and this may be the only way I can get you in."

He made me promise that, at the very least, I would agree to coach the junior varsity team. We shook hands.

"By the way, you are certified, aren't you?" he asked with a smile.

"No, but I am certifiable, I think." Although I had taught nearly all the courses necessary for state certification as a social studies teacher, I did not hold a certificate to teach in the state. University teachers are not required to have teaching certificates. My high school certificate would be granted five months later, based on a reciprocal agreement with a state in which I was certified. My career as a high school teacher would begin as soon as the board of education voted to approve my contract. Several days later, friends presented me with the Acme Thunderer, one of the more popular coach whistles.

I needed some time to think about the job. I drove back to the school to look for Paul and Troy, but they were no longer in the building, and the school was almost deserted. It was 3:10 P.M., and the school day had ended thirty minutes earlier. The hallways were empty except for a few custodians. Some, with portable vacuum cleaners on their backs, were cleaning up the accumulated debris of the school day; others were piling chairs on top of tables in the cafeteria and preparing to wash the floor.

The school was very hot and humid. The original design of the building had included air conditioning, but it was later considered excessive, and central air conditioning was left out. There was air conditioning in the administrative and guidance suites and in the resource centers, but none in the auditorium, gymnasium, cafeteria, library, or classrooms.

A lobby was the core of this thirteen-year-old building. It was a rectangle, approximately 60 feet wide and 110 feet long, that provided access to the major facilities of the school. Along the north side was the main entrance, which neatly divided the nearly identical suites housing the guidance and administrative offices. The library entrances were on the south side of the lobby, and large glass windows permitted a view of the books and tables. Along the east side of the lobby were the doorways to the 500-seat auditorium, and on either side were the entrances to two corridors that led to the music rooms, shops, art rooms, the cafeteria, and the stairways to the second floor. The west side of the lobby was the focal point of the school. A floor-to-ceiling glass wall invited a look at the gymnasium below. It was the most physically distinctive aspect of the school, which although only two stories high, was built on three levels. Half of the school was higher than the lobby level, and the other half was one story below it.

The lobby provided a captivating view of the entire gym from a vantage point above one of the glass backboards. It was a naturally attractive spot, and a small group of students was clustered around the windowed wall watching the action below. Instead of the athletic ballet of basketball or volleyball, the action that day was the loud, rhythmic explosions of automatic hammers as construction workers fired nails into new hardwood flooring. During the school day, the noise punctured the classrooms surrounding the gym.

On either side of the windowed wall were corridors leading to classrooms, appendages to the central body of the school. Along the northwest corridor were four doors, two dark blue and two light blue. The light blue doors were unmarked, and I later learned that these were rear entrances to the principal's office and the office of the assistant principal. This was a break in the otherwise perfect symmetry of the lobby area, as there were no rear entrances to the guidance offices. The two dark blue doors were clearly labeled Gentlemen, and Men Faculty. The faculty room contained one open-stall toilet and two sinks. No one was ever able to explain this architectural curiosity. The students' lavatory had a more balanced design of four urinals, four sinks, and two open-stall toilets. There were glass mirrors on the wall and towels in the dispenser. There were no cigarette butts, graffiti, or signs of vandalism. The other lavatories in the school were similarly clean, but they differed in that, except for the facilities off the lobby, none of the other lavs had doors. They had all been removed several years earlier so the faculty and administration could better keep an eye on things.

I returned to the office and asked the secretary where the social studies wing was located. She directed me to a lower level, behind the gym, on the far western side of the school. High schools often arrange subject disciplines in groups. While there was no academic reason why the French teacher could not teach next to the history teacher or the calculus teacher, most high schools dedicate wings or floors to specific disciplines. Troy had told me that the teaching position for which I had interviewed would be assigned to room 24. I had never been particularly interested in the rooms in which I taught at the university. I preferred those that were close to my office, appropriate in size and seating for the courses I was teaching, and air conditioned during the summer. Classrooms are of far greater concern in high schools. University teachers spend between six and twelve hours a week in classrooms and then retreat to labs, offices, or libraries to carry out their other responsibilities. High school teachers do not typically have offices, and they have few responsibilities other than teaching. They are likely to spend five or more hours in one room with five classes of twenty-five to thirty students, and they are understandably possessive about their classrooms.

Room 24 was one of five rooms on a corridor of all social studies classes. The room had a blue door set in a black steel frame, exposed I-beam construction being one of the nicer touches in the school's design. Through a small rectangular window, I could see that the room was being used for a meeting of the cross-country team, and although they were about to leave, I did not enter. Along the corridor walls were lockers which had not changed much since I had been in high school. Each student had a narrow rectangular box with hooks to hang coats, and a separate square for books. Both cubicles were controlled by a single combination lock. Some students decorated the insides of their lockers with photographs, old Valentines, posters, bumper stickers, or a few dried flowers. Couples often shared one another's lockers, particularly if they had lockers in opposite ends of the building; it was a bit like owning two homes.

An exit next to the room led to the outside and the athletic fields. The faculty and students were justifiably proud of the appearance of the grounds. Between the football field and the school were gentle hills dotted with fruit trees and other hardwoods. A particularly appealing willow tree grew at an unlikely forty-five-degree angle away from the building. On the outside perimeter of the school property, hardwoods mixed with cedar and spruce trees separated the school from the community. The school building was located on the highest land on the school property, and from the rear of the school it was possible to look down and see the all-weather track that encircled the football field, two baseball fields, and the two football practice fields. Concealed from view were other fields used by the softball teams and soccer teams.

The sights and sounds of a high school in autumn were everywhere. Coaches yelled at, encouraged, and teased their players. Cheerleaders, in their practice white tops and shorts, appeared attentive as their advisers admonished them to cheer for a touchdown only when their side had the ball. Painfully thin athletes from the cross-country team ran seemingly endless circles around the school. There were nearly as many female as male athletes. No longer limited to participating in field hockey in the fall, there were girls' teams in soccer and cross country working out on the field, and the girls' tennis team was practicing at a private indoor facility in town.

I walked toward the parking lot along the south side of the building and came upon a strange rectangle of land. It was demarcated by fifty-five-gallon drums painted green, and white chalk lines similar to those used on the football field. There were cigarette butts all over the ground, but no signs of other litter. A couple, dressed in faded blue denims and long-sleeve, colored T shirts, sat facing each other crosslegged on the ground.

"I guess this is the smoking area," I said inanely, noticing both of the kids with cigarettes in their hands.

"Yeah, this is the grove. They let us smoke here."

I glanced at this flat expanse of grass and offered the obvious: "I thought a grove meant something to do with trees."

"The old grove had trees. This is the new grove."

Their answers had been polite but cautious. They regarded me with some suspicion, and it was clear that they did not encourage me to ask many questions. I learned later that the smoking area had been in the grove of trees directly behind the school, but it had been considered a distraction to the classes and in the way of the construction crews, so it was moved to a far side of the building. Despite the move, the smoking area still kept its former name.

The students gave me directions to the main highway, and I drove around the community to try to get some feel for the area. I learned that Oldham and Webster are separate towns with distinct pasts. According to local histories, the area was once populated by peaceful Indians who initially welcomed the white settlers. There was a legend that an Indian chief interpreted the comet of 1680 to mean that "the Indians shall melt away and this country will be inhabited by another people." Oldham was founded in 1749 and Webster in 1799, and by the 1830s the Indians were gone.

Webster was originally settled by Congregationalists, Methodists,

and Presbyterians in search of a simple, pious farming life. It remained
a quiet farming community until the discovery of iron ore transformed
it into a robust little mining and industrial town. By the end of the
1800s, Webster boasted dozens of small, deep-shaft mines, forges,
distilleries, and lumber mills. According to one local history, the
wealthy people of Webster never lived as well as they did in that time.
There were carriages and coachmen, house and yard servants, a thriv-
ing business community, and a population of 2,400. The prosperity
was short-lived. When vast iron ore deposits were discovered close to
the surface in Minnesota's Mesabi Range, Webster's deep-shaft mines
became uncompetitive. The mines quickly and quietly closed, and the
prosperity ebbed. The area would not regain its popularity until its
rediscovery in the 1970s by those looking for new housing outside the
older suburbs.

The Websters (Webster Borough and Webster Township) had a
combined population of 6,631, according to the 1980 census. There
was a small shopping center, the area's only fast food hamburger place,
and one Oriental restaurant, which seemed to alternate between Chi-
nese and Vietnamese owners. The town boasted carefully restored
buildings along Main Street, some of which dated to the early parts
of the last century. A flea market on Sundays attracted thousands of
tourists and newcomers in search of Americana, antiques, and bar-
gains. While the 1880s may have indeed been Webster's heyday, a
century later it had a mean family income of nearly $34,000, placing
it about 50 percent above the state average, in one of the wealthiest
states in the nation. Only 3.4 percent of persons reporting in the 1980
census were described as living below the poverty level. If there was
a status problem in Webster, it came mainly from a comparison with
Oldham, its wealthier and older neighbor to the east.

Oldham had nearly 9,000 residents living in the borough and
township and a mean family income of almost $46,000. The First
Presbyterian church of Oldham was considered to be the oldest building in the area, dating its original construction to 1745. George Washington was said to have visited the area several times, and during one
winter of the Revolutionary War, troops of the Colonial Army were
quartered in nearby farmlands in what is now a well-preserved national park.

Perhaps due to more favorable terrain, the larger estates were built
in Oldham rather than Webster. Many of those in the state who made
great fortunes in the late nineteenth and early twentieth centuries
built huge estates on the crown of nearly every hill in Oldham. Some

of these were still standing, but they were more likely to be used as private schools and businesses than as private residences. Local people pointed to these estates with unreserved civic pride, but according to one local wag, most of the town's residents who dated their lineage to the estate period were far more likely to be related to those who had worked on the estates than to those who had lived on them.

Most of the area's residents did not pretend to long historic links to the area, but were more closely tied to the large corporations that had moved in since the 1970s. As major corporations abandoned the cities and moved their plants and headquarters to the outer fringes of the suburbs, Oldham became one of the areas that attracted the executives, managers, and engineers the corporations moved with them. That Oldham was synonymous with prestige in the state was only partially attributable to local boosterism. There was occasionally a real estate listing for an Oldham property in *The New York Times Magazine* in the "Luxury Homes and Estates" section. These ads typically described Oldham as "historic" or "nestled in the prestigious horse country" where one was able to "enjoy gracious country living" only minutes from "corporate centers and highways." It was not unusual to see homes advertised which boasted "horse stalls for six," "trainer's cabins," and "breathtaking California baths."

The township had some of the larger and more wooded properties in the area that displayed the name of the property more often than the name of the owner. A ride through winding country roads brought you to Tall Tree Farms, Juniper Jump, and Walnut Acres. Because the area was hilly and laced with streams, many of the larger property owners were able to build dams and create their own ponds. These, I was told, were far more prestigious than building a swimming pool.

Although only 2.1 percent of the population admitted to living below the poverty line in 1980, not everyone owned horses, lived on estates or debated the relative merits of concrete swimming pools versus natural ponds. The majority of people in Oldham lived in suburban subdivisions or older private homes with very little property. There were also some two-family houses, and a few garden apartments and townhouses. Oldham was a solidly middle class community, but not a very exciting town. There were no movie theaters, no ice cream stores, and the closest fast food hamburger was five miles away in Webster. There were two bars in town, three gas stations, four banks, and five real estate agencies. Students often joked that one of the highlights of their weekends was to come out at midnight and watch one of the traffic signals on Main Street change into a blinking light. (The other one did not change.) It was generally accepted that people did not move there to live life in the fast lane. It was a family-oriented community where people came to raise children and send them to good public schools in the hope that they would go to good colleges.

2

FIRST DAY,
FIRST IMPRESSIONS

Seven-thirty in the morning. It was the earliest I had arrived at work
since I had been discharged from the army. A bell would ring at 7:35
A.M., and another at 7:40 A.M. The first was to prepare students for the
second, which warned them they had five minutes to get to their first
period class. Twenty-two bells later, students would be herded onto
buses and sent home. School was dismissed at 2:40 P.M.; buses left at
2:50 P.M. From first bell to last, every minute was accounted for, and
everyone followed the same time schedule.

I found the main office and emptied my cubbyhole mailbox, which
had been crammed full with papers. There were a stack of notices to
give to students, attendance cards, absence excuses, a list of students
who had medical problems, a copy of the faculty handbook and a copy
of the daily bulletin. The secretarial staff arrived at 7:45; until then the
office was managed by the principals and the head of pupil personnel
services (guidance). The three men answered the phones, checked
which teachers were there, arranged for substitute teachers, and made
small talk. I smelled coffee coming from the workroom. One of the
secretaries got it ready the night before and set a timer for 6 A.M.
Although the administrators greeted me cordially, no one offered a
cup. This was their coffee, and there was no place to buy coffee until
9 A.M., no place to make coffee, no coffee unless you brought your own.
One of the teachers advised me to bring a vacuum bottle from home,
but he cautioned that drinking coffee in the classroom was a violation
of school rules.

I had five minutes now before the students arrived. It was enough
time to glance at the headlines, but not to read much more of my
newspaper. Teaching was not a job that allowed me to hide in an office
and linger over the mail or the paper in the morning. There were no

faculty offices, no places to be alone, and few quiet places in which to work. Teachers typically walked in and out of one another's classrooms in the morning before school began; and at 7:40, the students came pouring into the room, and we were on. For the next seven and a half hours, teachers were surrounded by people constantly, and they responded to thousands of questions from more than a hundred students.

Troy Thayer walked down to my classroom with me and gave me a key to the door. He wished me good luck and promised to return later in the day with class rosters, course outlines, and a book inventory. Room 24 was 24 feet from front to back and 30 feet wide. It was similar to the other rooms on the wing: cream-colored, cement block walls, black steel desk with a light gray Formica top, two yellow bulletin boards in the front of the room, a single blue bulletin board on the side, blackboards with aluminum chalk trays, exposed steel beams in the corner, and three lines of single-lamp fluorescent lights. There was no closet to hang my jacket or store my books. There were four large windows, but only two of them opened. I opened them as wide as I could to let in the morning air, and the wind rattled the venetian blinds. If I pulled the blinds up the rattle would stop, but they would not stay up. I put up with the rattle for a period or two until one of the students showed me that if I knotted the draw cord, pulled the blinds up, and slipped the cord under the horizontal grate of the heating units, the blinds would stay up.

My desk had two drawers on the right and three on the left in addition to a narrow center drawer. As I looked for a place to store my papers and books, I saw that the right-hand drawers were filled with books, pencils, and stacks of paper.

I noticed an adult enter the room, and I turned around to greet him.

"Hi! I'm Mike Werge," he said. "We're sharing this room. That's my stuff in the drawers."

"Hi, I'm Stu Palonsky." I extended my hand to a smiling Alan Alda look-alike who had just walked into the room. His face screwed up quizzically as I pronounced my last name.

"Palonsky," I said slowly, "as in Roman Polanski, you know my cousin, the famed rapist?" He looked a little troubled. "I assure you we have little else in common besides the name. I am not the least bit interested in girls until their fourteenth birthday."

"Oh, yeah. Nice to meet you. Welcome to Oldham. I have a whole bunch of maps and posters from my old school we can put up. This school has nothing. Put up anything you want. See ya later; I gotta go."

Mike was in his late thirties, and he too was in his first year at

Oldham High. He had taught social studies for eleven years in another high school, but he had been the least senior person, and when staff cutbacks followed enrollment declines, he was let go. He seemed to be sensibly dressed for the job: soft-soled shoes because he stood for most of the day; slacks and shirt rather than a suit because he was always carrying books and moving supplies; a tie because it pleased administrators. I was delighted to hear that he had posters and maps to tack up around the room. The walls were bare; it was just a plain vault of a room.

The warning bell rang. Mike popped his head in the door.

"Funny line about your cousin Roman. The desks okay?"

"Fine," I said.

He had arranged the room in two semi-circles of fifteen desks each. Virtually all the classrooms had desks in neat rows, and Mike seemed relieved that I had no objection to his seating design.

"I think it promotes class discussion," he said. "At least the kids can face each other. It's hard to argue with the back of someone's head."

I nodded in agreement. Mike smiled, and went back to his other room.

The desks had tubular aluminum frames with seats and backs of molded plastic. Some of the desks were green, others orange, and they were cheap and uncomfortable. The desk tops, all of which favored right-handers, were made of laminated plyboard covered with an easily washed, scratch-resistant surface. The seats were broken on at least six of them; screws were missing from another dozen; and the undersides of all the desks were dotted with spent wads of bubble gum in the currently popular flavors: strawberry, raspberry, and grape.

The students began to trickle in slowly. Some took their seats a few minutes before the bell rang, but most came through the door, or tried to, just as the second bell was ringing. There were twenty-five of them, and they were more alert and more animated than seemed reasonable for that hour of the morning. According to Troy, most of the students were juniors, although there were a few seniors who needed to pass this course in order to graduate. They looked clean, pressed, and country-scrubbed. Most of the girls wore whites and pastels; they seemed to like cotton tops with a few buttons left undone and the collars turned up. It did not seem to concern them that their outfits, though expensive, were often identical to those worn by other students. If one girl was wearing a top with "ESPRIT" printed on it, you could be assured that a dozen others would be wearing the same top. A few of the girls wore long, starched cotton dresses, and one or two sported the basic blues of denim jacket and jeans, often with a designer label.

Most of the boys wore T shirts and beltless, straight-leg jeans with no labels. Some of the T shirts were purchased at rock concerts; others recalled family trips to Aruba or Cancun. A few wore long-sleeve collarless shirts with elaborate, colorful scenes of surfing or sailing or skiing. High-top white sneakers with laces untied or workboots were the preferred footwear. One student told me that he did not feel completely dressed without a round container of smokeless tobacco stuck in a back pocket of his jeans.

American history 2C. Troy told me not to worry much about the C-level students. "They're a problem," he said. "No one really cares about them." C stood for "average," but no one explained what that meant, except a student who approached my desk shortly after the bell rang.

"You're the new teacher, right?"

"I look too old to be a kid, huh?"

"Do you know what kind of class this is?"

"American history?"

"Well kinda, we're C's."

"That means comely, candid cognoscenti, right?"

"I don't know any of those words, but I think 'candid' was one of my vocabulary words from freshman year. I could look it up, I have all my notes home since I was in fifth grade." I thanked her but said that it was not necessary. "I was just showing off," I told her.

"I just wanted you to know that we don't read much, we don't like to write much, but we'll talk in class if that'll make you feel better. We just wanted you to know, you being a college professor and stuff."

"Thanks. Do you plan to go to college after you graduate?"

"I think so, everybody here goes to college."

I thanked her again. The class quieted down when I asked them to. I let them sit anywhere. Most of the boys sat on my left near the windows. Many were jayvee football players. They spoke loudly, teased one another, and talked of sports and beer parties. One would be plagued the entire year by early morning flatulence, and he would regularly punctuate my class and scatter the students. Another mumbled badly, and every time he spoke, three or four students would mumble in a chorus behind him. This I could stop.

A few of the students regarded me sullenly, but most seemed cooperative. I asked them some questions from a standardized test to see what they remembered from the previous year. They did not seem to remember anything.

"It's not our fault," volunteered one student. "We had a very bad teacher last year."

"What about the year before?" I asked.

"He was even worse, a real scumbag. Oh excuse me, doctor, I forgot the summer's over."

I went on without comment. I had them read questions from the Gallup Poll on education partly to have some discussion and partly to listen to them read. I allowed those who did not want to read to pass. All but three of the students read, and most read fairly well although slowly and without interest, mispronouncing longer words and often ignoring punctuation. Those who had trouble were not teased. I asked the class to write a one-page paper explaining those things teachers did which made them angry and those things teachers could do which pleased them. They were not to put their names on the papers. No, they would not be graded, I told them. No, the papers would not count. Yes, I agreed it was work for which they would not be rewarded. I was just interested in their opinions.

The forty-two minutes were about up. It was Friday and I decided not to give an assignment. Each student had been issued a textbook noted mainly for its pictures and blandness.[1] Carefully designed to offend no one, it contained precious little interest or excitement. It rarely took a position on anything. Including maps, index, and pictures, it was 379 pages long. If I gave a reading assignment for every school day, each assignment would be about two pages in length. At that rate, it was possible to miss a week of school and catch up in thirty minutes.

A few minutes before the end of the period, the head custodian, John Churchill, walked into the room to adjust the ventilating unit. Mr. Churchill was appreciated for his curmudgeonly humor and general disdain for authority. He had a pot belly and few teeth. His right shoulder appeared to be five inches lower than his left, and he walked diagonally through the hall as though he were tacking into a strong wind. Whenever Mr. Churchill came into my room, all eyes would focus on him, and no additional enthusiasm on my part could recapture their interest until he left. Mr. Churchill never failed to remind me of his seductive charms. "You guys must be real dull if the kids are more interested in me changing a light bulb than in you!" he would say in his raspy stage whisper that could be heard by everyone in the class. "Maybe they should hire me to be the teacher, and you guys can change the light bulbs."

[1]The text, as well as others in American history, is discussed in Anyon (1979) and FitzGerald (1979).

Later in the year, Mr. Churchill brought a temporary halt to my teaching simply by coming into the classroom, standing in the doorway, and staring at the blinds. "Can I help you, Mr. Churchill?" I asked, noticing twenty-five pairs of eyes leave me and focus on him.

"We gotta do something about those blinds," he said.

"What's the matter?"

"This room can be seen from the athletic fields. Do you know what I mean?" he asked.

"No."

"The board of education people are always walking on the fields. One of them complained that the blinds on this wing were uneven at the end of the day. You know what I mean? It looks bad. Some are up, some are down. No uniformity. Can you leave yours up at the end of the day?"

"I'd like to, but I can't. Two of the four won't stay all the way up. Can we have everyone on the wing leave the blinds down?" I asked Mr. Churchill.

"Now there's a good idea. I'll bring it up at the next board meeting." He laughed and left.

The bell rang at 8:27, but no one moved. For the next five minutes there was an activity period. Troy had explained the procedures to me. My first activity, as mandated by state law, was to lead the flag salute. For the first six months of school, there was no flag in the room, but I explained to students that there was no cause for alarm. If someone found out we had not been reciting the pledge, we could chip in and buy a flag on the last day of the year, repeat the pledge 180 times in twenty-five-part harmony, and they would all be allowed to become seniors. They were neither amused nor concerned.

Later in the year, Mike Werge provided us with a huge flag that had once graced the S.S. *United States,* and we mounted it on the rear wall. I asked the class if they knew why we could not salute this "flawed" flag. After a few minutes they recognized that this was not an up-to-date flag, but an antique with only forty-eight stars. One of the students raised vociferous protests when I would remove the flag to project films on the wall. The kids called him "sarge," and he was headed for the Marine Corps. He believed that taking the flag down before sunset was unpatriotic. Another student, the one with the gas problem, said that saluting this flag would be too much of an insult to the missing states, "Alaska and the other one."

I agreed. I had nothing against rituals, but so many other things had to be done in this five-minute period that I welcomed any relief. Among my other responsibilities was the reading of the daily bulletin which heralded forthcoming athletic events, dances, lost and found notices, breaches of school etiquette (such as the smokeless tobacco fad), blood drives, and visits of college representatives. Students only partially listened to the bulletin. If it concerned something with which they were involved, such as football or modern dance, or a new smoking regulation, they would ask me to re-read it. It really did not matter; if it was important, it would be repeated several days in a row in the bulletin. There was no reason to pay attention to anything the first time.

My third responsibility was to take attendance. I had computer punch cards for each student and two envelopes. The instructions were unambiguous: "Keep all students' attendance cards together in the envelope marked 'not absent.' When students are absent, take their cards from the 'not absent' envelope and put them in the envelope marked 'absent.' Send this envelope to the office at 8:36 A.M." It seemed easy enough, but somehow I had a lot of trouble with attendance. I often missed a student, sometimes reporting some absent when they were present or present when they were absent. Once I put all those present in the "absent" envelope and sent them to the office. Sometimes I forgot to send any envelopes to the office, which would bring a call from the assistant principal's secretary over the intercom phone. The call alerted the students to my negligence, and they always rewarded me with good-natured teasing.

I did not enjoy the clerical chores of teaching, and I did not pay sufficient attention to those students who were tardy. "Tardy" means, of course, to arrive later than expected, but it is rarely used outside school settings. No one arrives fashionably tardy to a party, and airline arrivals are never tardy; people do not show up tardy for work or dinner, but tardy is a serious school concern. When a student was tardy, the teacher was to admit the student to class, record the tardiness in the record book, place the student's name on the "tardy slip," and include the slip with the attendance cards in the envelope marked "absent."

Tardiness was clearly explained in the *Student Handbook* under the first major section of the book, "Rules Pertaining to Attendance." It said: "Students are expected to be in school on time. Reasons for legal tardiness are the same as listed under state law for absences (personal illness, death in family, quarantine, sudden and extreme emergency, religious holidays). If a student comes to class tardy, but during first period, the student is to report to the class, and be subjected to the five-step schedule of penalties:"

Step 1 Reprimand by the teacher for the first three offenses
Step 2 Quiet study assignment by the teacher

Step 3 Counselor telephones student's home
Step 4 Teacher's supervisor telephones student's home
Step 5 Referral to the vice-principal

Only two students were ever tardy for my first period class, and it really did not bother me. They were rarely more than three minutes late, and they were not disruptive, but the other students demanded that I take action.

"You can't let them get away with it!" one student yelled out.

"If we have to be here on time, they have to be here on time," shouted another.

"It's not fair," added a third.

I ignored the problem as long as I could, then I became angry at the students for forcing me to deal with all the paperwork necessitated by the tardiness regulation. I decided to explain the reason why schools require punctuality. I droned on about the school being an agency of socialization which had to pass on the norms of society to new members—in this case, my first period class—as a means of anticipatory socialization for the world of work. It is not that the school cares if you're late, I explained, but AT&T wants its employees there on time, so they force the school to make tardiness a behavior problem punished by institutional sanctions. In this way punctuality becomes a socially valued, habitual behavior, and AT&T can be assured of employees with good work habits.

"Do you understand?" I asked.

The offender was a huge senior boy with a record of truancy, tardiness, and marginal grades.

"No," he said, "but I'm not really late. My father's Corvette wouldn't start; his girlfriend had to take him to work; and I had to walk to school. Anyway, I brought you some coffee."

Other teachers would not be bribed so easily, but I accepted his story and the coffee. As I sipped the coffee, I told him to consider this his first reprimand and I asked the rest of the class to make note of it. The students did not complain; they seemed to understand corruption.

Several of the teachers told me they had developed their own accommodations to the school rules. One math teacher fined students for minor infractions such as tardiness or coming to class without a pencil, and at the end of the year they had pizza and soda with the accumulated money. Another teacher made the students wash desk tops or do pushups. The metal shop teacher, an imposing bear of a man, would stop an offending student at the entrance to his shop, grab his hand, and repeatedly slap himself in the face with the student's hand. "It's an insult to come late to my class," he would tell the student. "It's like slapping me in the face. Do you want to slap my face? Do you want to insult me? Don't you ever come to class late!"

At 8:32 the bell rang, ending activity period. I had four minutes to gather up the clutter on my desk, erase the blackboard, urge students to throw away papers and rearrange their chairs, and run upstairs for the next period.

I passed Mike Werge in the hall.

"How did it go?" he asked.

"Fine. Do you have the rosters for this class?"

"No, Troy has them."

"Where are the books for the freshmen?"

"I don't know. I gotta go; talk to you later."

I was late for library duty, my second period school assignment. Every teacher in the school taught five classes and had one period for a school duty and one period for a department duty. My department duty entailed sitting in Troy's office and helping students who had trouble with social studies or proctoring a makeup test for a teacher in the department. "Proctologizing," one teacher called it. Library/lobby duty was considered a plum duty, often given to new teachers who did not know the students and could have trouble in the more difficult supervisory jobs of cafeteria duty or "quiet study." Troy walked upstairs with me and introduced me to the librarian, Sandy Weiss. Sandy, married with two children and in her early thirties, was in her first year at Oldham after several years as school librarian in another district. Sandy introduced me to the library secretary and began to explain my duties and the library rules.

"Students can come to the library without a pass, except freshmen who always need a pass, although later in the year they don't need a pass either, but I'll explain that another time. Students can sign books out themselves, but you should occasionally check to see if they did. There can be quiet talking at the table. . . . "

"Excuse me," I interrupted, "do I smell coffee? Can I buy a cup? I'll give you $100."

"You can't buy a cup. Just take one; use this mug, but bring in one when you have a chance. Keep an eye on the coffee, when we need some, buy some."

Sandy advised me of the school rules. It would be all right to drink coffee in the library workroom, but not in the library itself. Faculty and students were to be treated alike; no food was permitted outside the cafeteria except in authorized faculty areas.

I thanked her, and she went on: "At the end of the period, walk around, see that the books are put away and the chairs are under the table. . . ."

I tried to listen, but I could not keep up. The job of library duty was new to me. In my other public school teaching experience, the school had hired aides to supervise the library and the cafeteria. When Troy told me that I had library duty, I thought it was an academic responsibility, helping students learn how to use the library and assisting them in finding sources for homework assignments and papers. I had envisioned myself assisting students with the microfiche reader and *The Reader's Guide to Periodical Literature;* directing them to the volumes on literary criticism and the *Encyclopedia of Bioethics.* I soon realized that library duty meant supervision; students could not be left alone. They had to be watched wherever they were; the school was responsible for their physical well-being, not only their education.

"Can I go to the bathroom?" a student asked, interrupting Sandy's orientation lecture.

"Sure, why not," I said.

Sandy laughed. I asked why.

"You looked at that kid as if it were a ridiculous question."

I had the power to approve or disapprove requests to use the lavs, and it would always strike me as a little strange. I sometimes advised them to wash their hands or to turn off the light, but I never said no. Mike Werge told me that he had once refused to let a student leave because there were only a few minutes left in the period, and she responded by throwing up all over the classroom.

I walked around the library, signing passes, saying hello to students, and looking at the books in the shelves. While most of the students were not studying very seriously, they were quiet. They collaborated on homework, read books, copied assignments, and chatted with their friends. Students asked me a lot of questions for which I had no answers: "Is this an overnight book?" "Can I take this magazine home?" "What time does this period end?" I referred them to the librarian, saying, "I know nothing; I just keep order."

Toward the latter half of the period, Don Brandt, the assistant principal, came in to introduce himself to me. A former coach, former supervisor of the physical education department, Brandt was a short, balding man in his early fifties. "I'm very glad to meet you," he said, cordially. "It's really very nice to have you here. I'd like to explain a few of the school rules about this duty. Nothing special, pretty obvious stuff."

We walked out into the lobby. Another teacher was on duty there now, but halfway through the year he would go inside the library and I would become the lobby supervisor. It was a step up in difficulty and control. Don explained the rules in pleasant, relaxed tones.

"Your job here is to maintain an atmosphere of quiet conversation," he said and then, looking across the lobby, he called out, "Mr. Wiebe, feet off the table, please. Thank you." His tone was firm, but not harsh. The rules were clear; the student had complied without a flinch or a sign of displeasure. The lobby could be used by students during their free periods, Brandt explained. Only freshmen had regular study halls, other students had free periods. My job, during lobby duty, was to make sure that students could study if they wanted to. Students were allowed to talk here, but they had to do so in a restrained manner.

"My rule of thumb," Brandt said, "is that if you can hear a murmur of conversation, everything is fine, but if you can hear one group speaking above the rest, they are probably too loud." I decided not to tell him about my service-connected hearing loss. Maybe this duty was too difficult for a disabled veteran and they would transfer me to cafeteria supervision, where the hearing-impaired would probably be at an advantage.

There were four round tables and five rectangular tables in the lobby. All students in the lobby had to be seated. If there were not enough seats, students had to go elsewhere. "Do you know how many students can sit at a round table?" Don asked me. I do not know now that I think about it, but at the time it sounded similar to the question of how many angels can dance on the head of a pin. I said that because a table has a circumference of three hundred and sixty degrees, and it is infinitely divisible, theoretically all of the students in the school could sit at one table.

"No. Four. Each round table is limited to four people. There are four chairs at each table, and they are not to be moved to another table. Do you know how many people can sit at a rectangular table?"

Not to make the same mistake twice, I admitted that I did not know.

"Seven. Three on each side and one on the end, the lobby end, not the wall end. If you let 'em sit on the wall end, they lean their chairs back and mar the walls. This way, too, the guys don't take the end chairs and just girl-watch all period. Okay?"

"Fine."

"Oh yeah, one more thing. You can't let kids stand by the windows and stare into the gym. It distracts the gym classes."

Looking up, we saw two students near the windows.

"Miss Scanlon, Miss Johnson, away from the windows, please."

The girls moved away from the window, and the lobby duty teacher, a nontenured member of the social studies department, cringed slightly when he heard Brandt's voice.

At a faculty meeting later in the year, the job of the duty teachers was expanded to include "policing the area," an expression I had not heard since the army. It meant that the teachers had to make sure the areas they supervised were free of paper and litter.

Another bell, another period. I found my briefcase and headed back to room 24. Along the way I spotted Paul.

"How's it going?" he asked.

"Fine. When do you have lunch?"

"Sixth."

"Me too, want to go out and get a bite?"

He laughed. "You can't leave school during the day. I thought you used to be a teacher."

"Silly me, I just lost my head, thinking about being an adult and going out for lunch. It won't happen again, captain."

"See that it doesn't. Talk to you later."

Freshmen, thirty of them, filled every chair. Two of the girls were huddled around an electrical outlet adjusting their hair styles with curling irons. At the sound of the bell, they mumbled something about just coming from gym. They quickly unplugged the curling irons, wrapped the cords around them, and jammed the hot irons into their handbags. Most of the other students became quiet and opened their notebooks at the bell. They all looked squeaky-clean and alert. They seemed to crackle with youthful energy, and they were remarkably attractive kids. They all seemed to have good posture, clear complexions, and sparkling eyes. It also seemed that nearly every one of them had braces. I thought it must be wonderful to be an orthodontist in the suburbs.

Unlike the juniors, this group of students seemed to remember everything from the previous year and the year before. This was their first year in the building. Most of them came from four separate middle schools, three public and one parochial, and they had all studied different subjects in an unorchestrated curriculum. Some had just moved into the area, and a few were prep school transfers. I asked them questions to find out what they had studied and what they knew. They were unrestrained in their enthusiasm. Every question was greeted by at least twenty waving hands, each arm supported at the armpit by the other hand so their zeal would not cause an arm to be pulled out of joint. They were anxious to impress me, and they did.

We talked about the books they had read over the summer, trips they had taken, films they had seen. They volunteered to read from a handout I gave them, and they read very well, with enthusiasm, understanding, and apparent enjoyment. They asked questions about the course requirements and the papers (neither of which was planned at that point). They asked about grading, and easily filled up both sides of a sheet of paper when I asked them to write about the kinds of teachers they liked and disliked.

I held up some of the books we would be using and tried to describe some of the things we would be doing that year. I had sixty freshmen, and there would not be enough books for all of them to have one to take home. In fact, for most of the units we would have to read in class and double up on books, as there typically were fewer than thirty books of any one set. Some of the books were good, but over ten years old and out of print. The psychology book was twelve years old and discussed "hippies" in the chapter entitled "Adolescent Rebellion," but there were enough of them to assign one to every student. The sociology book was older than they were and had a section that discussed the "Negro Problem."

I held up each of the books, asking students if they knew what each field was concerned with, in an attempt to develop definitions for the field and have them induce what it was that united all the social sciences. One book I held up was greeted with tightly controlled giggles and a few red faces. I looked at the back of the book and saw an unsigned pencil drawing of an erect penis with the title "Suck a Big One."

"Well, we won't be reading this one," I said straight-faced, "I'll be sending this to Mr. Brandt for handwriting analysis in the morning."

The students relaxed and laughed. I wondered how old the artist was now, late twenties perhaps, maybe teaching somewhere. The lesson could not be completed, we had 170 more days, so I gave the students the last five minutes to talk to each other as I gathered up my papers for another move.

"Excuse me, doctor, but do I detect the faint traces of a New York accent?" The question came from a dark-haired, smiling student dressed in black and sporting a mouthful of braces.

"Indeed you do," I told him, "but could we make this our secret? I think it is grounds for dismissal out here in the country."

"It's music to my Bensonhurst ears. I'm Aaron Finklestein, Brooklyn, New York. Welcome to Oldham." He extended a pudgy hand in my direction and gave me a firm but sweaty handshake. "Will you be taking off for Yom Kippur, or am I being too personal?"

"You'll have to forgive Aaron," another student interrupted, "you didn't let him talk enough today in class. He's Jewish, and if you don't let him talk, he'll burst."

I thanked him for the tip, told them both that it was a pleasure to meet them, and assured Aaron that I would do whatever I could to prevent him from bursting.

Cal came in as the bell was ringing.

"How's it going? Here are your class lists. If you wait for Troy to give them to you, you may never get them." He smiled and left.

Another duty period, followed by another American history class. This class was smaller; the students were less interested and less cooperative. It was getting close to lunch, and maybe they were hungry or getting tired. I was not yet ready to consider that the problem might have been with me. I asked them to do the same reading, writing, and recalling I had done with the morning class.

As they wrote, I had a chance to read through the papers written by the students in the morning classes. They claimed that they did not like teachers who gave hard tests, had favorites, did not keep their word, and made fun of students. Some students did not like to talk in class, others did not like to read in class. No one liked homework over the weekend. The juniors and seniors had a hard time describing those things a teacher could do that pleased them. Desirable teacher behaviors were typically expressed in the negative—no homework, no failures, no ridicule, no yelling. The freshmen said they liked teachers with humor and wit. They reluctantly admitted they did not mind papers—if they were not too long. They liked debates. They liked reading. They liked projects, and some of them liked group work. A few claimed that social studies was their favorite subject.

Twelve-twenty-six. A bell ended the class and announced the time for my scheduled lunch period. I was lucky. This was not a bad time to eat lunch; some teachers ate as early as 10:54 A.M., and others as late as 1:12 P.M. Due to a scheduling quirk, I had a full lunch period followed by a preparation period, giving me an hour and a half block of time to eat and work. Many of the teachers had only a twenty-one-minute lunch period. If they walked to the cafeteria and bought lunch, they would have about ten or twelve minutes in which to eat.

On my first day, Mike Werge, Paul De Faro, and I went to the cafeteria together. Later in the year, we ate in Paul's classroom; it provided our only time during the school day to talk. There were two serving lines in the cafeteria, one for the hot lunch, the other for sandwiches and soup. Sandwich choices included hamburgers, cheeseburgers, fried fish, tuna fish, and egg salad. Ice cream cost 30 cents;

sandwiches sold for a dollar. The students and teachers stood in an orderly line at each entrance, and few teachers cut in. Paul was scheduled for the short lunch period, but he declined to use this as an excuse to cut in front of the students, and he stood with Mike and me at the end of the file.

The lunches were served efficiently by a small cafeteria staff augmented by a few student workers. I glanced at the hot lunch and quickly grabbed a sandwich and some yogurt. School food did not seem to have changed much over the years. It was cheap, abundant, and starchy; the meatloaf, spaghetti, and pizza tasted exactly the same as they had when I was in high school. It was as if there were one secret recipe, available only to public schools, which was handed down from one generation of cafeteria workers to another. Eating the school's meatloaf made me think of people I had not seen in twenty years. Mike Werge, staring at a square slice of pizza and a pile of limp green beans, deadpanned that this was the way his wife always served pizza, and when it was accompanied by a container of chocolate milk, it was one of his favorite meals.

There was one dining area for students and another for the faculty, and we quickly headed for the sanctuary of the faculty room. Lunch was one of the few times during the day when teachers could talk with other adults. The faculty room was divided into two parts by a paneled wall divider. The rear section, reserved for smokers, contained one oblong table and seven chairs. It was connected to the nonsmoking section by an open doorway. The air conditioner was in the smoking section, and closing off the doorway would have kept out the smoke, but at the expense of the cooled air. There was a telephone on the wall of the smoking section that could be used to call out of the building. Officially, teachers were expected to use the pay phones in the lobby unless they were calling on school business. In practice, the teachers used the school phones for private calls, but their conversations were overheard by everyone in the room. It was the way in which we learned about colleagues' family illnesses, car problems, and marital disputes.

There were four small, round tables in the nonsmoking section. Formality was at a minimum. Teachers squeezed in where they could, pushing lunch trays in any open space, grabbing for napkins, salt, and pepper. Conversations were not private; teachers yelled from table to table and interrupted each other without apology. The faculty room was no place to make private phone calls or have private discussions; serious conversations were typically avoided. The teachers ate quickly. Those teachers with only twenty-one-minute lunch periods had little time to talk, and those who had full-period lunches talked mainly about cars, children, and sports.

There was not enough room in the nonsmoking section, so Mike, Paul, and I grabbed seats in the back room and ate amid the fumes. The teachers welcomed me, wished me well, and expressed the hope that I would enjoy myself. Troy came into the room and tapped me on the shoulder.

"Greetings. How are things going?" he asked.

"Fine," I said, "but I couldn't find a wine list."

"We'll straighten that out tomorrow. Oh, by the way, do you have a Ph.D. or an Ed.D.?"

"Ph.D. Why?"

"Some of the teachers were asking me," Troy said. "I didn't know, so I thought I'd check with you. I'm glad it's a Ph.D.; Ed.Ds are not held in high regard here."

"Okay, you may want to keep it a secret, but my degree is in education. By the way, did you find the course outlines yet?"

"No, I probably have them at home. I'll put them in your mailbox. See ya later."

I ate quickly. I had what seemed like a million things to do. I wanted to set up my grade book, find out what resources were in the library, figure out how to use the photocopying machine, and write some lesson plans. Troy wanted copies of weekly plans handed to him on Mondays. Members of the social studies department told me that Troy began every year by requesting plans, but most teachers ignored him. They told me not to worry about it, but I needed to make some plans for myself.

On the way out of the dining room, a teacher stopped me.

"Hi, I'm Sal. I heard you were going to be the new varsity wrestling coach, and I just wanted to introduce myself to you and let you know that I would be happy to be your assistant."

I shook his hand, and thanked him. Sal did not look like a jock. He taught physics and bore a somatic and behavioral resemblance to Don Knotts. Sal was very thin, and he moved with small, tense, jerking motions. He wore a short-sleeve green polyester shirt and a wide patterned tie that extended two inches below his belt. Sal had been an assistant wrestling coach for about five years. Every year he threatened to resign, and every year he came back, always for a different reason. That year, I was among the first to learn that he was again willing to coach. Sal told me that he could make an extra $1,600 as assistant wrestling coach; he was newly married, planning a family, and he needed the money.

"Sal, have you ever considered being a varsity coach?" I asked. "Five years as an assistant certainly qualifies you as a varsity coach."

"Yes, I've considered it," he said, "but I want them to ask me. I want to feel as if the effort I give is appreciated. Do you know what I mean?"

I told him I understood, but Sal would never be asked to be the varsity coach. Cal Bullinger had confided to me during my job interview that although there were two assistant wrestling coaches in the building, he did not think that either of them was right for the job of head coach. One, he said, did not project the right image to be a coach at Oldham, and the other did not command the respect of the kids and the parents. I was not sure into which category Sal fell, but I told him that I would be happy to have him work as my assistant. I also admitted to him that I was looking for a way out of the coaching assignment, and encouraged him to consider the varsity job. The word spread quickly that I was having second thoughts about coaching. Sports and coaching were not things about which one could speak lightly in the high school.

Two more classes. I looked forward to psychology. It was an A-level class, and in many high schools the students in these college prep courses can do the work expected of undergraduates. There were enough textbooks for all the students, and although we were not using the most current edition of the text, it was a fairly well-regarded high school book. The librarian's secretary had a bibliography of resources the library held for the teaching of psychology, and it looked adequate. There were no supplementary books or novels or monographs, but Troy said if I could give him a book request, he would see what he could do.

My neighbor in room 25, Gus Poulos, was the other psychology teacher. Gus was in his late twenties; he had taught in another school, and he was unusual for Oldham. He wore a beard, dressed very casually, typically wearing sneakers and eschewing ties and jackets. I doubt that he owned a suit. Gus talked out of the side of the mouth, a behavior he claimed to have picked up from a youth spent in places more urban than Oldham. His 135 pounds were distributed evenly over a 5'11" frame, leaving no excess of fat anywhere. He combed his straight dark hair forward, exposing an oval of baldness in the back. The students teased him good-naturedly about his hair style and he took it well, apparently enjoying the attention.

We would both be teaching a course called Principles of Psychology, a one-semester course. In the second semester, I would teach Sociology (A) and Gus would teach Contemporary Psychology (A).

Some of the students I taught first semester would take the second psych course with Gus, and I felt an obligation to prepare my students for the second semester. I asked him for a copy of the curriculum, and he gave me the Curriculum Guide, which described the course:

Principles of Psychology (A-Level). An introduction to the scientific study of human behavior including topics such as learning, personality, intelligence, biology, motives, emotions, and social influences on behavior and the concept of mental health. Student research and experimentation as well as extensive use of library resources and writing exercises are integral parts of the course.

"That's it?" I asked. The curriculum was sufficiently broad to include virtually everything that had ever been written about psychology, but too vague to give me any help in determining how much time to spend on individual units or what it was that students were supposed to take away from the course.

"That's it," he said. "Teach whatever ya wanna teach. There's a lotta freedom here." As Gus spoke, he extended his long arms to his side; he turned his palms inward and rocked back and forth on his heels. With his head cocked at an angle, he compensated for speaking out of the side of his mouth, and he was able to aim his words directly toward me.

"Hey, have a good time here, man. The kids are great. Everything else is bullshit. Close the doors and enjoy the kids. Don't worry about what you teach, the second semester course doesn't really follow the first semester course, anyway. See ya later."

For most of the first semester, Gus avoided me and gave me very little help. He told me later that he had feared that I was an "administration spy" who had been sent there to check up on the teachers. I did not know it at the time, but Gus was the other assistant wrestling coach. He was also one of the three teachers in the department being considered for tenure. This was his third year at Oldham, and if he taught for three years and a day, he was virtually assured of a lifetime job unless he was convicted of some crime or a moral offense, or the enrollment declined.

Although my classes were at least a week behind everyone else, no one indicated that it was necessary to rush and catch up. So I decided to play some get-acquainted games with the class until I was able to find a more specific outline of the curriculum. I also wanted to get to know the students a bit before I planned any work for them. I introduced myself to the small group of twenty-three juniors and seniors.

I decided to play a values clarification[2] exercise with them that I had learned at a free school in Michigan in the early seventies. The students were given the following scenario:

> There is a terrible storm and a ship is wrecked at sea. All those who survive the shipwreck are stranded on one of two habitable islands. The islands have fruit trees, coconut trees, and fresh water. On one island are Alice, her mother Bertha, and a black naval architect named Carlos. On the other island are David, Alice's boyfriend, and Ernie, a mutual friend of Alice and David. When the storm clears, Alice walks down to the beach and sees David on the other island. She is ecstatic. If only she could get to the other island, they would be together, perhaps forever. But she is unable to swim well, and the waters appear to be shark infested.
>
> Alice tells Carlos of her discovery, and he agrees to help her build a raft and to take her across on the one condition that she consent to sleep with him. Alice decides to think it over, and asks her mother what she should do. Her mother tells her that it is her life, her decision, and since she must live with the consequences of her actions, she must decide what to do by herself. Alice thinks it over and agrees to Carlos's proposition.
>
> Carlos, true to his word, builds the raft, takes her over to the other island, and then paddles back to the first island. On seeing Alice, David is overjoyed. They run to each other in slow motion and embrace. Alice decides to tell David the story of how she managed to get to the island. She explains that she has always wanted to be honest and open with him and she wants to continue to be. On hearing her story, David becomes enraged. "Do you have no morals, no standards, no values?" he snarls. He goes off to live the life of a hermit, saying that he would rather be alone than live with a woman like her. Ernie, having overheard all this, tells Alice that David has always been a bit of a hothead and a fool, and that she was too good for David. Perhaps, Ernie says, as the only two people on the island, they should get it on as a couple.

The students were then asked to rank-order the characters, in terms of personal preference, from 1 to 5. After a few minutes, they compared their rankings with someone else in the class and explained why they rated the people as they did. I walked around talking to students and asking them questions. After about ten minutes, I wrote all the responses on the board, and we compared the class rankings, and examined what caused them to rate the characters as they did.

[2]This teaching strategy follows a values clarification model (see Raths et al., 1966) that aroused controversy in the 1970s. It was accused, with some justification, of encouraging moral relativism if not handled with care, and many schools directly prohibited teachers from using these strategies. Troy Thayer was familiar with the controversy, and at a later time he observed a class in which I used this teaching technique, but he offered no objections.

I used this exercise to get students to talk, to take a position and defend it, and to examine human behavior and the influences on behavior. After the first round, I changed the sex of the principal characters. Instead of Alice, there is Allen who is propositioned by the raft-building Carla, and has to ask his father, Bob, for his advice. I then asked the students to evaluate the characters again, and examine if it is all right for a male to seek his father's advice before sleeping with someone.

In the middle of the game, one student asked me if he could draw on the blackboard. I asked him if we could finish the activity first.

"I already did, you wanna see my rankings?"

"No, not now. Could we wait till everyone's done? Do you want to compare yours to someone else's?"

"No, can I draw a face on the board?"

"Okay."

"What face do you want me to draw. Any face at all. I can draw anyone!"

"How about Santa Claus?"

"Okay, Donald Duck. You got it."

The teachers called him a "sick bird"; one of the guidance counselors referred to him as a "hurtin' buckeroo." Paul laughed when I told him about the student, and said that he was probably crazy, but likable and harmless. He seemed to have few friends but the other students usually put up with him, although sometimes they threatened to end his life. He often came to class with bruises and scrapes which he sometimes attributed to "extraterrestrials" or "a fall." He caused no trouble, came to class regularly, and remained cooperative and friendly even after I failed him.

Many students acted strangely in class. I did not know it at the time, but psychology had earned a reputation as a "gut." It was one of those courses upperclassmen took to balance out calculus and physics and Western civilization. Some of the brightest students in the school took psych. A few of them were enrolled in my section and were bound for the best colleges in the country, but they were in the course for a midday rest. They intended to take psych because it required little work; it would protect their grade point average; and it was different—you did not have to memorize a great deal, and you could explore feelings and attitudes that are usually avoided in high school. After the first unit test, which nearly the entire class failed, the students explained their expectations for the course. It would be hard to change them.

Ninth period, last of the day. Although four of my five classes were in room 24, I did not have two periods in the same room and every bell signaled a change of location. I grabbed my briefcase, papers, and books and ran up the stairs to my next class, another freshman social studies. No time to talk to students, no time to check my notes, no time for coffee or the lavatory. I had to shift gears from senior psychology to freshman social studies and be prepared for thirty new people in four minutes.

The class met on the main floor in the last room of an English wing. The desks were arranged in rows, and there were posters of kittens, a rabbit racing a tortoise, and television actor John Ritter. I opened my briefcase, searched for the class rosters, looked for my pencil, and fumbled with everything. I signed a program sheet for a new student, told her to take any seat, and promised her that I would get a book for her. The bell rang. I sought organization; the students talked loudly in a half-dozen small knots in the classroom. I wondered if I should have them rearrange their desks for the period, and then spend time at the end of the period returning them to their original rows. I decided against it. All this took too much time. My students were noisy, and the typing teacher next door stuck her head in my room.

"Everything okay?"

"I guess so, thanks for asking."

I had committed a minor sin: My students were disturbing other classes. I went to close the door. The halls were empty and quiet. Up and down the corridor, teachers had gotten their students under control and, I could only assume, engaged in something worthwhile. My classroom was the only one from which noise was coming. The teachers would begin to wonder, was the new guy having a discipline problem?

Indeed, I was. The freshmen by ninth period seemed to have had enough of school. Perhaps the point of diminishing returns on academic investment had set in after the eighth period; no matter how hard I tried, and how well I prepared, the results here would be considerably less than with my other freshman class. I had a great deal of trouble getting the students to quiet down at the beginning of the class, and more trouble holding their attention during class. There were three or four sections of the room that caused problems. A small knot of guys in the front constantly teased one other student. When I turned my back on them, they would knock his books to the ground or write obscene comments on his papers, causing him to turn around and respond. Students knew the timing of classes, and it was the victim who would be caught and yelled at as I turned back from the board and caught him in his acts of retaliation. It took me a while to regain my own timing as a classroom teacher and figure out what was going on.

Another group of three boys answered and asked questions with intelligence and insight, but regularly threw papers, pencils, and books at each other. They sulked when I reproached them and always apologized to me after class, promising to mend their ways, but they did not until I moved their seats. One student continued to talk no matter where I moved him, but I did not have the heart to send him to the assistant principal for my inability to interest him in the subject at the end of a long day. His behavior reflected less malice than boredom. As he said, "It's nothing personal; it's ninth period."

It was not only the boys who gave me trouble. Two girls talked all period unless we did something especially interesting in class. One girl's parent insisted that she was a "brilliant student," involved with the "gifted and talented program" every year, and that last year she "loved her social studies teacher" and he loved her. She and I were never to share this love. Another girl would take out a paperback and read it quietly whenever she lost interest in the class. She was a straight A student and I never stopped her, but I felt rejected. The struggle for the attention of the students would go on for most of the first marking period.

It was a long class. The forty-two minutes, which flew during the other periods, now seemed interminable. The material which I had barely covered in an earlier class filled little more than half of the ninth period, even with the interruptions necessary to get the students back on task. By the end of the day, I had lost my enthusiasm. I was tired of talking about the subject, tired of writing the same things on the board for the fifth time, and tired of talking to a parade of students who, by that time, had become just a blur of names and faces.

As the year went on, I noticed that few of the teachers seemed to have much energy by the last period of the day, and many of them ended class five or six minutes early. I often did the same, but whenever I did so, a small group of students would crowd around the door waiting for the bell. I did not like this, and I would use teacher-speak and teacher-logic, telling them to "Please keep your seats until the bell rings."

"All of you teachers are the same," one student told me. "Why do you care if we hang around the door? You're the ones who ended the class."

"I know, but we are gentle, sensitive people, and we are easily wounded."

"Huh! You're just afraid that it would look bad if one of the principals walked by."

They were right. It did look bad for half of the class to be straining at the harness, sniffing at the freedom behind the door. While I later admitted to them that my behavior was entirely self-serving, I demanded that they remain in their seats anyway. Some of the students had digital quartz watches which were synchronized precisely with the master clock in the office. These students could get up, walk to the door, and as I was saying "Please keep your seats until . . . ," the bell would ring, and they would leave without breaking stride.

When the final bell rang at 2:40, the students ran out with a flurry of energy unmatched by anything I had seen that day. All the classes in the school were emptied simultaneously, and the halls were crowded with gleeful, shouting students, running to lockers, greeting their friends, and embracing their lovers. The students and I shared a mutual sense of relief. They did not have to play student and I did not have to play teacher for another day, and it was difficult to tell which of us was happier. I, however, had a few more chores to complete. I had neglected to ask the students to straighten out their desks and close the windows, so the jobs were left to me. The rooms would be vacuumed every evening and the blackboards would be washed, but that was the extent of the cleaning. If the windows and desk tops were dirty, or the erasers needed cleaning, the teachers had to do it themselves or get the students to help. I turned off the lights, locked the door behind me, and walked down to the office to file my daily attendance report.

Keeping track of cuts and illegal absences was the teachers' responsibility. At the end of each school day, teachers had to compile a list of the students who were absent but who were not listed as absent on the attendance sheet. These were potential cuts. We were also to list the names of the students who were on the absentee list but who were in class. These students were the system beaters: They did not report to their first period class; they would be marked absent for the day, and their names would appear on the absentee list. Unless the teachers turned them in, they could cut classes with impunity, showing up only at those classes they enjoyed. Teachers were also to list students who were "proven cuts," and students who were "behavior problems." The assistant principal would track these students down, determine their guilt or innocence, and the teachers would have to apply the proper punishment. I was not at all sure what the punishments were; I did not have class rosters for most of the day; I had no idea who was there who was not supposed to be there; and I did not want to admit to all my "behavior problems" in the last class, so I did not turn in my daily report. A record would be kept of all the teachers and how many times they did not turn in a report. Subject supervisors would be given this information, and they would inform delinquent teachers.

I went back to room 24 to get my jacket. Mike Werge was picking up papers, rearranging the desks, and washing off the desk tops with a sponge and a cleaning solution he obtained from Mr. Churchill. I felt guilty that I had not thought to help him, although my students no doubt had contributed to the problem. He told me not to worry about it. It was just part of the job, he said, and he had gotten used to it.

Paul and I sat down in the lobby to review the day. I told him that my last class had soured an otherwise pleasant day. Satisfaction with teaching seemed to be very fragile; one bad class out of five could make it a bad day. Paul offered some advice.

"Tell 'em, if they won't quiet down, you won't teach."

"You're kidding," I said, "that works here?"

"Sure, most of them are worried about getting into college, and if you don't teach, they think they could miss something that will help them on their SATs. Try it."

I had my doubts, but I was willing to try it.

Several teachers invited us out for a drink; it was something of a Friday ritual. A group of teachers would go out to a local bar, and spend a couple of hours drinking and talking about school politics and personnel. I thanked them for the offer, but the football coach had told me that it was all right to use the weights room. I wanted to lift weights and run a few laps; if I had to coach, I should be in better shape.

Working out in the gym provided the first quiet moments of the day, and the first chance to reflect. I was anxious to establish the proper climate in class so I could teach and the students could learn. The first day, the first impressions were important for them and me. I wanted to be able to engage smart students in serious, thoughtful activities; I wanted to work on skills with slower students; I wanted to teach subject matter in a legitimate way to everyone; I wanted students to enjoy school; and I wanted them to like me. It was difficult to be a new teacher in the school. I did not know the bell schedule; there were no familiar faces; and I had no personal history with any of the students. Until I got to know them, I would be spending my entire day with strangers. They did not know what to expect from me, and for some of the students, these were difficult times. They wanted me to know how smart they were, and how their other teachers had appreciated them and rewarded them, and they wanted me to know that I was to do the same. For other students, it was a relief to them that I did not know of their past failures and problems.

I had done more teaching in one day than most college professors do in a week, and I looked forward to a weekend filled with lesson planning. I had never taught the freshman social studies course, and I had not taught psychology on a high school level. I had to prepare to teach three separate courses for five days. Not only did I have to decide what content to cover, but I also had to develop teaching techniques that encouraged students to learn that content. The students had confirmed in writing what I had already suspected: They did not like teachers who lectured all the time; it was "boring." They enjoyed classes, they wrote, in which they could talk freely and "do different things." I had to develop those different things.

As a teacher, the easiest thing to do is lecture. You find a book that has more information than the student text; you make an outline of the content; and you present it to the students, writing salient facts and names on the board and inserting a few jokes. By the time students get to high school, they are able to write notes while thinking of other things, and they can usually spring instantly from deep daydreaming to answer a question when a teacher calls on them. Troy had told me that Oldham encouraged teachers not to rely too heavily on lecture. Students could not be expected to listen to six or seven lectures a day. It was necessary, he told me, for teachers to develop strategies that encouraged students to play a more active role in the class. As someone who had spent ten years teaching the much-maligned methods of teaching courses to undergraduates, I felt a special obligation not to be boring. Preparing for class would take me at least eight hours a week, and this did not include making up and grading tests or marking papers.

After my first day of teaching, I was hot and I was tired. It had been an abrasive day. The sound of the automatic hammers penetrated my classroom, and I wondered how much longer it would take them to complete the gym floor. There was other construction going on: The roof of my wing was being retarred, and by late afternoon the stench was unbearable. An auxiliary gym was being constructed, elevators installed, and the ground behind my classroom was being landscaped. For the first six weeks of school, we would have to put up with the aroma and shout over the noise.

My contact with teachers had been limited to one lunch period and a series of four-minute conversations between classes, but my initial impressions of the faculty were positive. They seemed hardworking and proud of the school, and I was pleased that they had invited me out for a drink. I looked forward to teaching at Oldham. As I ran around the track, I counted laps. Four laps to a mile, fourteen laps for my usual three and a half miles. I thought about the day and what one of the teachers had said to me earlier that morning: "Two thousand, five hundred to go." Someone later explained that he counted every day until retirement, and during the course of each day, he would announce how many periods were left: "Six down, three to go." I decided to stop counting laps, and I ran through the town and along the shaded back roads. My first day as a teacher was over, but I did not want to start counting.

3

THE GRIND

"Hello, Mike. This is Stu. How are ya? Good, thanks. May I speak to one of your daughters?"

"Okay. Sure. Is everything all right? You want to talk to one of the kids?"

"Yeah. Beth or Jennifer, it doesn't matter. I need some expert advice and information."

"Hello."

"Hello. Jennifer? This is your Uncle Stu. What's a Smurf?"

The other end of the phone dissolved into giggles, and I asked her to put her older sister on the line. I realized that the eleven-year-old knew, but I would have to get a more sober explanation from a thirteen-year-old. Beth was able to tell me that "Smurfs are little blue people—cartoon characters," and she added, condescendingly, "You don't know what a Smurf is?"

"No, of course not. If I knew, would I call long distance to ask you? Tell me, Beth, is Papa Smurf a good guy or a bad guy, and, more important, do you think I look like Papa Smurf?"

In between laughs, she explained that Papa Smurf is the head of the Smurf clan, which populates Saturday morning television and graces the sides of lunchboxes, notebooks, and a thousand other things. Papa Smurf, I learned, has a pot belly and a white beard. He wears a red stocking cap, red leotards, and yes, she said, I did remind her of Papa Smurf. I was not overjoyed at this, but I was relieved to hear that he was generally a good guy, although he occasionally exhibited the petulance and exasperation common to those who regularly deal with the young.

After the first month of school, one of my students had playfully taunted me with "I betcha ya don't know what the kids call ya behind ya back." I admitted that I did not, and that, yes, I was curious. The students, I was told, referred to me as Papa Smurf.

The teachers feared that I would be offended, and they reassured me that nicknames were an inevitable part of the job and that most nicknames were not favorable. I imagined many other cartoon characters with whom I would not like to have been compared. Papa Smurf also sounded better after I heard one teacher referred to as Ratman, for what students considered his rodentlike features, another as Dr. Strangelove, and one vilified as Ms. Poly for flaunting the unwritten Oldham prohibition against wearing synthetic fibers.

When the students found out that I did not mind my nickname, Smurf posters, dolls, and figures appeared on my desk and on the walls. In class, the students called me Dr. P. or Doc, but in the halls some of the freshmen would yell out, "Papa Smurf, do we have any homework?" One of the posters tacked on my wall showed Papa saying, "To Smurf or not to Smurf, that is the question."

I enjoyed the decorations. They added personality and life, and I encouraged the students to bring in other things from home to put up around the room. I liked classrooms that were visually stimulating, with lots of things to look at, and read, and write on, but I had not accumulated much of this kind of material over the years, and I felt badly about depending upon the other teachers to provide decorations. The freshmen brought in posters of animals and rock groups in addition to the Smurfs. The upperclassmen said they were tired of helping teachers decorate, and the room reflected the freshmen more than the other classes. I brought in a few posters and borrowed some photographs from the library. The more often things were added and changed the better I felt about it, and the students always noticed even the smallest additions to the room. I said, without giving it very much thought, that we could put up anything that was in good taste.

One morning, before classes began, a quiet freshman boy asked me if he could put up a poster. Two or three of his friends were with him, and they all looked vaguely uncomfortable. I asked them to show the poster to me before they put it up, and he sheepishly unfurled a life-size reproduction of a blond Hollywood ingenue wearing a tiny bathing suit that revealed a great deal of skin, and showed erect nipples protruding through the body-hugging material. I was less than delighted, but I allowed them to put it up. I decided not to make an a priori judgment about community standards. If my classes thought that the poster was not offensive, overly sexist, or unnecessarily provocative, we would leave it up. If anyone objected, I would take it down. I informed the student of my ad hoc ruling, and he agreed. He seemed more than a little surprised and very pleased. His mother had told him to remove the poster from his bedroom wall, and he had kept it in his locker for two weeks, working up the courage to ask me if he could display it in class. I felt like a champion of free expression.

The girls regarded it with disdain, and they asked me if it was my idea. The freshman girls thought that it was sexist, and that it was exploitative, but they did not think it was necessary to take it down. Instead, they vowed to retaliate with posters of their own. In a few days, a delegation of girls presented me with a poster of a male body builder posing in a black bathing suit, and flexing his biceps and pectorals. The two posters now graced the front of the room, the male on the right and the female on the left, and I declared a truce in the poster war, since we had satisfied both sides.

Initially, some of the freshman boys were very uncomfortable with the body builder, and they refused to admit that the girls had an equal right to "pinups." One of the boys secretly took the poster down after school and hid it. It became a minor incident. Two of the girls had overheard him telling his friends about the theft, and they insisted that I intervene. Although we had studied the rights of citizens accused of crimes, this was real life, and I simply confronted the student and told him to give back the poster or the girls would "punch his lights out." I was prepared to tell him we had videotaped evidence, fingerprints, and sworn testimony, but it was not necessary. He returned the poster without much fuss, and then challenged me with, "How can ya let 'em put that stuff up? Waddaya, some kinda homo?"

At that point, I realized that the posters may not have been a bad idea. After all, we were studying psychology, and as social scientists we could discuss the different reactions of males and females to the posters. Were people represented as objects? Were the boys more threatened than the girls? How did the psychological conditioning of men and women differ in our society? It led to some good discussion, some agreement, some arguments, and it helped convey a message that we could talk about a great many topics as social studies students. After a few days, the posters became part of the room, blending in with the maps and bulletin boards and, for the most part, fading into the background. On more than one occasion I caught a student's eyes drifting toward one poster or the other, but I doubt that students would have thought about sex any less frequently if I had not put them up.

The posters troubled Troy, my department supervisor. He gave them both a quick examination, but his eyes returned to the barely covered starlet and he shook his head. "Well, that's something," he said. I explained how they came to be part of the decor, but I could tell that he was uncomfortable with them.

"I'm not sure they're appropriate," he told me. "I'll have to come out with a memo about what should and should not be on the walls."

"Too titillating?" I asked, taking advantage of his discomfort.

"Don't misunderstand me," he said, "I have nothing against this stuff, but schools are funny. . . ."

I did not want to take the posters down, but I realized that I had put Troy in an awkward position. He wanted to give the greatest possible latitude to the teachers, and he seemed to understand that we had dealt with the posters in an academically responsible manner. On the other hand, he was worried that if some parent or board member came into the room, they would see only the lasciviousness and not the legitimacy of our decorations. I decided to wait for the memo.

Weeks went by and no memo was sent. Although Troy had suggested that other members of the department also had "questionable" material in their rooms, no one else seemed to expect a warning. I had forgotten about it and I thought that he had too. However, on returning to school after a day off for illness, I noticed the posters had been taken down. Troy had not said anything to me about it, but the students told me what happened. On the day I was out, Troy had come into the class, before school, and quietly removed them. The incident served to reinforce the primacy of the teacher-student relationship in schools. The students and I became allied against the school and its administrators. We thought of ourselves as the good guys who celebrated the First Amendment and our ability to handle delicate issues; *they* were the bad guys, the censors who made us take our decorations down. They underestimated our maturity and sophistication. They did not understand us. We would have to stick together and fight it out against them.

MOST OF THE KIDS ARE NICE, BUT DON'T LET THE WISE GUYS GET OVER ON YOU

Slowly, through dozens of incidents, hundreds of complex interactions, and thousands of verbal and nonverbal exchanges, the students and I were able to forge a solid working relationship. Before the students could extend their trust to me, they had many questions to answer: Does this teacher keep his word? Will he make fun of me if I say something dumb? Can I talk with him? Can I confide in him? Can I be honest? One bad experience with a teacher could undo dozens of good experiences, and it was hard for me to develop good classroom rapport with no previous history in the school.

It was difficult to get to know students when you deal with them in blocks of twenty-five or thirty, but as my personal relationships with students developed, my satisfaction with teaching increased. At its best, high school teaching allows you to drop into the lives of adolescents and develop powerful connections that encourage their intellectual, personal, and emotional growth. Relationship building, however, was not easy, and I knew that students probe the limits of their dealings with high school teachers, these unusual adults who choose to work in the adolescent's world. I was warned, as are all new teachers, to be careful. Some teachers and administrators said: "Don't get too friendly with them or they'll lose respect for you." "Keep your distance." "Don't let the wise guys get over on you." "Be on your guard."

Early in the year, I kept a close watch on student behavior. Sometimes I misread the signs, thinking that they were testing me or being disrespectful when they were just playing. On one occasion it had unpleasant consequences. The students in my first period class typically talked and clowned around during the activity period. It rarely bothered me, and it gave me a few minutes to take attendance and fill out the tardiness forms. It was usually easy to quiet them for the few minutes it took to read the daily bulletin. One morning in late September the students were noisier than usual, and I had to ask for their attention several times. I glanced at the loudest student that day, Jeff, and saw that he was not looking at me, but was nervously fooling with a Spanish book while he talked. Not thinking much about it, I asked him to be quiet in Spanish.

He looked at me, and he yelled out in Spanish: "Suck my cock! Your mother is a whore!" He stared at me and smiled, and the rest of the class laughed, and one said, "That's telling him, amigo."

I walked over to Jeff, a tall, skinny, blond junior, and told him to come out in the hall with me. He followed me out into the deserted corridor as the class watched in stunned silence. I did not know Jeff very well. He sat by the window with the jayvee football players, but this was only the second week of school, we had never spoken outside of class, and I knew only a few scattered things about him: He would cut school to attend rock concerts; he wore preppy clothes; he usually drummed his books with his fingers in an abundance of nervous energy; and he did very little school work. I was furious, and when we were out in the hall, I jabbed my finger into his chest and demanded an explanation for his language. He fell back against the locker with a loud crash.

"Whatsamatta! What'd-I-say? What'd-I-do? I can't talk Spanish!

I'm failing! Honest! Ask my teacher! Ask anybody! Did I say something wrong?"

I translated for Jeff, his face turned pale, and he apologized. He really did not know what he had said. He felt bad about his language; I felt worse about my anger. I apologized to Jeff for shoving him up against the lockers. He accepted my apology and we shook hands. We spent a few minutes in the hall talking, calming ourselves, and eventually laughing about the incident. The students were absolutely silent when we returned to the class, and I finished reading the daily bulletin. I am not sure if it was as a result of this experience, but Jeff took up weightlifting that year and by June he had added about twenty-five pounds of muscle.

The noise of Jeff crashing into the lockers had drawn several of the social studies teachers out of their classes. Gus Poulos glanced at us and raised his eyebrows, and I assured him that everything was all right. The other teachers said nothing, but the story spread throughout the school in one period. The athletic director saw me during second period in the lobby, and asked me how many times I had hit Jeff. By sixth period, Paul had heard about "the fight" and wanted to know if I had hit Jeff before or after he hit me. Another teacher asked if I had hit Jeff with an open or a closed hand. Everyone seemed a little disappointed when they found out that no blows had been struck. Paul told me I had done the right thing. "It's good to show 'em that you're a little crazy, and that you won't take any crap from 'em." Another teacher reminded me that if Jeff complained, it would no doubt cost me my job.

Jeff did not complain, and he and I developed a good relationship after that day. We had experienced an unpleasant incident for which we were each partially responsible, and it seemed to bond us. He worked hard in class, and he gave me absolutely no trouble for the rest of the year; I gave him extra time and extra consideration. It left an impression on the students in the first period as well. They never mentioned it in class, but late in June, while I was chatting with Jeff in the lobby, one of Jeff's friends asked us if we recalled that day. We both admitted the vividness of our recollections, and in the scatalogical lexicon of adolescents, the student summed it up very well: "Yeah, that was really something, Jeff was shittin' and you were pissed."

By the second month, I was beginning to be more comfortable in the school, and I was less concerned about students testing me. I knew the names of all my students, some had begun to stop by my room before and after school to talk. I knew most of the teachers by sight, and I had spoken to those with whom I shared a lunch period or a preparation period. I was getting accustomed to the routine of getting up at 5:30 A.M. and letting bells run my day.

LIBRARY DUTY

My schedule was well suited for a new teacher in the building. With only two classes back to back, I had time during the day to prepare work, grade papers, and photostat tests and material for handouts. Second period library duty was a good time to prepare for my third period freshman course. I could drink coffee, review my lesson plans, and gradually wake up. I liked the library. It had 10,000 volumes, microfiche and microfilm readers, and it served as home to the school radio station. The library was light and airy, although, like most of the school, it was cold in the winter and hot in the summer. The 900s were on the left, the 500s, on the right, and biographies were in the center. It was a microcosm of the world, a bit incomplete, but more ordered than the real world and certainly quieter.

The library rules were straightforward. According to the *Oldham High School Faculty Handbook,* those on library duty were to "move about the library at least once every ten minutes to make the students aware of (their) presence," enforce the seating rules, "execute random checks" of books to see if the students had signed them out, and maintain a studious atmosphere and a low noise level. This was an easy duty. Students did not need to come to the library to hang out. If they did not have a class, they were free to go to the cafeteria, the grove, or the lobby, and this increased the likelihood that those in the library were there to study or do homework. Because there was only one faculty room, and it was typically noisy and smoke-filled, many teachers worked in the library during their free period, making the supervision of students easier for the duty teachers.

Students regarded me cautiously as I walked around the library. I was a new and therefore an unpredictable teacher. They could not be sure how I would interpret their noise level or the extent to which they were complying with the school rules.

"I'm just making sure you're aware of my presence," I explained to one student, thrusting my faculty handbook at him. He read it, smiled, and said that I was doing a great job maintaining the Oldham atmosphere, for a new guy. I admonished another not to think about sex in the library, but I walked off when he demanded to see the section in the handbook which contained that prohibition.

Students were observing the seating rules; no one was sitting on the floor; no feet were on the table. I signed passes, told kids to return magazines, and surveyed the library with some satisfaction: Everything was in order. I made a quick decision. The library was quiet enough for me to run fifty yards to the cafeteria, get something to eat and return before any harm came to the library or the students. The cafeteria served snacks from 9:00 A.M. until lunchtime. Students and faculty could stop in during their free periods for cookies, bagels, or soft pretzels. There was mustard for the pretzels and butter or peanut butter for the bagels. It was hardly gourmet fare, but the thought of a warm bagel slathered with melting peanut butter and washed down by a container of chocolate milk was enough to seduce me.

I was gone for no more than five minutes, but Sandy, the librarian, noticed that I had been missing, and when I returned she whispered out of the side of her mouth, "You just made a no-no."

"Leaving my post while on duty, ma'am? Is this similar to desertion under fire? Not a capital offense, is it?"

Sandy laughed. "No, you just can't carry food out of the cafeteria," she said. The cafeteria was for eating, the library for studying, the gym for running, and the lobby for chatting. It was a neatly ordered world, and it was one in which the teachers and students shared common prohibitions. Sandy did not mind if I drank coffee and munched bagels. She invited a relaxed atmosphere in the library and encouraged the teachers to work there and to bring classes in. She enjoyed gossip, school politics, and guess-who's-sleeping-with-whom and guess-who's-cheating-on-whom stories.

Sandy had inherited a library that had been run well, and very strictly, by a woman who had retired the previous June. From what I understood, the former librarian was quite scholarly, but a bit of an academic elitist. According to the other teachers, she was convinced that only A-level students should use the library, and then only for specific assignments, not just to browse. She ran a taut ship, as the teachers said. There was no talking, no nonsense, and no fooling around. Library duty under the former librarian was said to have been more difficult; those on duty had to enforce the rules more stringently. Sandy did not pretend to be especially academic. She could not get admitted to the state university's degree program in library science, so she matriculated for a graduate degree in educational administration at a college not noted for its strong programs. She admitted to reading mainly novels, and she described herself as a "media person," someone who was more interested in nonprint materials than in books.

Under Sandy's predecessor, the library was not well used by the math or science teachers, but for most of the teachers in other subject areas, the library had been the academic center of the school. Serious study and intelligent conversation were prized, and it was one of the few areas of the building in which teachers felt encouraged to discuss subject area topics. The former librarian was said to delight in getting obscure reference books and information into the hands of the teachers, and she encouraged the more able students to think through research assignments. Her role in the school was largely a function of her personality, and while it was nowhere stated in her job description, she provided the intellectual support and the scholarly emphasis many of the teachers needed.

Sandy may have been an adequate librarian, but to the disappointment of the teachers, she could not play the role of the scholar. The administration too seemed to be unhappy with Sandy. Don Brandt, the assistant principal who supervised her, claimed that his concern was not with a blurring of the academic focus of the library, but with what appeared to be a change in the atmosphere. There was more talking, more papers on the floor, and fewer chairs pushed under the tables at the end of each period. Don Brandt brought these problems to Sandy's attention. She knew that her job was on the line, and she decided to crack down on the duty teachers.

On a Monday morning, Sandy handed me a memo that redefined the role of the duty teachers. It read:

> As duty teachers, it is your job, first and foremost, to maintain order and quiet and remind students to put away all materials not signed out. This is not the time to grade papers, have conferences, tutor students, do lesson plans or read newspapers. It is imperative that you do your intended job, or I will have no choice but to bring these matters to Don Brandt's attention.

The teacher who had library duty just prior to mine quipped, "You can tell she's working on a degree in administration: She's begun to communicate by memo."

Sandy apologized for the memo, saying that it was not her idea, but that it had to be done. Most of the teachers agreed. "The library has to look like a high school library," one of the teachers told me. Sandy's adherence to the new policy varied from day to day. At times she allowed the library to be informal and relaxed, and at other times she seemed to expect martinetism from those on duty. On one occasion, she interrupted my conversation with a student because he was resting his leg on the seat of a chair.

"I hope that there is something wrong with your leg," she snapped.

"I have bone chips," the student replied meekly.

"Good," Sandy said, and without another word, she marched off to scold someone else.

On another day, Sandy threw two girls out of the library because she thought they were laughing at her and mocking her authority. The girls had been laughing at a joke told to them by a teacher, and I explained this to the assistant principal to save the girls embarrassment and punishment.

"You have to support the staff, sometimes even when they are wrong," he told me, but he promised not to enter the incident in the girls' records.

The new, stricter library policy caused some problems for me when I brought my own classes to the library to work. I encouraged students to work in pairs, and I allowed them to talk quietly in the library, but the noise of their conversations would sometimes get me into trouble with the teacher on duty who, according to the school rules, had the responsibility to maintain quiet even if the classroom teacher permitted talking.

"Dr. Palonsky, will this student be coming back to the library?"

"I assume so," I told the duty teacher.

"Not unless he keeps his feet off the table. I had to speak to him twice today about putting his feet on the table." The duty teacher, Willa Green, had yelled across a crowded library to tell me of this violation of the library rules. The students stared up at us; teacher-teacher conflicts were the best possible entertainment.

"If this happens again," I yelled in mock outrage, "we will not let him have children! I believe this is an unfortunate genetic defect which can be abolished in one generation if we have the courage to act. I'll bet his father did the same thing."

The class laughed, and the student said that, yes, much to his mother's chagrin, his father did put his feet on the coffee table at home. I told Ms. Green that this proved my point, but I promised her that I would speak to the student. I yelled at him privately for putting me in that situation against so formidable an adversary as Ms. Green.

Willa Green saw it as her obligation to enforce all the school rules, and she let other teachers know, in no uncertain terms, when they were lax in their adherence to regulations. Ms. Green was barely over five feet tall, and in her fifties. She was one of those hardworking, grimly serious teachers who are the backbone of public schools and other rule-governed institutions. Students would not dare to split infinitives or dangle participles in her English classes, and she would not allow them to break the school rules outside class. She followed the tardiness and attendance policies with the strictest interpretations.

Students risked a reduction in their grades if they were late to class or failed to bring a pencil or the right notebook.

One Thanksgiving, the students had constructed a fall harvest scene in the lobby with pumpkins, cornstalks, and a scarecrow dressed in a man's clothing. Someone had placed a banana in the fly of scarecrow's trousers, and Ms. Green was outraged. She fumed and fussed to anyone who would listen. Although she would not remove it herself, with all the students watching her, she ordered one of the male teachers to remove the offending fruit. Willa saw all teachers as being in need of her assistance. She scolded some about their grammar; she chastized others about their dress and she regularly offered me unsolicited advice about school policy. One day, as we walked through the lobby, we noticed two students embracing.

"Do you see that?" she asked me.

"Yes, but let's not stare. It's impolite."

"Get along to class!" she yelled at the students, and to me, she whispered: "We must all work together. We can't let those things go on. How would it look to someone from outside?"

Willa was right; it would look to outsiders like we were condoning these behaviors by not trying to stop them, but breaking up embraces or telling a couple not to hold hands always made me feel silly. Because teachers had to remind students of proper school behavior dozens of times a day, many grew to ignore common politeness and good discipline techniques. Instead of walking over to students and speaking to them privately, teachers often yelled to them across a crowded lobby or lunch room. One of my freshman students, who had just begun dating, told me of her embarrassment. "Do you know how it feels," she asked, "when one of your teachers yells at you in front of half the school for kissing your boyfriend on the cheek?"

CURRICULUM AND RESOURCES

Among the first teacher complaints I heard were that the resources were not sufficient to teach the subject matter, and the curriculum was in disarray. Members of the social studies department who taught the same courses regularly asked each other where they were in the chronology of history courses, or what unit they were teaching in topical courses. Mike Werge and I were both teaching American history and the freshman course, but we had no common planning times, nor did we teach the same courses at the same times. Because I was scheduled to coach wrestling and Mike was slated to coach track, we had commitments for two-thirds of the year that made it impossible for us to get together after school. Usually our discussions about the curriculum and resources took place during the four minutes between classes.

"What are you doing in history?" I asked him one day.

"Fascism," he answered. "There's nothing in the book. Paul De Faro gave me a couple of good articles; I'll photostat thirty copies tomorrow. I'll be done Wednesday if you want them."

"Okay, I'll stretch the New Deal; maybe I'll elect FDR to a fifth term. How much longer will you be using the anthropology books?"

"Don't use them; they're unreadable. Find something else. Talk to you at lunch."

We taught those units for which there were adequate resources. If someone photostatted an interesting article, it became part of the curriculum; if we found a good film, we used it. It was hardly a careful plan of instruction; it was a curriculum of serendipity rather than design. I discovered that I could borrow sixteen copies of B. F. Skinner's novel, *Walden Two,* from one of the English teachers. I was able to get two copies from the library, one from another school, and I had enough for a psychology unit in the accidental curriculum.

C- and E-level classes were not given very much attention. I asked Troy if it would be possible to take a topical rather than a chronological approach to teaching C-level American history. I wanted to teach topics such as immigration and war, for example, rather than trace the history of the twentieth century year by year. Troy had no objection; there was no detailed written curriculum indicating what was supposed to be covered or in what order. "Use whatever works," was his advice for the C classes. There was no master plan of instruction, although several teachers were working on "courses of study" for the courses they were teaching. Mike and I were writing the course of study for the fundamentals of the social studies as we taught it, and whatever we taught therefore became the curriculum. There was a great deal of freedom in curricular chaos.

Mike Werge had retrieved some books and supplies literally out of the trash heap of his former school. Among these resources was an excellent, if somewhat fragile, map of Japan. The department had thirty copies of *Hiroshima* by John Hersey and twenty copies of an edited reader that offered varied perspectives on the decision to drop the A-bomb. Because we had these materials, the Hiroshima Decision became the longest unit of the year, lasting well over six weeks. In contrast, the textbook had fewer than six pages on Vietnam; we had no novels to read, and no films to show. The Vietnam unit lasted only five days, and it probably would have been shorter if we had not had a videotape borrowed from Mike Werge.

Mike was a video hobbyist. He had a videocassette recorder (VCR) and a good collection of tapes, some purchased, some recorded off the air. Mike informally proposed a plan to several members of the department by which he would supply us with videotapes and a VCR for classroom use if we chipped in $10 a person. While it probably violated copyright laws to show these tapes in class, we eagerly took advantage of his offer. It gave us fresh and powerful teaching materials, and it provided us with the resources we needed. The teachers appreciated the VCR. It was certainly better than the filmstrip projector, which beeped every ten seconds to tell the teacher to advance to the next frame, and it was easier to use than the antiquated 16mm projectors, which seemed to eat films. Without question, several members of the social studies department abused this with regularity and showed any videotape even remotely related to their courses. Teachers from other departments teased that a social studies teacher would be rendered catatonic if the VCR broke in the middle of class.

The students liked the VCR, and occasionally they would suggest videotapes for class. My American history classes spent about three weeks reading Dalton Trumbo's World War I novel, *Johnny Got His Gun*. The students were intrigued and horrified by the story of a faceless, quadruple-amputee victim of the war. It took us a long time to complete the short novel because much of it had to be read in class, and parts of it were confusing for the students. There were flashbacks, mixtures of fantasy and reality, and often confusing imagery. It was a very provocative and unusually controversial book to read in a public school, and I was delighted to use it, and pleased that the students enjoyed it. The students told me that a videotape of the film version could be rented from a store in town and suggested that we watch it, and I agreed to rent the tape.

I had not seen the film since it had first been released in the early seventies. I recalled only that it was faithful to the book, having been directed by Trumbo, and I could think of no reason why we could not use it in class. I did not have a VCR at home, and I did not preview the film before using it in class, a potentially critical mistake. One of the early scenes in the movie is a flashback in which the young soldier tells his girlfriend that he is going into the army, and with her father's permission they spend the night together. It had been an interesting scene to discuss in class when we had read the book. We had compared the fictional father's reaction with speculations about their own parents' reactions, and we discussed the effects of war on moral behavior.

In the film version, however, we were all treated to one of the taboos of public school: nudity. Not a sound was heard as the girl slipped off her nightgown in full view of the draftee, my first period class, and their anxiety-filled teacher. There it was: nakedness, before

8:00 A.M., in a suburban high school. Would I have a chance for a last bagel, or would the board of education relieve me of my responsibilities immediately after class? I was seated in the back of the room, and I did not move my head, but my eyes darted from side to side and checked on the class. A student seated next to me whispered, "Are you sure we're supposed to be watching this movie?" but no one giggled; no one talked; all eyes were riveted on the monitor. They seemed to know that we were sharing a historic moment.

The videotape would take two class periods to view, and it could not be completed until the next day. I stopped the VCR about ten minutes before the end of the period to discuss some of the similarities and differences between the book and the movie, and to give a writing assignment. No one mentioned anything about the nudity. As the bell rang and the students filed out, one girl nudged me and whispered, "Aren't you proud of the way we handled that? Real mature." Although they would later claim they had seen "this sort of thing a million times, every weekend," many of the students were a little shocked; they seemed to know that school is supposed to be discontinuous with life. Before the next classes viewed the tape, I warned them of the potentially offending scene.

Despite videotapes and borrowed books, resources were a constant problem. Mike Werge became frustrated having to spend so much time "scrounging around" for materials. "We're just entertainment for the students. Without enough books and articles to read, we're reduced to doing monologues about history. It's like putting on 900 shows a year."

Troy blamed the central administration, claiming that his requests for materials were met with indifference. The building principals agreed with Troy, but they argued that we had a photostat machine, so resources should not be a problem. Ultimately, they said, the teachers should "make do." The recommended solution was to photocopy everything needed for class. We were encouraged to copy magazine and journal articles, newspaper editorials, and even whole chapters from books. When I asked Troy how we could get extra copies of *Walden Two,* he only half-jokingly suggested photocopying them. The budget for photocopying seemed limitless, and it was the linchpin for all teaching. If the math teachers did not have enough workbooks or language teachers needed additional texts, they were told to copy them. English, science, math, social studies, special education, and industrial arts all competed for the photocopying machine.

Meeting the demands of sixty-six teachers, three administrators, five guidance counselors, two nurses, eight auxiliary personnel, and seven members of the office staff was too much for the ten-year-old machine, and we became quite friendly with the repairman. Each teacher had one preparation period, and it was often spent pacing up and down outside the photocopying room waiting for the machine to be free or repaired. Six-thirty in the morning or six-thirty at night, no matter when you got there, the machine was being used. You began to regard your colleagues as hostile competitors who could keep you from preparing a test or class materials. Midway through the year, the inevitable occurred: The machine suffered a serious breakdown. The cataclysmic news was greeted with mourning and outrage, and it seemed as if the entire school was coming to a halt. With no photo-copying machine the school could not function, and the panic was not relieved until Cal Bullinger announced the acquisition of a new im-proved machine that could automatically copy on both sides, reduce in two sizes, collate, staple, and copy blue originals. He stood behind it, smiling like a proud parent, as each teacher was given an instruc-tional briefing by a company representative.

C-LEVEL CLASSES

During one department meeting, I expressed dissatisfaction with the texts. "If we took everything worthwhile in that C-level American history textbook," I said, "and multiplied it by 100, we could still fit it all inside a thimble!" I was exaggerating, but for emphasis I added that the major benefit of the text was probably as a sleep inducer for chronically insomnious students.

Troy did not say anything about my comments at the meeting. He seemed to understand that I was just blowing off steam during one of those rare times when teachers have a sympathetic audience. Later he told me that I had offended some of the teachers who had been part of the book selection process, and he explained it had been the best book for the money. Funds for new texts were always limited, he told me, and this text was selected because it was the least expensive. He admitted that it was dull, but it had the dates and facts spelled out, and there were good graphics. I asked for the names of the offended faculty members so that I could assure them that my attack was academic, not ad hominem, but Troy said it was better that I did not know. Several members of the department later told me that Troy had selected the text without faculty consultation.

If there were limited funds, the selection of an inexpensive book might be understandable, but it was sadly ironic that the students with the least interest in the subject, and probably the least interest in reading, were given the dullest books. There was little else available to supplement these texts. There were no special materials and no special programs for the C-level students. It seemed to confirm Troy's view that "no one really cares about the Cs." According to the district's curriculum policy, "students were placed in homogeneously grouped courses according to ability, achievement, interest, and goals." There were four designations:

H = Honors
A = Above average
C = Average
E = Skills emphasis

Homogeneous groupings were used only in certain courses: English, mathematics, social studies, sciences, and foreign languages. These were the courses used to determine class rank, a comparative listing of all the students in the class. Letter grades were assigned for each course, but they were transposed to numerical grades and a weighting factor was used to determine rank in class:

Weight Factor

GRADE	HONORS	A	C	E
A	7	6	5	4
B	6	5	4	3
C	5	4	3	2
D	4	3	2	1
F	0	0	0	0

If a student received a final grade of B in a C-level group, for example, his or her grade was assigned a weight factor of 4. Weight factors were multiplied by the credits assigned to each course (typically 5.0 for a full-year course). The product was called the "rank points," and for every student the total number of "rank points" was divided by the total number of qualifying class rank credits the student had taken. The school referred to the quotient of this division as "rank points weighted." These were then arranged in descending order to indicate where a student ranked in class. The greater the "rank points weighted," the higher the student ranked in class.

The system of rankings and groupings was considered complex but necessary for a district in which the students knew there was life after high school. Between 85 and 90 percent of a typical graduating class at Oldham High School attended some type of postsecondary institution, and the class ranking formula was designed to make the competition for college more equitable. Some teachers, administrators, and board members feared if there were no weight factors, students would take mainly C-level courses, pad their averages, and look better to competitive colleges than students who had taken more of the difficult A-level courses but received grades of B. Many students at Oldham had good grade point averages, but unless they took honors or A-level courses, they did not rank very high in their class.

I was told by Troy and by several members of the guidance department not to be concerned if I gave my C-level students high grades, because the weighting system would take care of it. The C students could please their parents every academic quarter and still not fool the more selective colleges. I was also told by some of the teachers that because the C-level at Oldham was equal in ability to A-level in most of the other schools in the state, giving them good grades might not be inappropriate. The C-level students at Oldham were said to look bad only in contrast with the A-level students. Compared to other students in the state, they were said to be of the highest level.

The origins of this myth were difficult to track down. The students repeated it often and seemed to believe it. A few of the teachers claimed they had read it, perhaps in some State Education Department document, they said. But most of the building administrators, guidance counselors, and teachers who had taught elsewhere knew this was not true. The story was probably started by a classroom teacher who wanted the C-level students to feel better about themselves. In fact, Oldham C students read a shade below grade level, and their Scholastic Aptitude Test scores typically were at, or below, the national average.

Nearly half of all the students in the school were enrolled in C and E-level courses, and according to the head of pupil personnel services, far more belonged at these levels. He told me that because of parental pressures and unreasonably high levels of aspirations, there were too many C-level students in A-level courses and too many A-level students taking honors work. The E-level designation tended to disappear after the freshman year, but it was not because students' skills had improved. When students first entered the school in their freshman year, they could be convinced to enroll in "skill development" courses. Parents were presented with the evidence of their child's deficiencies in mathematics, reading, and writing, and E-level course sections were created. By the sophomore year, students and parents learned that those in E-level courses suffered a great deal of ridicule from other

students, and students refused to take courses with an E-level designation. There were no E-level courses in social studies in the sophomore
year.

As a new teacher, I did not know of the stigma attached to the
E-level. I taught two C-level history courses and they were over-
enrolled; board policy limited class size to thirty students. We were to
divide the classes into three sections, one of which was to be an E
section that I would teach. The students were adamant in their refusal
to go into a designated E-level. They admitted they needed help with
basic skills, but it was better to get less help in a C-level course than
suffer the ignominious designation of an E. The building principals
and I agreed to split the classes into C-level sections, one a lower level
C than the others, but the board refused. They wanted a designated
E-level class or a split based on random assignment. The students
insisted on the latter.

As in most schools, the Oldham teachers had a preference hierarchy for grade and ability levels. Most of them favored seniors, followed in descending order by juniors, sophomores, and freshmen.
Clearly a majority of teachers preferred A or H-levels to the C and
E-levels. There was compassion in their eyes when I told them that I
would be teaching two C-level courses and two freshmen courses. One
teacher sighed and looked toward the ceiling. "Good luck," she said,
"that's an awful thing to do to you. At least you do have one senior
A course."

Most of the teachers spoke glowingly of the students who were
accepted into Ivy League schools and the "seven sisters," although
these students typically represented less than 5 percent of the class.
Between 20 and 25 percent of a graduating class, most of them C-level
students, could be expected to enroll in the two-year county college.

There were more C-level students than H-level students, but they
were largely invisible; few teachers seemed to pay much attention to
them. Although they dressed and looked not unlike the A-level students, there were differences between the two groups. The C-level
students were absent more frequently than A-level students. The daily
absence rate for the entire school was about 10 percent, but A-level
students had an absentee rate of about 5 percent and C-level students
had an absentee rate of over 20 percent. There were days when between one-fourth and one-third of a C-level class would be out. They
cut class more often; they caused more trouble; and they were less apt
to be forgiven when they were caught. Substitute teachers would leave
a note for me indicating those students and classes that had caused
them trouble. Typically, they would name the C-level.

Some teachers had been assigned C and E classes as chastenment. After teachers are awarded tenure, it is very difficult to get rid of them or punish them. At Oldham, poor teaching or failure to follow the rules could result in a tenured teacher being assigned to cafeteria duty and all lower-ability classes. In a few cases, the board of education had voted to withold teachers' annual raises, resulting in the loss of several thousand dollars. One social studies teacher had his increment withheld and was assigned two C-level freshman classes for weak teaching and failing to turn in adequate lesson plans.

"What do I think of Cs? Keep the best, and shoot the rest," he said, but there was no malice in his voice.

Paul De Faro and Larry Silverman were among the few teachers who told me that they liked working with C classes. Paul had grown up in a working class community and was the first person in his family to have been graduated from college. He was completing a graduate degree in medieval history; he held down a construction job in the summers; and he enjoyed teaching the harder to teach students. "The kids are almost too good here," he told me. "If I didn't teach some of the slower classes, I'd think I was stealing money."

Paul taught a special group of C and E-level students known as the learning community. The students in this class were the most disaffected students in the school. Not only did they have trouble academically, but they were not the least bit compliant with the Oldham tradition. They did not like the school, its regulations, restrictions and courses, and they let their teachers know about it. Paul had volunteered to work with these students in a team teaching program with an English teacher and a mathematics teacher. Said Paul, "These are more like the kids I grew up with. I like them."

Larry Silverman had grown up in a small town in the coal mining region of central Pennsylvania. He admitted that he had not done well in high school, nor had he enjoyed it, but he believed that his background and personality made him a good teacher for the slower students. He claimed the secret to teaching C-level students was the ability to motivate them. "I was a turned-off student, and I know what it's like to be bored in school," he said. "I'm a big believer in a variety of motivational strategies. You gotta know when to speed up, when to slow down. You have to know how to push these kids without frustrating them. I understand the C kids better than most of the teachers here do."

Larry was a big man. He stood a few inches over six feet tall; his 270 pounds were unevenly distributed on his body, with the midsection receiving a disproportionate share. He assumed a heavy load of

C-level classes after he became the supervisor of the mathematics department. He had given the teachers in his department their choice of classes to teach. To accommodate his teachers, all of whom chose A-level classes, he had to pick up more of the C classes, and he learned to like them. Larry was enormously enthusiastic about teaching, and he claimed the classroom was his stage. "Hey, I love it," he said. "You couldn't get me out of the classroom. I'm happiest when I'm in front of the class. You know, I do anything, I mean *anything* to get a kid's attention. I yell. I jump around. When they're not paying attention, I lay down on the floor and kick my heels. I'm telling ya, ya gotta be an actor to be a teacher."

He liked to teach the C-level students because he felt he could have the greatest impact as a teacher with these students. Larry taught algebra and geometry, and he believed the A students would succeed with or without any special effort on the part of the school. He regarded the C students as the marginal students; they were the people the school could affect with good teaching. It was with C students, he felt, that teachers could make a difference, and it was in those classes that he would put his energies. "If the smart kids don't learn calculus here, they'll learn it in college," he said. "If the C kids don't learn math here, they'll never get it!"

Several members of the faculty said that Larry was a teacher who gave a great deal to his students. They credited him for his unflagging support of the C-level students and his ability to get a lot of work out of them. When I arrived at Oldham, Larry was still teaching C courses, but he was no longer the supervisor of the math department. When one of the sending districts withdrew from the Oldham-Webster Regional High School District, Larry found himself with less seniority than the supervisor in another high school. That person replaced him as the supervisor of Oldham under the same seniority rule that brought Troy Thayer to the school as the supervisor of the social studies department.

New teachers inevitably got the least desirable courses. No one in the department had more C-level classes or more preparations than I. "It could have been worse," groused another teacher upon hearing my schedule. "They could have given you E-level fundies! There's nothing worse than that."

Most of the teachers agreed that would be the least desirable course to teach, but the athletic director interrupted. "Hey, I teach the E-level fundies. They're okay. Hey, there's really nothing wrong with them. I kinda enjoy them; they're funny. Listen to this, you'd enjoy this, Stu; probably happened a lot when you were teaching college. I had my E kids in the library for freshman library orientation, right. In the middle of Sandy's lecture, one of the kids barfs all over the table, just gets up and pukes his guts out. Now what's she gonna do, huh? One kid barfing his guts out stops the whole show. Funniest thing you ever saw. Now that's what an E class is all about."

Most of the other teachers could not muster even this kind of enthusiasm for the lower-ability groups, and they repeated their favorite regurgitation stories.

"Remember the kid who puked at the basketball game. . . ."

"That was nothing. The greatest barf I ever saw was in Madison Square Garden," said one of the teachers. "Some guy from a college team threw up all over fifty people. . . ."

The C students knew that very few of the teachers delighted in them as students or enjoyed them as people.

"Boy, did they ever screw you," a C-level senior boy said to me before class.

"How's that?" I asked.

"Givin' ya us. Why didn't they put you in an honors class. You're a good teacher."

"Thanks, but don't you guys deserve good teachers?"

"Yeah, but that's not the way it works around here. You got screwed."

The C-level students had trouble expressing themselves in class, and they did not like to write. The district had embarked on a program to encourage writing in every class. We had inservice workshops and guest speakers to help us with our writing assignments, and all the teachers had to keep a log of their writing activities. Few teachers participated in the decision to include writing as a new curricular emphasis, and some resented it. "Every year they discover a new crisis! Three years ago it was reading! Now it is writing! What will it be next year? Why can't they just let us teach?" asked a French teacher.

I tried to combine the teaching of writing skills with reading and library skills in the C classes. I gave each student carefully chosen, discrete bits of information to look up, and a series of short writing assignments. I told them they could not use encyclopedias, but I allowed the students to work in pairs. Library work gave me a chance to help students individually, and not let them "fade out" as they did in the classroom.

One day in the library I noticed one of my students sitting and staring out the window.

"John, what's the matter?" I asked.

"I can't find anything," he whispered. "My partner's absent. I don't know where to start."

"Did you look at the card catalog?"

"Okay, good idea."

"John, do you know how to use the card catalog?"

"Can I wait until my partner comes back? He'll be back tomorrow. He's got all the notes."

I showed John how to find the book he needed. John and many other C students had tremendous difficulties in the library. They had all been shown several times how to use the card catalog and the various commercial indexes, but it was hard for many of them to remember from one year to the next. For some, it was easier to sit all period than to expose their ignorance; the library was just one more frustration.

"Doc, I looked everywhere," a student told me. "There's nothing on Roosevelt in this whole library! Ya gotta let me use the encyclopedia! I'm serious."

"Do you know what they call a book written about another person's life?" I asked.

"Yeah, a biography."

"Right. Did you look in the biography section? There's an alphabetical arrangement of books according to the last name of the subject. Look under the Rs."

"It's not there. I'm serious. Can I go to the bathroom? I'll look again when I get back. Really. I'm not kiddin, I gotta go."

I let him go. Under the best circumstances, not much was accomplished in any one period in the library. By the time the students got there and located a book, encyclopedia, or microfiche, they had little more than fifteen or twenty minutes before they had to put things away. There was a lot of motion, but not much action. There was a nice microfilm source for *The New York Times,* and microfiche of many magazines and periodicals, but there was only one microfiche reader and two microfilm readers, and a lot of time was spent waiting for a machine to be free.

I enjoyed the time with students away from class. The C students were interesting and fun to talk to whenever we could leave the narrow focus of the subject matter. Many of them worked after school; they had interesting experiences and insights; they were certainly less academically pretentious and less concerned about impressing their teachers than the A students. One student came up to me in the library, laughing, with her finger pointing to an open page of a history book. "Did you know that the *Maine* was a battleship?" she asked. "I just read that. I used to think that the Spanish blew up the state!"

"Yeah, Dale, I think I did know that, but thanks for reminding me."

"Do the Cubans speak Spanish or Cuban?"

"I don't know, Ellen. Ask Jeff. He's the Spanish expert."

"Hey Doc, that film we saw in class, *All Quiet on the Western Front.* Was it about Germans or Americans?"

"They were American actors portraying Germans."

"Are you sure, Doc? They didn't talk with German accents."

"Trust me on this one. By the way, what's for lunch?"

"Dog. We had cat yesterday. They never serve cat two days in a row."

I thanked him, and noted the time. "Okay," I said loudly in my authoritative teacher voice. "We have two minutes to go. Put your books away; push the chairs under the tables; straighten up the encyclopedias; pick up the papers around the table; put away your hacky sacks; don't throw the gummy bears around the room; thank the librarian for a wonderful day; see ya tomorrow. Quietly, please, quietly."

I would have liked to spend two or three days a week in the library, but that was not possible. There were many other social studies and English classes competing for library time. My classes averaged about two visits every third week. We prepared for debates, looked up material to be discussed in class, and did some "research." The C students had a narrow range of interests, and the library provided a greater array of materials, and offered a better chance of interesting them than I could in class. Although most of the C-level students could read and write, they operated on a literal level. They had a great deal of difficulty dealing with abstractions. Books and films that jumped from past to present to future confused them, but they could be touched by the good films and the good books.

The school had a copy of the 1940 Darryl F. Zanuck film version of John Steinbeck's *The Grapes of Wrath.* When I discovered the film, it became part of the curriculum. It had been purchased for the English department with funds from a student money-making project. My classes enjoyed the film and did not object to the writing projects I assigned every night. I told them there was one Academy Award winner among the cast, and I asked them to write a letter nominating the person they thought most deserved it. We also wrote letters to President Roosevelt recommending solutions to the Depression; we wrote alternate endings to the film; we cast the film with contemporary actors, and we talked about the Joad family. The film and the problems of the Joad family seemed to capture the imagination of most of the students. It took a week to view the film, discuss it, and write about it; and it may have been the most satisfying week I spent as their teacher. I had found something that had legitimate content for the C students to consider; they worked very hard; they did good work; and they seemed to enjoy it.

There was, however, a shortage of materials that could whet the curiosity of those who were not especially excited by school. I had no other films to rival *The Grapes of Wrath,* and no other books to match *Johnny Got His Gun.* Students liked the videotapes, but sometimes these were confusing. I showed the Public Broadcasting System's "Time Was" series so often that many of the students probably thought Dick Cavett was their regular teacher. I also showed them an illegally taped version of "FDR: That Man in the White House" starring Robert Vaughn in a one-man show, but the many references to historic personalities, foreign heads of state, and political rivals confused the students, and I had to stop the tape often to explain the characters.

"Okay, do you know who 'Babs' is?" I asked.

"Yeah, his wife. Who's Lucy Mercer?"

"His lover," yelled out another student.

"That's awesome! Didn't Kennedy have a lover?" asked the first student.

"We'll get to that," I said. "Are there any other questions about this videotape? Do you understand who all the characters are? Do you know which party is which?"

"No. Was Roosevelt a Democrat or a Republican?"

"Democrat," I said.

"Okay. Kennedy was a Republican, right?"

"No, he was a Democrat, too. Remember Harding, Coolidge, and Hoover were Republicans. Reagan was a Democract, but now he's a Republican."

"Doc, I'm having trouble keeping all this straight. Can you give us an easy way to remember it?"

"I'll try. Remember, Democrats have more affairs than Republicans. If you can't recall if a president was Democrat or Republican, ask yourself, 'Would anyone sleep with this man?' "

"Okay, no problem. I got it. Now which one has the elephant?"

"Will this be on the test?"

The students laughed. They knew that I had been kidding, and they were glad of the opportunity to tease me in return. We talked about party affiliations during the New Deal period and during the present time, and we went back to the tape. Whenever I presented new material, the C students in particular were concerned with the extent to which they had to learn it. They would ask, "Are we responsible for this stuff?" "Will it be on the test?" "Do we have to write this down?" "Do we have to know this?"

A large number of the Oldham students did not know how to take notes from classroom discussions. The C-level students in particular seemed confused about what was important or what to write down. They seemed to write only those things I wrote on the board, and in the beginning of the year, they asked me to write everything in outline form so they could take it down more easily. In other schools I had observed teachers who handed out a ditto sheet with a content outline before every class, but the Oldham teachers did not resort to this. I tried to get the C students to decide what was important after every period by asking different students to summarize the class discussion. Initially, this was difficult for them, and one student, unable to find the right words, angrily told me this was my job, not his. Another student asked me if I did this with my A-level classes.

The C students were self-conscious about their academic abilities, and they were curious to know if I treated them in the same way that I treated my A-level classes. On several occasions I combined classes with other teachers to show a film, or for panel discussions involving several teachers. If the other classes were composed of A-level or honors students, my usually gregarious and uninhibited C students would neither ask questions nor make comments. They sometimes did not understand the humor of A-level students, and they occasionally had trouble following the verbal interactions. Referring to the students in the honors class, one of my C students warned me, "Never bring that type of kid in here again."

Very little content was covered in C-level classes, but I had to vary my methodology a bit so one day could be distinguished from another. Sometimes we used simulation games, debates, role-playing games, and class presentations. Other times there were films, videotapes, and the library, along with in-class reading and discussions. It was not easy for me to think up writing projects that would interest them, and harder to find the time to read them. It was also frustrating to spend ten minutes writing comments on a paper that had not been written seriously, and then have a student look only at the grade and toss the paper away. I tried correcting papers with the student looking over my shoulder, but this was very time-consuming. It would take me a week to correct and comment on one class set. I seemed always to be buried under an avalanche of student papers; I was rarely sure if they had learned very much; and I wondered if the things they were learning were worthwhile.

A-LEVEL FUNDIES

The freshmen were at the bottom of the teachers' list of preferred students. Most of the teachers responded that the freshmen were "too young" when I asked how they liked teaching them. The freshmen were born in the same year I was drafted into the army, and teaching freshmen was a constant reminder of aging. The Vietnam war did not touch most of them more personally than the Spanish-American War. They could not recall when fast food hamburgers were cheaper, and they could remember no president before Jimmy Carter. The teachers preferred the older students too because they could talk to them about a wider range of subjects. Freshmen had few experiences; they did not often date; and they did not drive cars.

One social studies teacher presented a cynical analysis of teacher preferences. "Look who goes into teaching," he said. "They were just average shnooks in high school. They were the kids at the bottom of the A classes; the kids with B averages; the second-string jayvee basketball players; the band fags. Now they're teachers and they can hang around with the best athletes in the school, the best-looking kids in school, and the smartest kids in the school. It's their chance to be what they were not in high school: Now they can be cool for the first and only times in their lives. If you're cool, why would you want to hang around with freshmen?"

The freshmen understood their low status and they tried hard to please their teachers. The A-level freshmen had a long history of doing well in school, and they expected their teachers to like them. There was no H-level in the freshman year, and the A classes represented the brightest and shiniest students in the grade. It was from the A classes that all the freshmen class officers were elected. Students in these classes ran the student council, and organized the dances, money-making projects, dance marathons, and candy sales. The A-level freshmen were competitive, grade-conscious, and under pressure from home to do well. They quickly learned the Oldham game called "grade grubbing." Any grade of less than a B was considered unacceptable, and students would appeal, whine, moan, pout, and protest as long as the teachers would listen or until they raised the grade. At least 15 percent of the freshmen had taken some form of privately administered intelligence test, and many of them claimed they were in the "near genius" range as measured by IQ tests. They could discuss the entrance requirements of Ivy League schools and the Scholastic Aptitude Test scores necessary for admission to a dozen other schools.

There was no shortage of hubris among some of them. During Sandy's library orientation lecture, two of the girls in my third period freshman class decided they understood the Dewey Decimal System and the rest of the library well enough to close their notebooks, tune out, talk, and brush their hair. Loud enough for me to hear, they discussed their scores on the SAT exams they had taken the previous year. This test, usually administered to college-bound seniors, is also given experimentally to a large number of twelve-year-olds who show unusual promise. Although the form of the exam differs somewhat from those given the seniors, both girls had scores more than adequate to gain automatic admission to the state university, and I mentioned it to them.

"Well who wants to go there?" one asked. "I'm shooting for Yale, Princeton, or MIT."

I wilted, and when Sandy told me to ask them not to brush their hair until the bell rang, I was glad of the opportunity to reproach them.

They were smart and they knew it, and while on occasion they could be nasty and arrogant, they were generally passive and cooperative. The guidance counselors said they placed a very high value on compliance. When these students did not like what was going on in class, they retreated inwardly; they withdrew and became quiet rather than challenge the teachers. Some of them wrote notes to me indicating that while they might appear not to be paying attention in class, they probably were. One student wrote, "I'm real smart and I get bored easily. I hope it doesn't bother you if my mind wanders."

During a psychology unit, we discussed the nurture-nature controversy as part of our consideration of intelligence. We read the text and a few articles that gave opposing views. One side indicated that intelligence was a heritable trait determined largely by biology and only slightly affected by the way an individual is raised. The other side argued that intelligence, as measured by standardized tests, was influenced by heredity, but the greatest single variable determining scores on IQ tests was the environment in which the individual grew up.

For homework, I asked them to decide whether they supported the nurture or the nature argument, formulate a hypothesis which reflected their view, and design an experiment that would test their hypothesis. The next day, one student suggested we surreptitiously take 100 newborn infants from the inner city and randomly place them with families in Oldham and Webster to be raised. At the same time, he said, we would take 100 newborns from this area and have them raised by city families. After fourteen years, he continued, we could measure their IQs, and compare them to the average IQ in the areas in which they grew up. If the individuals' IQ scores were similar to others in the areas in which they were raised, we could assume that intelligence is primarily a function of environment. If the IQ scores were more harmonious with the average IQ in the areas from which they were taken, we could assume heredity is the primary determinant of IQ.

The class enjoyed the student's research proposal and gave him a round of applause. The students were very good with this type of mental gymnastics. They enjoyed academic games and challenges, and they would light up and come alive. After class, two students told me how much they had liked the exercise and complimented me: "Good class, Dr. P. Very well done." I was surprised to feel so buoyed by the compliments of fourteen-year-old students, and in the future, after classes that I thought had gone unusually well, I listened for, but rarely heard, similar approbation.

We studied the social scientific method and read a fairly complex book that introduced them to the problem-solving techniques of social scientists. The text was out of print, and there were not enough copies for all my students, so we had to read it in class. The book introduced students to inductive and deductive logic, hypothesis formation, statistical analysis, and prediction. All but the brightest students had to wrestle pretty hard with the the ideas in the book. To reward their effort, and to see if they understood some of the book's more difficult concepts, I had them read excerpts from Joe McGinnis's book, *Fatal Vision.*

The book, which was then a best seller, told the story of Dr. Jeffery MacDonald, who was accused and convicted of killing his wife and two children. MacDonald was serving a life sentence, but was appealing his conviction. I asked the students to hypothesize about his guilt or innocence, and present their data and arguments using either inductive or deductive logic. I may have been catering to their interest in violence, but they became highly involved in the case. They discussed the book and the assignment with their parents, and I heard them argue about it in the cafeteria. I found several of them reading trial testimony in the library during their free periods. They pored over documents, drew floor plans of the house in which the murders took place, and made careful presentations in class. They were further intrigued when I told them that Dr. MacDonald, his wife, and I had gone to high school together, and that we had been tracked in academic honors classes similar to those in which they now found themselves. Could I bring him in as a guest speaker, they asked. I had to admit that while I may appear pretty powerful to freshmen, I could not grant pardons.

These were the activities with which I started the year, and if the students thought this was a promise of things to come, they could have had me arrested for false advertisement. The curriculum guide for the fundamentals of social studies course was a single page that listed the seven units to be taught (critical thinking, behavioral sciences, political science, economics, geography, area studies, and ancient history) and the duration of each unit. Books had to be shared with the other teachers, and the scheduled time of the units had to be adhered to, but we were free to teach anything. We used some of the textbooks in their entirety, parts of others, and photocopied articles and anything we could find that looked as though it would interest students.

We spent a lot of time on political and economic learning. Troy reminded me several times "to hit the isms very hard in the freshman year." The isms were capitalism, communism, and socialism, and students had to be told that capitalism was good and socialism was bad; democracy was good and totalitarianism was bad. The harder I hit the isms, the more the students slumped back in their chairs. Some of the students had covered this same material in the eighth grade, and they were bored. All the students disliked the book we had for this unit, and with little supplementary material for them to read, I had to lecture or take them to the library. The freshmen were a tough audience; they paid reasonably good attention, but it took very powerful materials and enthusiastic teaching to keep them with me. Most of the time the books were not provocative or even interesting, the classes were not that exciting, and the students sat back and politely observed what was going on.

To try to get the students more actively involved in the course, I assigned several research papers during the year. The first paper asked them to choose some social problem, describe it, and develop several hypotheses that could lead to its solution. I allowed them to select their own topics. The most frequently selected topic was child abuse, followed by adolescent suicide, runaways, alcoholism, divorce, drug abuse, and teenage prostitution. The assignment called for a paper that was to be eight pages in length, and we spent one day a week for five weeks in the library. I allowed students to work in pairs to make the assignment easier for them and for me. There were twelve separate parts to the paper, and the students could divide responsibility for each section between them; teaming up on the assignment would also reduce the number of papers I had to read by one half.

About two weeks before the papers were due, a delegation of students from both of my freshman classes came to see me.

"Dr. P., we have some questions about the paper."

"Okay," I said, confidently, pretending that I had answers for an assignment that I was, for the most part, making up as I went along.

"Is it true that both people will get the same grade for the paper?"

"Yes, that's true," I said, although I had given this no thought at all.

"That isn't fair. What if one person works hard and the other does not. They both get the same grade. That's like socialism."

"You're right. But ultimately the hard worker's investment in labor and capital will pay off, and he will be rewarded. You know, like the three little pigs. The students who do not work hard now will be devoured by the wolves of ignorance when they get to college. Anyway, I think you're complaining because you chose the wrong partner. Next time you can all work alone or choose someone smart to work with on the projects. Okay?"

"Okay. One more question. You said that the papers had to be typed. Does a word processor count as a typewriter?"

I thought that the students would ask permission to turn in handwritten papers, and I was prepared to agree (if they were neat), but a request to turn in computer-typed papers was new for me. I told them that it was all right and, yes, they could use word processing paper if they ripped off the perforated edges. A few students asked for an extension until January 1, because they had been promised a computer for Christmas. (The school conducted a survey which found that 25 percent of all the students, and 40 percent of the freshmen and sophomores, had a computer at home.) Several students had their parents or their parent's secretary type the paper, and about half of them banged the keyboards themselves. No one asked to turn in a handwritten paper.

Their academic skills and intellectual abilities were invigorating. The A-level freshmen were capable of more rigorous thought than the C-level juniors and seniors, and they were more willing to take risks than the A-level upperclassmen. They were not afraid of making mistakes, and some of their classroom questions, guesses, and opinions could shake me from the dulling routines of teaching to consider the social sciences in new ways. We also talked about topics that were tangential to the subject, such as politics and current events, and some topics that had nothing to do with the subject, such as music and computers. They loaned me record albums and diskettes of computer games, and groaned when I shared my tastes in music with them.

I enjoyed the freshmen as people. I found myself looking forward to my freshman classes and waiting at the door before class. They would enliven my day, and I was genuinely glad to see them. We would exchange greetings and smiles, and make whatever small talk the four minutes between classes allowed. Some of the students were shy and would slip by, mumbling hellos and glancing at me only through the corners of their eyes, while others would slap hands and give "high fives," seeming to enjoy being physical. They were open and enthusiastic, and they would bring in wonderful stories, experiences, and bits of information. One day a student asked me if I wanted to see what she had just learned in biology. I nodded yes, and she grabbed my arm and pulled some of the skin from the back of my hand and then released it.

"See how slowly the skin goes back to its original shape compared to mine?" she asked as she performed the same experiment on her arm. "That means you're getting old, Doc. Your skin loses its stretchiness! Isn't that neat?"

Real neat, I admitted.

I was eager to begin my freshman classes, and I often skipped taking attendance formally and just looked around to see who was absent. It was fun to work with open, enthusiastic students. They knew how to please teachers. They handed in their work on time, and it was well done; they were typically quiet even when they were bored; if you were moderately interesting, they rewarded you with rapt attention; and they would usually pull you out of a jam. If no one initially volunteered during an in-class reading, someone would eventually raise a hand and read, even if it meant removing an orthodontal retainer from his or her mouth. Whenever I was observed by Troy or one of the administrators, the students put on a show they called "Let's play perfect kids." They would pretend excitement for everything I did; they would laugh at every joke; and they would fight to answer every question, and pretend to appreciate everything I said. It was a performance they had rehearsed many times for their parents, but it never failed to impress administrators.

I relaxed so much with the freshmen that it occasionally put me in conflict with the school rules, especially toward the end of the year. School became less formal by spring. By then, teachers had developed relationships with their students; they knew what to expect from one another, and they could relax more than they could at the beginning of the year. Students and teachers could wear shorts to school (if they were not too short). The emphasis on covering material decreased. Proms became major topics of conversation and interest; students were excused early on prom days, and teachers could be talked out of giving an assignment just before or just after prom weekends.

On the first warm day of spring, water pistols seemed to materialize with the crocus and proliferate like crab grass. Everyone from the president of the senior class to the lowliest and most demure freshman seemed to have at least one water pistol. A student in my last period freshman class had a small black water pistol, wrapped in a plastic baggie, in her handbag.

"Mary, can I see that, please?" I asked her.

"Oh, don't take it away. School's almost over."

"I won't take it away. Stop whining, I just want to see it."

Mary handed the water pistol to me, and I admired the style and quality.

"These are similar to the water pistols I had in high school," I said. While pretending to admire the gun, I pointed the barrel toward her, squeezed the trigger, and squirted her. "Oh, I'm sorry, Mary, I had no idea that would happen."

She knew better, and when I gave the gun back to her, she squirted me once. The word soon spread among the students: Papa Smurf had a water pistol fight with his class. Other teachers were confiscating them and smashing them under their heels, and I was using them and returning them in direct violation of school policy.

By the next day, my third period class seemed to be armed with enough water pistols to put out a major fire. I feigned anger and seriousness of purpose. I confiscated all the water pistols, but promised to return them at the end of the period. A few minutes before the bell rang, I drenched the entire unarmed class with their own water pistols. I returned the guns to them, as I promised, and they emptied into the halls to reload. The windows were open in room 24. The ground sloped away sharply from the building and what appeared to be about a ten foot drop to the ground was, in reality, less than four feet. A freshman girl, with a mischievous gleam in her eye, led the charge, brandishing a reloaded water pistol. I taunted her and at the last minute, I jumped out of the window as the stunned class watched and squirted in impotence. The next day, I imposed a truce that held for the last month of school, despite numerous cease-fire violations by both sides.

SENIORITIS

I had not expected to enjoy teaching the freshmen as much as I did, but psychology turned out to be somewhat of a disappointment for me. About half of the students were eager and interested in everything we talked about, and the other half, mainly seniors, admitted they were there as a way to coast painlessly through their last year. One student told me, "Ya shoulda known us when we were freshmen, Doc. We worked hard; we studied; all our teachers loved us. It's been downhill since."

Another student agreed, saying that "Senior year is a reward for putting up with school for eleven years."

The students were open and reasonably attentive, but they were not interested in doing much work. During what I thought was a pretty good introduction to Freudian dream symbolism, one of the students interrupted me. "Pssst, Doc. Look at this picture. Isn't she cute? Twenty-six, four foot eleven." I was stopped in mid-sentence to pass judgment on the comeliness of a red-headed girl in a blurred photograph.

"Very pretty," I said, hoping to return to my lecture.

"I told her about you; I think you two would make a cute couple. She's living with her boyfriend, but they plan to break up. Can I tell her you're interested?"

"Yeah, sure," I said to her, and to the class, "I'll get back to Freud tomorrow, unless you want me to hurry through this today."

"Save yourself, Doc," called out one college-bound senior boy. "Ya got one more period to go today. Pace yourself or you'll burn out. We can wait."

The students were informal, relaxed and willing to discuss their phobias, dreams, and defense mechanisms, but they did not want to write a paper, and they nearly panicked when I announced a test.

"Is the test going to be multiple guess or essay?"

"I plan to have some objective questions and two short essays."

One student yelled out, "Hey, Doc, why don't you use the 'scam-tron machine'?"

Psychology had a reputation as a course in which the students did not have to do much work, and because I was a new teacher, the students felt it was their duty to teach me the rules. The school had a Scan-tron brand test-scoring machine that was able to read and score a multiple-choice test in two or three seconds, giving the teacher the items most frequently missed and the mean scores. The students liked the machine because it encouraged teachers to give multiple-choice tests; the students could guess at the answers, claim some of the questions were ambiguous, and plead for a curve. Some of the teachers liked the machine-scored tests because they were easy to make up and grade. The psychology book came with a test manual of standardized test questions for each chapter in the book. If the teacher took tests from the manual, used the photocopying machine and the test-grading machine, tests for 120 students could be produced, run off, and graded in less than an hour. The students encouraged me to use "scamtron" tests out of a sense of fairness: They did not plan to work hard, and they did not expect me to work hard.

We worked out some compromises: There would be no paper in the course, but there would be essay exams. We could talk about anything in class, and get off the topic as much as they liked, but the students would still be responsible for the material in the text and readings. The course evaluations at the end of the semester were very favorable. We had covered less material than I would have liked, but the students did more work than they had bargained for, and they seemed to have learned some psychology and enjoyed the course. I had enjoyed the negotiations and the students.

In the second semester I taught sociology in place of psychology, and things did not go as well. For the most part, I had the same students, but now they were in the second semester of their senior year, a time when, even in the better high schools, very little goes on of academic consequence. To make matters worse, the textbook was not very good.

The book was part of a series prepared by the American Sociological Association, supported by the National Science Foundation, and placed on the market in 1972, about the same time my students entered kindergarten. The most current data on population, income, voting, and infant mortality were from 1969. There were pictures of Richard Nixon and Spiro Agnew as president and vice-president, John Lindsay as mayor of New York, and a man in a "gray flannel suit," which the caption identified as "the symbol of upward mobility." The text was part of a multibook series, but the student workbooks were missing; there were no supplementary materials; and most of the student readers had been lost. The instructor's manual encouraged me to use strategies and handouts that were nowhere to be found. It was not unlike reading a book in which every other page was missing: It was impossible to make sense out of it or maintain interest in it.

Troy knew things were bad, but he did not want to cancel the course for fear that once it was off the schedule, he would have trouble resurrecting it. He had been promised new books for the following year, and he suggested that I use the eight or nine sample copies he had received from publishers and book salespeople. This would have meant that every student had a different text, and fifteen students would not have had texts. He realized this was not a perfect solution, and he added, "There's always the photocopy machine."

I photostatted some articles and sections from texts; I sent students to the library; and I asked them to conduct surveys and sociological interviews; but the course was a dismal failure. By my own count, one class in every five was worthwhile, and very little work was done. A few students wrote good papers; one drew Donald Duck faces on the blackboard every day; and most students had a period in which to relax. I told the class they had the dubious distinction of being in the worst class I had ever taught. One student told me that "It had been an honor to take part in such a historic occasion," and he shook my hand. I planned to pass everyone in the course, largely out of embarrassment, but I could not. The only major requirement of the course was a six- to eight-page paper, and one student had not handed it in. I told him it was not possible to pass the course unless he turned in the paper, and I gave him several extensions of time. On the day of the final exam, he handed me a nine-page paper with one word written on each page: "This-is-my-paper-I-hope-you-like-it."

* * *

The school day sped by quickly. There was little time to think about what you were doing or reflect on the consequences of your actions. From the first bell to the last, we were always rushing. There was always work to do, papers to grade, tests to run off, and materials to duplicate. When I first started teaching in the school, I noticed that most of my colleagues were always busy with papers and grade books. By the second week, I no longer noticed because I was consumed with my own work, much of it clerical. I had to check attendance lists, prepare homework assignments for absent students, keep track of tests and makeup exams, and maintain a record of those students who were failing and those who were not working hard. Grades were sent home every ten weeks, and at the five-week point, "progress reports" were sent home to parents (unless the student was eighteen years old, in which case they would be given directly to the student). At times I thought I did more grading and testing than teaching.

For the most part, one day blended in with the next, with little to distinguish one from another. I saw the same students at the same time every day. I passed the same teachers and students in the hall at the same place and time every day. I said hello to the same people as often as a dozen times a day, but rarely engaged any of them in more substantive conversation. I arrived at school at the same time; I ate lunch at the same time; and I left at the same time every day.

I found it was difficult to teach well. Preparing for class, devising strategies, finding materials, and presenting them to students took more time and energy than I had. It was hard enough to teach thirty students well any one period, and perhaps too unrealistic to expect to do it five times a day. I tried to keep a tally of the classes I taught well and the days on which I taught all five well. If I really tried hard, I could teach three to four good classes a day, and I could usually do this about two or three days a week. I told one of the teachers of my frustration. He told me that if I were a baseball player and went two for five every day, I would be a .400 hitter. No one has hit like that since Ted Williams, he said by way of consolation. Who did I think I was anyway?

The students seemed to be enormously forgiving and tolerant of bad teaching. Sometimes I wondered why they did not scream out "Come on, teach better! You can do it! You've done it before! We'll help!" But they never did; they would compliment me on a good class, a good reading assignment, or a good videotape, but they rarely complained.

When my teaching did not go well, I felt terrible, but there was seldom anyone to talk to about it. For the most part, my job as a public school teacher was spent in isolation from colleagues and superiors. Most things occurred away from other adults. When I had a particularly good or bad class, no one knew about it but the students. Only two periods of the nine period day were spent in the company of other teachers, and during these periods I often had too much work to do to talk. Teachers rarely talked about their classes at any time. When teachers were having lunch or preparing material, they seldom discussed teaching.

Once in a while something would happen in a class that compelled teachers to seek out a sympathetic colleague. One day, Mike Werge stopped me in the hall between classes. "I've got to tell you this story," he said. "There's a new student in my fourth period freshman class from Iran. He's fourteen years old and he came to the United States because he had been drafted into the army. I asked my students if they had any questions they would like to ask him. No one asked any questions, so I asked some questions. I asked him what would have happened if he had refused to go into the army. He said he would have been arrested and executed. The class did not react. I asked him what differences he found between life in Iran and life in the United States. He said 'sex.' In the United States, he saw boys and girls holding hands and kissing in public; in Iran they would be whipped for this. The class said nothing; they sat there like stones, as if they had not heard anything the least bit out of the ordinary. What do you make of it? There is nothing I do with that class that gets a reaction. There's nothing I can do that interests them and it sometimes drives me crazy!"

"You're obviously a bad teacher," I told Mike. "What made you think that high school kids in the United States are the least bit interested in sex and violence? Teach the isms. That's the bell. I have to go. I'll talk to you at lunch."

I had no idea what was going on in Mike's class, and I am not sure that I could have helped him, but I was not expected by the school to help, and I was not free the period when he taught to stop in on my own. The best we could offer each other was sympathetic commiseration. The job of classroom teacher was defined very narrowly. I had five classes to teach, one library duty, and one department duty. Mike had five classes, cafeteria duty, and a department duty. We did the same job in the same building, and two of the courses we taught were the same, but we worked separately and alone. We were to teach and maintain order. There were no other formal requirements of the job. I was not expected to help my colleagues, nor was I told to expect any help from them. The schedules were made for us; the curriculum was designed for us; and the textbooks were selected for us. Administrators made decisions, and supervisors gave assistance when they could. If we wanted to exert a greater influence over our jobs, we would have to become administrators.

As a classroom teacher, the job seemed largely out of my control. It was a physically tiring job, but there were few decisions to make, and very little pressure. Some teachers said that the best way to accommodate to teaching was simply to "go with it." They advised me to teach the classes, enjoy the kids, and not worry about anything else. They said that because we had no authority, we had no responsibility. For those teachers who wanted to bring about some change, or to try some new ideas, or exert a greater control over their teaching, the job could be very difficult. As Mike Werge said, "It could be a very easy job to do, but a very hard job to do well."

4

FACULTY AND STAFF

THE FACULTY ROOM

The faculty room was the center of the teachers' social world, the scene of most of their interactions with colleagues. It served as lunch room, workroom, and a place to relax and unwind. It was also the teachers' sanctuary; it was one of the few areas of the school where the students could not go.

The room was small, always filled with smoke, and usually dirty. The windows were unwashed; the tables were strewn with crumbs, and there were flies everywhere. Early in the year, teachers complained about the conditions of the room, and Don Brandt, the assistant principal, promised to investigate. After several weeks, he reported to the faculty that he had found the room to be clean at the beginning of school, but that it became dirty as the day wore on. By the third lunch period, he noted, the tables were soiled and the trash basket was overflowing. He concluded that because only the faculty used this room, it was they who were creating the mess. He suggested that if the faculty picked up after themselves, there would not be a problem. The teachers were less than enthusiastic about his findings and recommendation.

Don conceded that the flies were a problem for which the teachers were not directly responsible, and he decided to purchase five rolls of flypaper and put them up himself. "If this will make the teachers happier, then I am glad to do it," he said as he scanned the room for the best place to put the spirals of sticky paper.

In an attempt to improve the appearance of the faculty room, the school purchased matching tablecloths and curtains. The tablecloths were washed infrequently, and they contributed to the problems of the room. The teachers circled food and coffee stains, noting the day and date so they could determine the interval between washings. "Look at this one," shouted an incredulous wood shop teacher. "That's

84

a spaghetti stain, and we haven't had spaghetti in a week! Who's supposed to take care of these things? What do we have administrators for?"[1]

Don Brandt ignored the question offered in the playfully contentious spirit of the faculty room, and he sat down with Paul De Faro and me. Paul rarely spent time in the faculty room, and whenever he did, he could expect some teasing from Brandt and the other faculty room regulars.

"Welcome to the faculty room, Mr. De Faro," Brandt said. "We're honored to have you here. Did I ever tell you about my high school basketball team?"

"Six times," Paul De Faro answered in a soft voice.

"Well, let me tell the story again. Maybe Stu didn't hear. You know, I was the only white guy, a 5'7" guard, on an all-Italian team. Every practice they would wear those—what do you call them?— guinea-Ts, with their hair all slicked back. I, of course, had a crew cut and a really good two hand set shot, if I say so myself. . . ."

Paul would bristle at Don's intentionally provocative humor. Later he told me: "Up to a point, I'm willing to take this stuff from Brandt because he's an administrator, and I like him. But I'll only take it up to a point, and I won't take it at all from another teacher."

Most of the teachers told me not to take too seriously those things said in the faculty room; it was a place to "bust chops," they said. Paul resented ethnic humor and distrusted those who used it. He tried to avoid the faculty room, but in a small school with few other work areas it was not always possible. One day, in the faculty room, Paul and the head of the related arts department got into an argument about stereotypes.

"What's wrong with stereotypes if they're true, Paul? A lot of these stereotypes are based in fact. Let's face it, Italians are involved in organized crime; they do wear their shirts unbuttoned to the navel; they wear a lot of gold chains and skin-tight pants; they . . . "

"What about WASP stereotypes?" Paul interrupted. "They hold true as often as Italian stereotypes."

"What WASP stereotypes? There are no WASP stereotypes."

"Bland food, bad sex, and no personalities!" offered Paul. "Every

---

[1]The job of cleaning the tables and laundering the tablecloths had been assigned to the cafeteria staff, and they were not enthusiastic about it. They served food to 1,300 less than appreciative students and staff; all day long they heard complaints about the quality and selection of the food. The starting salary for the cafeteria workers was just over minimum wage, and they were promised only a 5 cent hourly increase for the following year. They thought that many of the faculty were snobs, and that the students were spoiled. They felt that laundering the tablecloths was an unnecessary imposition on an already overburdened staff.

time I go to one of your WASP weddings I have to stop off to get something to eat on the way home! You should be ashamed. You people starve your guests!" Paul said this calmly, but he was angry and he started to leave the room. Don Brandt was coming into the faculty room as Paul was leaving.

"You look very nice today," Brandt said. "What kind of outfit is that, Paul? Is that some Italian city-boy look?" Paul was wearing a flannel shirt, knit tie, and corduroy slacks. "I remember when I was in the service. . . . "

"Don, this is preppy," Paul interrupted, his usual tolerance for Brandt temporarily exhausted. "How can you work in Oldham and not recognize preppy clothes?"

Don laughed, and turned his attention to me and the toothpick I had in my mouth. Don gave me a gentle punch on the arm and asked, "Is that the U. L. Washington look? Do you know who he is?"

"Let me guess," I said. "The guy who got an Ed.D. in educational administration for inventing the late pass?"

"No, smart ass," replied Don. "U. L. Washington, for your information, was a shortstop with Kansas City, and he chewed on a toothpick too until he decided that it was a bad image for young ballplayers."

"Oh, I know this may not be a good image, but it replaced my smoking habit some years ago, and that was a poorer image for kids. Anyway, you know it's just an oral fixation, and how would it look if I walked around with a breast in my mouth all day."

One more punch on the arm, this time not as playful.

"Psychology teachers give me a pain. Have a good day, gentlemen," Don said. "I have to get back to work."

"Hey Brandt," one teacher yelled out, "you little bag of shit. What is it that you do around here besides giving teachers a hard time? Is your son still in chiroquackery school?"

The good-natured attack on Brandt came from a member of the English department who prided himself on his crude, sexually charged humor. His huge arms suggested his background in the building trades, and his more than ample girth reflected his physically easier work as a teacher.

"I won't dignify that with a response," Don responded, finding it impossible to ignore the attack on his only child who was in chiropractic school. "I'm just surprised," he said, referring to his tormentor's outfit, "that anyone wearing a pink sweater would be so bold." The teacher laughed and then focused his attention on one of his colleagues in the English department who was having trouble putting coins in the soda machine on the far side of the room.

"Put it in slowly, dear," he bellowed across the room. "Don't put it in upside down. It's hard to put it in upside down."

Don was uncomfortable with this type of humor, and he turned his attention to the metal shop teacher who was in a bad mood.

"Hey *paisan, come sta?*"

"Cut it out, Brandt, I've had enough crap from people today."

"What's the matter, *goomba,* bad day today?"

Without another word, the metal shop teacher picked Brandt up in his arms and placed him gently on one of the tables. Brandt was smart enough not to resist, and he gathered himself, adjusted his smile, and left the faculty room.

Loud banter dominated the room, but quieter conversations did go on. Willa Green claimed that it was only the men who joked and talked endlessly about sports and sex. She said the women's conversations, in a room in which the men and women rarely sat together, were more lofty and less crude. Willa enjoyed talking about art, the opera, and trips she had taken to Europe, and she often invited me to join her table. Most of the women did not discuss sports, but their conversations rarely were serious or cerebral, and in a sex-segregated school, it was easier for me to sit at one of the men's tables.

One day, Sal and Gus, the two wrestling coaches, and I found ourselves at the same table at lunch. We had little to talk about, and after five minutes of polite conversation about wrestling had ended, Gus decided to break the uncomfortable silence with a joke:

"I went out to get a hamburger yesterday in a restaurant near where I live," he said. "I was sitting at the table but there was no catsup at the table, so I went up to the counter to get some. When I got back to the table, there was this big black guy, maybe 200 pounds, getting ready to eat my hamburger. I said, 'Hey, that's my hamburger.' He says, 'Does it have your name on it?' So I called the manager, not wanting to confront a 200-pound black man, and he throws the guy out. The manager says that this guy does this all the time, sits down and scoffs up somebody else's food. So, I sat down to eat my hamburger and the guy comes back in. 'Hey,' he says, 'I left my paper bag under the table.' I looked down and sure enough there was a paper bag under the table. 'Is that your paper bag?' I asked him. 'Yeah,' he says. 'Well how do I know? It doesn't have your name on it.' The guy started to yell at me, but the manager threw him out again."

After a short pause, Sal asked, "Did you look in the bag?"

"Yeah, I did," said Gus, "and do you know what was in it?"

"What?"

"Bullshit. Just like the rest of the story."

We laughed politely. Gus excused himself. Telling jokes was not part of his conversational style. He claimed he had little in common with most of the teachers in the school, and he chose not to associate with them when he was not forced to. Although they worked together, coached together, and had wrestled in the same weight class in high school, Gus and Sal had few other similarities. Gus was relaxed and informal, and he enjoyed the students more for their personal qualities than their academic abilities. Sal was intense, insecure, and convinced of the importance of science. He liked academically rigorous courses and "the more capable students." Gus believed that he provided students with a relaxed course in psychology so they could explore their feelings and motivations. Sal thought the purpose of school was rigorous academic preparation for college, and explorations of feelings were perhaps frivolous, if even remotely appropriate for secondary schools. They each derived separate pleasures from being a high school teacher, and defined teaching differently. To avoid conflict, they did not discuss their substantive differences in outlook.

DON'T JUDGE THE TEACHERS BY WHAT YOU HEAR IN THE FACULTY ROOM

The bulletin board in the faculty room was used to tack up school notices, baseball pool results, and clippings from the local papers. Mike Flynn glanced over my shoulder as I read a copy of an article one of the teachers had photostatted and put up on the board.

> Amputated penis resewn. Doctors attached the penis of a man who virtually severed the organ with a circular saw and he was reported in good condition yesterday. . . .

Mike told me that the faculty room was not a good reflection of the teachers, but a sample of the population more skewed toward the complainers, the jocks, and the profane. Mike wore several hats in the school. He was an English teacher, the coordinator of student activities, and the coach of the golf team. It was he who had loaned me the extra copies of *Walden Two* and the film *The Grapes of Wrath*. Mike coordinated the school's nonathletic extracurricular activities, which ranged from the modern dance club to the bowling club, and from the literary magazine to the needlecraft club. There were thirty-eight extracurricular activities with a combined enrollment that exceeded the number of students in school. Mike had to schedule activities, keep track of expenses, submit credit vouchers, and supervise the activity advisers. For his work as coordinator, he received a one-class reduction in teaching load.

The students considered Mike to be one of the best teachers in the school, and his humanities class was one of their preferred courses. Mike said that it was the "kids that keep me going." He liked most of the students at Oldham, saying: "Most of the kids are nice, but the A students are less challenging, less interesting." His greatest criticism of the students was that they "don't tend to question; they are too robotized and too compliant."

Mike taught in the learning community (LC), the classes for those juniors who did not like school or school work. He was teamed with Paul De Faro and a geometry teacher, along with one guidance counselor. The program was designed to improve the students' attendance, attitude toward school, and academic achievement. The LC teachers were the only teachers who openly discussed students and teaching. They had common problems and a common meeting time every day to work on programs, curricula, and student progress. They had a block of three classes, back to back, for two hours of teaching. They could break up the time as they saw fit, and were not constrained by the bell schedule. Some days they would break the periods into three parts, while other days the entire two-hour block would be used for math, social studies, English, a guest speaker, or a field trip.

Mike Flynn decided that the hallway in which his classroom was located looked too institutional, and he encouraged the students to bring in plants and art reproductions from home. The "humanities hallway," as they called it, took on more charm and life than most of the others in the school, and damage to the plant shelves and the art was minimal. Mike and Paul De Faro shared one of the more interesting classrooms in the school. Paul was a collector, and a partial sample of his treasured junk was displayed in the room. There was a large American flag, an Italian flag, and a flag from the Soviet Union. The back wall was covered with a huge replica of a 1040A income tax form, publicity posters of the National Ballet of Cuba, a vintage James Dean poster, and more recent film posters. There were photographs of the U.S. *Intrepid,* a Marine recruiting poster, and assorted blowups from the front pages of *Variety* and *The Wall Street Journal.* Lying on his desk were a photograph of his wife, a World War I gas mask, and the nozzle of an oxyacetylene torch.

Both Mike and Paul were trivia fans, and every day they wrote trivia questions on the board. They felt if they asked students to "name the Seven Dwarfs," or "who was the heroine King Kong carried up the Empire State Building in the original movie?" students would be more likely to come to class on time. There was also a graffiti board on the side wall so students would not have to write on their desks.

De Faro and Flynn got along well, but they were the odd couple. Paul described himself as a "neat freak" who walked around straightening chairs and picking up paper whether he was in school or at home. Mike admitted that he could more easily tolerate disorder. "I'm willing to water the plants," he said, "but that's about it." Desks out of line and paper on the floor did not seem to bother him, and he and Paul often bantered about the cleanliness of the room in front of the students. As a hyperbolic extension of their disagreements, they divided the room in half by running a masking tape line along the carpet and up through the chalkboard. Paul warned Mike, in front of the students in the LC, to keep the mess on his side or there would be trouble. Mike scoffed at Paul, challenged him to a boxing match, and brought in two sets of sixteen-ounce gloves.

The fight was timed so there would be a lot of bravado exchanged, but no blows were to be struck. According to their plan, Larry Silverman, the assistant principal, was to come in and break up the fight before any damage was done, but Larry was late. Despite a great deal of stalling, Paul and Mike had to stage a fight for a few rounds. They each stood about six feet tall, but at 180 pounds, Mike was at least thirty pounds heavier than Paul. Neither of them was an experienced fighter; they did not know how to pull punches, and they both walked around with bruised ribs and sore arms for a few weeks. The LC students never knew if the fight was real or not, nor did they ask. Asked why they did it, Paul explained, "It's a way of keeping yourself sane in this crazy job."

Mike's major project of the year was the organization of the Hum Fest (humanities festival). For one day, in early May, regular classes were suspended, and in their place were workshops, presentations, and exhibits by faculty, students, and members of the community. Sal spoke about extraterrestrial life; Paul gave a demonstration of rock climbing; Mike Werge made a presentation on wilderness camping. There were poetry readings, judo exhibitions, and discussions of careers in architecture, photography, and merchandising by parents of students and other community residents. There were six one-hour sessions, and about sixteen presentations in each session. Teachers were assigned to supervise, and while behavior in the sessions was very good, student attendance was not. Nearly one-third of the students cut school. Mike was terribly disheartened. He and the student organizers had put a lot of energy into preparing for the day, and he said if students were going to reward their efforts by cutting, there would be no more Hum Fests. Although they had been running every year for six years, the Hum Fest was canceled for the following year. He wanted to make school more interesting, but the students' attitude made him pessimistic about changing the way in which schools were run.

Mike Flynn was graduated from a public high school and a state college, but he had a strong Catholic upbringing. When asked why he went into teaching, Mike explained: "The nuns had told me to pray for a vocation." Mike put a lot of energy into his teaching and his preparation. After fourteen years in the classroom, he had lost none of his enthusiasm for his work, but he was tired of his co-workers. He said that when he first began as a teacher, he would go out of his way to get together with other teachers to develop new strategies and to plan new courses, but he no longer had the time or the enthusiasm for it. As the single parent of two boys, he put his energy into his family, not his colleagues.

Mike shared an office with the athletic director, and he had a place to work that allowed him to avoid the faculty room except for a brief solitary lunch. He ate quietly, graded papers in the smoking section, and he checked on the soda machine. Mike refilled the machine and kept track of the profits, which were used for a student scholarship, but he kept out of most faculty discussions. He speculated that teaching may be such a personal art, such a private enterprise, that it was too hard for people engaged in it to work too closely with others. He did not think this was necessarily detrimental to the school. He suggested if enough talented teachers were hired, the school would run itself.

Many of the teachers avoided the faculty room. One of the brightest and the best read English teachers in the school typically ate lunch in the custodians' work room, claiming that he learned more there than he did from the teachers. "If I went to the faculty room, I would wind up fighting with half a dozen teachers every day. Who needs the aggravation?" he asked, adding sarcastically, "I'm a married man. I get all the fighting I need at home."

One member of the science department also avoided the faculty room. Lou Smith taught biology and coached the school's science teams, which competed against other high schools in academic competitions. He said that he did not like the faculty room because he could not accommodate the conversations and he did not have the time to waste.

"It takes me a long time to set up and break down labs, and I use my free periods to work," he told me. "The facilities are not adequate in science, and the equipment and supplies are so amazingly horrible that I have to work extra hard to prepare for class. I have a lot of plants to water and take care of, and anyway, I have student lab assistants, and I would rather spend my time with them than with the teachers."

Lou thought that the students were brighter and more interesting than most of the faculty. "All the teachers do is bitch about the job and the kids," he said. "I can have better conversations with the students."

Lou was one of the teachers who had retreated from the main-stream of the faculty, and he defined teaching personally and in isola-tion from other teachers. At one time he had played tennis with Sal, and he considered one of the French teachers to be his friend, but these teachers were now married, and Lou was divorced. He claimed he no longer maintained social friendships with his colleagues, and he rarely went to faculty parties. From our conversations, it did not appear that he liked most of the other teachers, but he enjoyed teaching. The advantages of the job for him were the vacations, the quality of the students, and the freedom to teach.

"I work very hard for ten months," he told me, "but I don't know if I could handle a real job with only two weeks of vacation. I'm addicted to my summers off. I like to travel to bizarre places. I'm thirty-five. I don't think I could find another job where I could make this much money in ten months. I'm in this for the summers, the vacations, and a segment of the student population. . . . The students are my social life. I go butterfly hunting with former students; I travel with former students; they really are my friends here."

Lou said he had a great deal of freedom once he closed the door to his classroom and labs and pursued the teaching of science. He complained about the lack of facilities, and while he thought his supervisor was less than strong, he said the supervisor was smart enough not to interfere with his teaching. He said, "If people leave me alone, I do fairly well in the classroom, and I'm pretty happy doing it."

Coaching the school's science teams put Lou in contact with many of the brightest students in the school, and he claimed the school left him alone because of the good publicity the science teams brought to the district. "It's a joke," he said. "This is not a strong department, but everyone thinks it is because the teams win state competitions. In

1978, the teams in biology, chemistry, and physics swept the state, and we usually have at least one winner a year, so we cover for the incompetents."

Lou said one member of his department could not control the students, another knew little science, a third was waiting to retire, and a fourth let his creationist views interfere with his teaching.

"We don't have enough lab time to teach science; in some areas, we don't even meet the state requirements. Students do not learn science by listening to a teacher, yet [one of the members of the department] doesn't like labs because the 'students make a mess' and labs take a long time to set up."

According to Lou, the successes of his science teams have, in some ways, hurt his department. "We have inadequate resources, but the kids do so well, [the members of the board of education] say that we don't need any more money." He attributed the victories of his teams mainly to the nature of the students. "We get academically oriented, middle class kids so we're bound to do well, but we beat other schools which are larger and wealthier, and so some of the credit has to go to the program." He wondered how much better his students would do if the science programs received greater financial support.

Lou's reputation among the students was that of a strong, demanding teacher who was very good for college-bound students. They were reluctant to rate him among the best teachers in the school because they knew him to be impatient with slower students. Among the faculty, he was known as an elitist and a loner. Lou claimed he felt good about the work he did as a teacher, but he was less than sanguine about the prospects for a change in teaching. He said there is so much wrong with high schools that in order to remedy the problems, the system would have to be dismantled and reconstructed. While he believed that good teachers were underpaid, he was not in favor of a salary increase for all teachers.

"I would vote against an across the board raise for teachers," he said. "It's too much like socialism to give everyone the same raise regardless of how well they perform. I blame the unions, in part, for the problems of teaching. I can't think of a thing that the state or the national teacher organizations have done for me or the profession except to protect incompetents."

Lou felt that at times it was embarrassing to be a teacher. He worked hard. He was proud of his advanced placement courses, for which students received college credit. He was the faculty adviser for the chess team; he advised and organized trips for the 170-member ski club; and he gave up much of his free time to coach the science team and to prepare for class. Yet he occasionally ran into members of the community who thought that teachers were lazy and overpaid. "Oldham High School has the reputation of being a country club, a school in which lazy teachers do not push compliant students nearly enough," he said.

Lou Smith thought that the reputation was largely deserved, but that his courses were rigorous, and he could not imagine working himself or his students any harder.

"Some guy in the English department gets an award from the librarian for showing 63 films a year! The social studies department is a sanctuary for coaches! I can't think of a bright person in PE," Lou said.

Lou Smith could not identify the best teachers in the school because, he said, he had no classroom experience with most of the staff, but he could name only four teachers he considered to be "very bright." In some ways, he felt it was tough to be a public school teacher today. "It's like being a cop," he said. "They have to take a lot of shit for bad cops, and good teachers take a lot of shit for bad teachers."

Like many teachers, Lou backed into the field. He had attended the University of Tennessee for two years, and then transferred to a school in-state as a pre-vet major. He could not get admitted to a school of veterinary medicine, and decided to try teaching for a few years. He liked it and decided to stay, earning two master's degrees from schools with good science departments. All his graduate coursework was in various science areas, not education. "Those courses," he said, referring to the latter with disdain, "are useless."

THE PROFESSIONAL EDUCATION OF TEACHERS

Many of the teachers disagreed with Lou's appraisal of the faculty and the strength of the science department, but most supported his view of coursework in education. In a survey I administered to the faculty, over 50 percent of the teachers claimed that their graduate and undergraduate education courses were "unhelpful" or "very unhelpful" to them. While the teachers indicated that undergraduate courses in education were more useful than graduate courses, many of them could not avoid taking graduate degrees in education. The only route out of the classroom was to become a supervisor, administrator, or guidance counselor, and the positions all had separate sets of state-mandated education coursework requirements.

Even for those teachers who planned to remain in the classroom, education courses had at least one undisputed value: money. A teacher with ten years of experience and a bachelor's degree earned about $19,000. With a master's degree and an additional sixty hours of coursework, a teacher could earn more than $25,000. Over a twenty-year period, the difference was $120,000. It did not matter if the coursework was in education or in subject fields. Most teachers claimed they could take no more than one course a semester in content areas, but it was not unreasonable to take two or more of the less-demanding education courses. Larry Silverman completed a master's degree in educational administration in two summers and one academic year of part-time attendance.

The teachers knew I had taught education courses, and they liked to give me a hard time about it. While I was grading papers one afternoon in the faculty room, one of the social studies teacher yelled out to me.

"Hey Stu, look at this," he said as he threw a college flier to me. "Wanna pick up a supervisor's certificate at MIT?"

"MIT?"

"Yeah, 'Miller Institute of Technology.' " He explained that Professor Miller was on the faculty of a small private college in the area, and he taught extension courses at the high schools in the field of curriculum and instruction. Teachers claimed that no one did any work in his courses, everyone received a grade of A or B, and everyone moved up on the pay scale. Professor Miller is reported to have asked his classes, "Who am I to stand in the way of your raise?"

The discussion of education courses attracted the teachers like flies.

"Why can't they speak English in those courses?" asked a French teacher. "They attempt to obscure the little they know with jargon, and our administrators take those courses and believe it. Look at Don Brandt, a PE major who took education courses and now considers himself a scholar. The man is a charlatan!"

"The whole field is a sham," agreed a German teacher. "Every course in education talks about Maslow and self-actualizing your prioritizations, and writing across the curriculum about your affective needs. . . ."

Willa Green said that she refused to take "educational courses" and did not have the time to take content courses in English, and consequently she did not have a master's degree. I agreed that education courses could be weak, but so too, I said, are many other courses. I tried to argue that teachers needed courses in education as well as in content, but I did not change anyone's opinion.

While coursework in education was discredited, there was a lack of sophistication about many areas of teaching and research. In February of my first year at the high school, Dr. Szabo and I discussed my future in the district. He said some members of the board were under the impression that I was to be there for only one year, and he indicated they were reluctant to reappoint a social studies teacher at my salary, especially one who did not want to coach. Dr. Szabo indicated that I could make myself more attractive to the board in several ways: by getting involved in the district's inservice program, working with the other high school in the district on a review of the curriculum, and by making a presentation to the board concerning the findings of the social studies assessment.

I agreed to make some inservice presentations and to work on the curriculum, but I told him I would have some trouble presenting the findings of the assessment program. I told Szabo something which I had shared with Troy Thayer, the social studies supervisor, several months earlier: The assessment lacked any semblance of validity or reliability. No effort had been made to determine whether the test measured the variable it purported to measure or the precision with which it measured that variable (see Cronbach, 1970; Ebel, 1972).

Each subject area was involved in an assessment process designed to document the extent of student learning. Departments from each of the two high schools jointly developed a test of academic content and administered it to the students. The social studies test, called a political awareness test, consisted of sixty-five multiple-choice and true-false questions. Multiple-choice questions asked students to identify the governor of the state, the United States senators from the state, and the vice-president of the United States. One question asked students to decide if the following statement was true or false: "When an individual lies under oath, he is committing *precedent.*" A multiple-choice question asked students to choose the best answer to complete the sentence: "A militaristic, ethnocentric, racist, ultranationalistic dictatorship that retains private property can be considered to be: (A) Democractic, (B) Fascist, (C) Socialist, (D) Communist."

The same test was administered to the freshmen and to the seniors. When the seniors scored higher on the exam, the increase was attributed to the social studies program. Szabo believed this indicated the social studies program was doing a good job. One of the textbooks used in his graduate program referred to this design as a "bad example" of research (Campbell and Stanley, 1966). For one thing, the assessment design did not account for the maturation of the students. A seventeen-year-old senior was more likely to know the name of the vice-president of the United States than a fourteen-year-old freshman by virtue of being older and having more life experiences. I told Dr. Szabo that the mean gain scores of the seniors over the freshmen could not be attributed to the social studies program with any greater degree of certainty than it could be attributed to radio, television, or the food in the cafeteria.

Szabo said it was better that I not be the person to present the findings of the social studies assessment to the board. He allowed that although one of the board members was a college administrator, the others were mainly businessmen and homemakers who would "not recognize the problems with the assessment" unless they were told. Dr. Mokowski, the assistant superintendent, had been in charge of the assessment programs, and admitted the social studies assessment was one of the weaker designs. She indicated that the math assessment had been particularly well done.

Pat Delaney, the math teacher who designed his department's assessment, chuckled up his sleeve when I told him about the social studies design. Pat taught a course in probability and statistics in the school and he understood research, but he would not volunteer to do any more work. He already taught five classes, and he was preparing an inservice program for teachers who would be teaching the school's computer programming courses. "Why should I volunteer to help them with research or assessments of other departments?" he asked in a good humor. "If they think I am of more use to the school guarding the lobby and picking up papers from the floor, who am I to correct them? After all, the superintendents have doctorates in education. I don't."

Ron Szabo did not think that it was essential for a chief school administrator to have a doctoral degree in educational administration. "A superintendent needs to know about curriculum and staff development, but most of the things a superintendent needs to know are not taught in school—they are learned on the job." Szabo recognized that although education courses were widely disparaged by his faculty, most teachers did not know enough about classroom discussion skills, test construction, evaluation, or the teaching of reading and writing skills. He believed a good staff development program was necessary to improve teachers' skills and attitudes. "Three-fourths of the staff is tenured," he said. "We're not going to fire anyone. We have to get the most out of the teachers we have, and make them feel good about the work that they do."

For three days a year (two half days and one full day), Oldham High teachers were given staff development training, usually referred to in public schools as inservice education. Students were excused from classes and teachers were required to attend workshops and presentations designed to improve teaching. Dr. Mokowski told me that the budget for all the inservice work was $1,000. That would be about $15 per person for the 66 teachers and supervisors at Oldham High School, but it also had to cover the cost of inservice for the other high school in the district.

"I hate inservice," said the wood shop teacher. "The only good inservice days are during deer season, and I can take the day off (as one of three personal days teachers get each year) and go hunting."

Not all the teachers were hunters, but most of them agreed with the shop teacher's appraisal of the value of inservice days. Over 90 percent of the teachers surveyed thought that inservice was unhelpful, uninteresting, and unstimulating. There was little variation among members of different departments, or among individuals in different salary groups.

"Inservice is useless," argued one of the social studies teachers. "It makes me feel worse about being a teacher. We all need help, but they never ask what it is that we need help with. They just organize inservice."

"I disagree," responded one of the English teachers. "I like inservice," he said, facetiously. "What other time can I catch up with paperwork and read the whole *New York Times?* You guys don't appreciate a day off, not to mention the free coffee. Ingrates!"

There was free coffee and free pastry. It was the same weak coffee they served every day, and the same pastry the cafeteria staff stored in the freezer and sold for 25 cents on school days. It was served at 8 o'clock on inservice days instead of the usual 9 o'clock, and the pastry did not always have time to thaw sufficiently. The teachers complained that weak coffee and frozen pastry were not a good start for an inservice day.

Inservice was a break in the routine, and it was usually a surprise. The teachers did not know what to expect or what the program would be about. Teachers did not plan the workshops or invite the speakers. While the majority of the faculty listened quietly, some teachers talked loudly and impolitely during presentations. Otherwise mature and responsible adults behaved like children and refused to be engaged by the speakers, some of whom were entertaining, well meaning, and informed. One speaker told jokes and funny stories, and tried to get audience participation.

"Raise your hands," he said, "if you ever felt that the superintendent did not understand your problems." A few teachers tentatively raised their hands. "Come on now," he continued, "don't be embarrassed by those little wet circles under your arms. Raise your hands high! This is your chance to speak out!"

A few more arms were raised and people laughed, but many teachers folded their arms tightly across their chests. The speaker was trying to address the communication problems in the school between administration and staff, and between students and teachers, but many of the teachers were not interested.

"The guy's a snake oil salesman," said Mike Werge. "Can they really believe that he is helping us? I've been listening to this guy for an hour. It's comic relief, but I haven't learned anything."

"I'm glad my husband isn't here to see this," whispered another teacher. "He thinks that the whole field of education is Mickey Mouse, and this would convince him."

Inservice days were difficult for me as well. When I had taught at the university, I had made a dozen or more inservice presentations, none of which was very different from those I was subjected to as a teacher. I was typically contacted not by the teachers, but by an administrator. I was never asked to find out what it was the teachers needed. Sometimes I was asked to make a presentation about a specific topic, such as classroom management or questioning techniques, but more often I was told to make a two-hour presentation on whatever I thought would be of value. In those cases I felt like a physician prescribing a remedy for a patient he had never examined, and whom he would never see again.

I admitted to the Oldham teachers that I had done this sort of work in the past, and I hoped they would not hold it against me. "Hey, how much does this guy get for this?" one teacher asked. I guessed about three hundred dollars. "For that money," groused one of the shop teachers, "they could hire buses and take us to Atlantic City to hear real comedians."

A staff development survey conducted by the school found that teachers wanted inservice work, but they wanted to plan it, and have it aimed more specifically at their needs as they defined them. Some teachers wanted to use inservice days to visit schools in other parts of the metropolitan area. Some wanted to spend the day at a major library collecting materials. Other teachers wanted to invite speakers from industry and universities. In its present form, they argued, inservice was insulting and demeaning. By providing inappropriate remedies for their problems, teachers felt inservice contributed to a decline in morale, and left them with a sense that no one understood their problems.

In general, faculty morale was a problem. Slightly over half of the teachers (52 percent) reported they had experienced "teacher burn-out," the feeling of being sapped by the excessive demands of the job and too few rewards. The teachers wrote that the symptoms of teacher burnout were: "giving fewer writing assignments," "anger," "frustration," "acceptance of the unacceptable," "I-don't-give-a-damn attitude," "apathy," and "not wanting to do anything in class."

It was a difficult time to be a secondary school teacher. Not only were teacher salaries low, but in the preceding twelve months, advance announcements of books and national and state reports had been issued which were critical of the conditions of secondary education. Among other things, teachers were told the nation was at risk, there was a rising tide of mediocrity in the high schools, and perhaps we were asking too much from schools and teachers.[2] The teachers did not discuss these reports or debate their findings.[3] Most of the teachers did not read more than the excerpts reported in newspapers. Some teachers said the criticisms probably were directed at other high schools, not Oldham. Other teachers said they did not want to be depressed by more criticism, and they did not want to feel worse than they already did about their choice of career.

Ron Szabo, the superintendent of schools, recognized the negative impact the reports could have on the faculty. He asked for a few minutes to speak at the regularly scheduled faculty meeting. Szabo told the teachers they were "appreciated," and he wanted them to know that he was more than pleased with their efforts. He said he regularly praised them behind their backs, and he wanted to take the opportunity to tell them in person that they were doing a good job. It was unusual for Dr. Szabo to address the teachers, and they were strangely quiet and unresponsive. There was no applause after he spoke, and it was clear that his words alone would not make them feel appreciated. If there was nothing tangible to show appreciation, they would give no physical response.

The next day, a new sign appeared in the faculty room. One of the foreign language teachers had taken a dollar bill and superimposed a photograph of Dr. Szabo over the likeness of George Washington. He

---

[2]For example, Ernest L. Boyer, *High School: A Report on Secondary Education in America* (New York: Harper and Row, 1983); John Goodlad, *A Place Called School: Prospects for the Future* (New York: McGraw-Hill, 1984); The National Commission on Excellence in Education, *A Nation at Risk: The Imperative for Educational Reform* (Washington: The United States Department of Education, April 1983); Theodore R. Sizer, *Horace's Compromise: The Dilemma of the American High School* (Boston: Houghton Mifflin, 1984); Task Force on Federal Elementary and Secondary Education Policy, *Making the Grade* (New York: Twentieth Century Fund, 1983).

[3]During the year after I left the school, I asked some of the teachers if they had read the books and reports which had by that time appeared in their entirety. No one had.

made several photocopies of it and posted them in the faculty room and in the main office with the following caption: "You are appreciated. Redeemable at your favorite store!! To be issued soon to all staff! Watch your mailbox for details!"

Dr. Szabo seemed more frustrated than angered by the teachers' response to his speech. He admitted there were only limited ways in which to demonstrate approval to the teachers. "What can I do to reward teachers beyond granting a few professional days (for them to attend conferences) and verbally praising them whenever I can?"

THE UNDERGROUND GAZETTE

The faculty room was a good place to catch up on sports, gossip, and the latest school news. One morning Willa Green burst into the room with a greater than normal exuberance. "Did you see this?" she screamed to everyone, but to no one in particular.

Willa was clutching volume 1, number 1 of the *Underground Gazette,* an unauthorized student newspaper that described itself as "The paper that doesn't care." I read through Willa's copy as she fumed and fulminated to others in the room.

> Welcome to the first monthly issue of the *OHS Underground Gazette! The Underground Gazette* is a periodical written and edited by a small group of OHS students seeking to delve behind the scenes and report what really goes on in the everyday lives of OHS students and faculty. . . . It should be noted that we try to write with the highest degree of integrity. Please keep in mind that our humorous accusations and incriminations are just that; while our serious articles are written with responsibility and supported with facts. We are exercising our Constitutional right to freedom of the press, and if we offend anyone, tough shit.

The anonymously written three-page paper poked fun at students, and the physical features of the school (such as the lack of stall doors in the lavatories), but teachers were the main target. The lead article, entitled "Teacher Scouting Report," caught my attention. Citing a Spanish teacher by name, the unsigned article read:

> Señora is the worst teacher in the worst department at OHS. She does provide a topic for lobby discussions, however. Students will debate what her worst trait is: could it be her atrocious lesson planning, her pathetic teaching techniques, or her arrogance? Regardless, the *Gazette* applauds the administration's nixing her pay hike.

"This is an outrage!" declared Willa.

"What's that?" one of the teachers asked.

"How did they know that her increment was being withheld? That is a teacher matter and none of their business! Someone is feeding these kids inside information! One of the teachers must be a spy! This is unprofessional!"

In fact, we later learned, the teacher's increment had not been withheld, but no one knew it at the time, and Willa was genuinely upset and could not be mollified.

"What do you think of this?" she asked me.

"What can you do, Willa? They probably are protected by the First Amendment. Look at the good side, the students are practicing their writing skills!"

Willa took the paper from me, and stormed off. There were only three of us in the faculty room, and we were not a very sympathetic audience. One of the teachers chuckled as Willa left, and handed his copy of the student newspaper to me.

"Look at the last paragraph," he said. "Willa's not worried about the poor Spanish teacher being hurt by 'inside information.' The students went after her, too."

"Willa is a very good teacher," the article said, "BUT, unfortunately, she is a lady with very strong and definate [sic] beliefs. For some reason, she seems to be deeply prejudiced against people whose beliefs are different than hers."

The paper did not explain what Willa had said or done to offend them. One teacher said they were probably referring to the time that she ripped a Christmas tree from the lobby and threw it out the front door, declaring that religion had no place in a public institution. Another said the students were recalling the scarecrow and the banana incident, while a third said it was just a constellation of the small things she says and does in class every day.

The school was divided over the paper. Virtually all the students loved it, and greeted each of its five editions with great excitement. It was their only chance to strike back at the teachers and administrators who controlled their inschool lives. It was hard to think of the Oldham students as the downtrodden masses, but given the context of public schools and the lack of student power, the paper could be regarded as the voice of the voiceless and disenfranchised. Several of the teachers delighted in the paper as much as the students. There is no uncertain joy in having someone held up to public scorn when you have been privately scornful of them for years. Other teachers found it as offensive as did Willa. They were angered that the privacy of faculty knowledge and faculty conversations had been violated, and they did not like students doing something in school over which they had no control.

It was a proud time for social studies teachers, who had a chance to prove they knew something of practical value. When other teachers questioned us about the students' right to publish and their own right to privacy, we had answers. I read some old school law casebooks, and I was ready when the teachers asked me if the *Gazette* was "legal."

"It is fairly well established in law," I intoned, pedantically, "that this type of student literature is considered an exercise of freedom of the press, and as such it enjoys First Amendment protection regardless of authorship. The schools can regulate the distribution of the paper, but they cannot stop it."

I was pretty sure that Cal Bullinger and Ron Szabo knew these cases as well. School law is typically a required course for school administrators, and those cases that supported the students' civil rights over the schools' authority were studied carefully. Most of the teachers did not seem to know very much about the substantive and due process rights of students.

"At what point does the right of students to publish this trash infringe on our rights to privacy? That's what I want to know," asked Willa, who would know no peace throughout the short publication history of the *Gazette*.

"From what I understand," I said, having read it the night before, "student literature may be censored only if the school can demonstrate that the literature had created, or would have created, a threat to the orderly processes of schooling."

"It is creating a climate of distrust in the staff, and I believe it is a threat to the orderly processes, right?" asked Willa, looking for support from other teachers.

While most teachers did not feel as strongly as Willa, the paper was not clear in its distinction between "humorous accusations" and "serious articles." The paper had gotten a lot slicker by the fifth issue. It was well-typed and reproduced; there was an attractive masthead, graphics and photographs, and they had uncovered a "scandal." According to the paper, cafeteria workers were told to add pork to the chicken salad if they ran out of chicken. The *Gazette* declared that "the repercussions of this conspiracy are grave in nature . . . [for] people of the Jewish persuasion [sic]."

The students were still as casual about the truth as they were about spelling. Volume 1, number 5, of the *Underground Gazette* contained a short section that cost the paper a good deal of faculty support:

Faculty Quote of the Month: "OHS calculus is the old ten pounds of shit in the eight pound bag."

by Chet W.

Rebuttal of the Month: "If brains were shit, Chet W. couldn't draw a fly."
by calculus mentor Patrick D.

Chet W. said it was possible that he said something similar to the quote in the paper. Chet was an experienced math teacher, and a well-liked one, but he did not have tenure, and he could easily lose his job. The students failed to appreciate his vulnerability. Patrick D. flatly denied offering the rebuttal quoted in the paper, and the students later admitted that it was a fabrication. Pat Delaney was one of the most respected teachers in the school, and widely regarded as one of the brightest. In his early forties, Pat had recently found new interest in teaching with the addition of computers and courses in programming to the math department. Pat had taught himself several programming languages, and he had written a few programs for use in schools. Pat was upset by the quote. He immediately apologized to Chet, and complained to the building administrators about the paper. Many teachers agreed that the paper had overstepped its bounds by defaming Pat.

Larry Silverman, acting as assistant principal since his appointment in October, rounded up all the usual suspects. (With only three or four Jewish students in the senior class, the pork article narrowed the field considerably.) In a private meeting held in his office, Larry made them promise not to attack nontenured teachers. Only Larry and perhaps a dozen other teachers knew who the editors were; most of the faculty, including Willa Green, did not.

In December, Willa brought the issue to the attention of Dr. Szabo and the board of education, and demanded that something be done about it. She planned to attack the paper at the next PIE session. PIE was an acronym for Professionals in Education, a series of informal discussions among the faculty, administration, and board members that had been instituted to improve communication within the district. The PIE sessions were held several times during the year, and teachers were invited to the conference room during their free periods, to ask questions, answer questions, and voice dissatisfactions.

According to the written summary of the PIE session, among the eighteen topics discussed were: whether coaches felt appreciated (yes); new teachers' impressions of Oldham High (favorable); concern over the renovation of the athletic fields (a high board priority, as soon as finances permit); and "the environment of distrust." Although the summary did not cite her by name, it was Willa Green who had brought up the issue of the paper. She declared she had had enough of the paper's "vilifications and vituperations," and that the continued publication of the *Gazette* was, as she put it, "a threat to my mental health." Dr. Szabo assured her that no members of the administration were involved in the paper, and she received similar assurances from the three women representing the board of education. Don Brandt's administrative summary of the meeting referred to Willa:

Environment of Distrust
Some staff members expressed a concern that OHS had an environment of distrust within the staff. A great deal of this was perpetrated by the fact that some people thought staff members may be providing information to the underground newspaper. The overwhelming feeling of those present during this discussion was that this was not so. The majority felt that the environment was a positive one and that the opinion of distrust was a part of the normal spectrum of staff impression.

In fact, the students did not have any inside information from members of the staff, and the paper was written and printed independent of faculty involvement. One of the contributors to the paper was the son of a school board member, but he claimed his father did not know of his involvement until after he was graduated. Officially, I was told, the *Gazette* had never been discussed at a board meeting. Szabo knew who the editors were, but he secretly enjoyed the paper and thought that Willa, whom he considered to be an excellent teacher, was a bit too sensitive. The paper ceased publication when the contributors joined the freshman classes at Harvard, the University of Michigan, Syracuse University, and the University of Virginia.

The publication of the *Gazette* embarrassed some of the teachers by holding them up to public ridicule and criticism which they could not refute, and to which they could not respond. The Spanish teacher who had been attacked in the first issue said, "They are talking about me in the community, and I have no way to set the record straight; I just want to tell the parents what really goes on in my classes."

The teachers had no direct means of communicating with the parents. They had no newspaper of their own, and few regular contacts with the community. Teachers knew that parents drew conclusions about them based on fragmentary evidence, and during that year much of the news about the school was not good. In addition to the underground newspaper's condemnations, the community learned that a member of the English department had resigned in September when it became known she was selling marijuana to some of the students and getting high with them. Later that month, the police had been called in because some students had driven their cars over the athletic fields, damaging the turf. As one of the teachers said, "This is not good public relations; our football team will have to go undefeated to counter this."

BACK-TO-SCHOOL NIGHT

The negative publicity put additional emphasis on the need for success in the school's back-to-school night program, the only formal contact most of the parents would have with the teachers. For two hours on a weekday night, parents were invited into the school to follow their child's schedule of classes and to meet the teachers and the administrators. Teachers were to give an overall description of their courses and what they expected from the students. One of the teachers told me that if I gave out a lot of handouts, passed the books around slowly, and made some general comments, I could slide through the eight-minute classes with little trouble. "Keep it light and breezy," he told me. "It's just a little p.r."

Cal appeared to be especially nervous before back-to-school night, and he was anxious to have everything go smoothly. He knew that negative publicity would not help his chances for tenure. At a Monday faculty meeting before we met the parents, Cal advised us to be optimistic and to insert some humor into our presentations. "Try to be enthusiastic and interesting," he implored, like a coach before the big game. "I'm sure you'll all do just fine."

Troy too seemed nervous and disorganized, although this would be his eleventh back-to-school night as supervisor. He sent out a last-minute memo reminding the teachers to straighten out their bookshelves, and to make sure the desk tops were clean and that the room was neat. He ran off multiple copies of the course objectives for us to distribute, and this was the first time I had seen them. Troy explained: "These were done for the state some years ago. They're pretty general and not very helpful as a day to day guide, but you can use them tonight if you want, but don't feel obligated. . . ."

I thanked him, and told him that I would read them over.

"Oh, by the way, a lot of the teachers wear jackets and ties on back-to-school night," he said, glancing at my jeans and open neck shirt. "It's not a requirement, but you may feel more comfortable."

I thanked him again. I stayed after school to wash the desk tops, and clean the blinds and the windowsills. I planned to grade some papers, workout in the gym, and then have dinner with Mike Werge.

Most of the faculty commuted a long distance to work; many lived more than an hour away from one another, and back-to-school night gave the teachers a chance to socialize outside of school. On my way out of the building, I ran into Cal Bullinger, who was straightening the chairs in the lobby and tacking some posters on the bulletin board. I asked him if he had plans for dinner, and invited him to join me. He thanked me but declined. He explained that he was diabetic and had to be careful what he ate. He had brought some food from home, and he planned to heat it in the microwave oven in the home economics class and eat alone.

"I have to be here two or three nights a week, and I can't afford to eat out that much. By the way," he said, "if you've got a minute, I need to talk to you about something. I've got to tell this to you, although I may be violating the chain of command. I got a call from Szabo this morning. He said one of the parents called a board member to complain about something you did in a freshman social studies class."

"What was it?"

"According to Szabo, you wrote a word on the blackboard which was supposed to trigger something in the students' minds, and they were supposed to write about it."

"That sounds like something I might do, but I don't remember it specifically. What was the word?"

"He didn't say."

"He didn't say? What's the complaint? Was it a dirty word?"

"No, that's not it. It is just that the parent said that her child . . . and I don't know if it's a boy or a girl, or who the parent was . . . did not understand the assignment, and it might be that you are teaching over the heads of some of the freshmen."

"Well that may be true, but I'm not sure what this is all about. Do you want me to call Szabo or the board member to straighten this out?"

"No," Cal said, "it's not necessary. Szabo just calls up regularly and yells, and this is one of the things he yelled about this week. I was supposed to tell Troy who was supposed to tell you, but I get so tired of this petty crap. You may be on the lookout for something tonight."

I thanked Cal for letting me know. I had not heard him use such strong language, and I realized he was under pressure. I never heard any more about the incident, and when I asked Szabo some months later, he claimed he did not recall it specifically, but that it was the type of thing the community expected of him.

The choices for dinner in the area were not extensive. There were two or three expensive restaurants, an Oriental restaurant, a diner, and a few bars that served food. Most of the male teachers preferred a small bar in town that featured hamburgers and a few daily specials which were listed on a blackboard. Waiting for Mike Werge, I joined several teachers at the bar. I told them about my conversation with Cal, and they were not surprised. Parents in the community had little reluctance about calling board members, they said. Board members are proscribed by their own code of ethics from making direct contact with teachers or school administrators other than the superintendent of schools. The superintendent simply acts as the bearer of complaints and bad news. The teachers said Szabo had earned a reputation for responding to every parent complaint by blaming a building adminis- trator or a teacher.

"He's not going to defend a teacher; there's no percentage in it; teachers have no power," said the political science teacher.

"I agree," said Gus Poúlos, the psychology teacher. "Cover your ass because when you're in trouble, you'll find out that you're all alone. Szabo will hang you out to dry."

I thanked them for the advice, and excused myself to join Mike Werge, who had just been seated at a table with Larry Silverman, the assistant principal. This was my first social contact with Silverman. He had a reputation as a controversial character, and his appointment as assistant principal the previous month had shocked Cal Bullinger, Don Brandt, and some members of the faculty. It was rumored that Szabo and the board were grooming him and testing him as a prospective replacement for Cal. Teachers had no direct formal contact with the board or the superintendent, nor were they involved in policy deci- sions, but there had been no shortage of rumors in the faculty room, and it did not take long for Larry to offer unsolicited confirmation. Before we ordered dinner, he said, "Hey, you guys may be looking at the new principal of Oldham High School. Maybe by January, but definitely by June."

Larry was a large, intense man who smoked heavily and was in constant motion. While Larry was not known for his subtlety, Mike and I were more than a bit surprised that he was confiding in two nontenured teachers who had been in the district for less than six weeks.

"Cal's a nice guy," Larry continued with little prompting, "but he's not strong enough for the job. He's afraid to stand up to Szabo and the board; they just push him around. The board was only willing to spring for $32,000, and Cal was the best they could get for the money. He really was better than the other candidates. Now he just runs scared. Did you see that guy in the lobby picking up papers and straightening up chairs?" Larry chuckled, and covered his mouth with his hand. "I'd never do that! If I become principal, I wouldn't do those things. I would be the same as I am now; I couldn't change. I would never cow tail to Szabo or to the board of education the way Cal does. I would have no compulsions about telling Szabo exactly how I felt. . . ."

His closest friends on the faculty said that he was a bright guy, and a quick study who enjoyed the intense competition of tournament bridge, but his use of language was legendary among the teachers. One of the English teachers labeled him the "master of malapropisms." Silverman was aware that he might not have presented the ideal image for a principal in this district, but he had the zest for the job and a good understanding of teaching.

"Hey," he said, "I'm a Jew from the coal mining region of Pennsylvania. A certain fraction of this community wants a WASP with a sophisticated, intellectual image. Some people don't think that I have the social enemities for the job, but I understand the politics of education, and I know where the bodies are buried in this district."

Larry claimed that he had always wanted to be a math teacher, and that he had picked up his administrator's certification only when he realized Cal was not a strong principal. He said some members of the board suggested to him that they would look favorably at his candidacy for the principalship.

"Cal's in big trouble," Silverman told us. "The school suffers without a strong principal to fight for it. I seriously think that I could do the job."

Some of Cal's problems were evident at back-to-school night. The evening was scheduled to commence with a welcoming speech to the parents delivered by the principal. I had decided to skip the speech, and was heading down to room 24 to await my first class of parents. Mike Flynn stopped me.

"You're going to miss the speech by our fearless leader?"

"Is he a good speaker?" I asked.

Mike advised me to judge for myself, and I decided to stay for the speech. Cal looked terrified and self-conscious in front the large, friendly crowd. He stooped over the lectern, stumbled over his words, and had difficulty maintaining eye contact. He welcomed the parents in a halting voice, and he seemed very unsure of himself. His face grew red, and his voice trailed off as he explained the agenda for the evening. He spoke in a rich baritone, but he left awkward pauses in the middle of his sentences, and he seemed to be engaged in a prolonged, futile struggle for the right word. He concluded his ten-minute address by wishing the parents an enjoyable evening, and inviting them to stop by his office for a chat when they were free. His discomfort was apparent, and everyone seemed relieved when he ended his address.

It was not possible to judge the reaction of the parents, but the faculty was embarrassed by Cal. They wanted someone who projected a stronger, more articulate image. Cal was probably a bright person, they said, but whatever skills he had were masked by so many insecurities and fears that he could not be an effective principal. The teachers felt he was indecisive, and that he hid in his office to avoid problems. They wanted the principal to be strong, visible, and involved in the daily operation of the building. "He should be in the halls between classes keeping an eye on the kids, checking on the janitors and running the school," said one of the teachers.

"I need to be able to talk to the principal a couple of times a day," another teacher told me. "I don't have time to fight through his secretaries; he should be out in the lobby where he can be accessible to the teachers. I want someone who makes quick decisions," the teacher said, pounding her fist into her hand.

Cal seemed temperamentally unsuited for the role of principal. He was unsure of himself, ill at ease in large groups, and he did not mix comfortably with the faculty or the students. He told Paul De Faro that when he first began his career as a music teacher, he was so nervous that every morning before school, he would have to pull his car to the side of the road to throw up.

During back-to-school night, some of the teachers were nearly as agitated as Cal. Although teaching is a verbal job, most teachers rarely speak to groups of people with adult status and intellect, and there was some excitement and discomfort among the staff. The athletic director stopped me in the lobby.

"There are a lot of heavy hitters here tonight."

"Heavy hitters?" I asked.

"Big bucks. Corporate execs. See that guy over there?" he said, out of the side of his mouth. "On the board of two corporations, 100 acre horse farm in the borough. Nice guy, thinks he knows a lot about sports. He doesn't know diddly. I humor him."

The athletic director elbowed me in the side, and we chuckled. Without a program, it was hard for me to tell who was who. The parents were dressed in business clothes that looked well-tailored but not excessively showy. As a group, the teachers dressed better than they did ordinarily, but because teachers rarely dressed up, more often than not they wore out-of-date styles. Ties and lapels were too wide; colors and skirt lengths often were not current. However, the students, who were there to serve as guides for the parents, teased us about our dress style. Pat Delaney, the calculus teacher misquoted in the *Gazette,* was one of the few male teachers who did not wear a jacket and tie.

"Look," he said, "I want to be judged by the way I teach, not by the way I dress. Let them ask me about mathematics or how I teach it. I was not hired for my fashions." Pat did not seem to care very much for clothes, and he claimed his wife and daughter had "given up" trying to upgrade his image. "I am what I am," he said.

I wore a jacket and tie, although I rarely dressed that way in school. A few of the teachers stopped by room 24 to ask me how things were going.

"Okay, I guess. They laughed at my jokes and no one has hit me so far."

One commented, "It's really a crock of shit, isn't it?"

The teachers looked around uncomfortably. They may not have disagreed with that evaluation, but you had to be careful what you said and how you said it in public schools.

There were more mothers than fathers at back-to-school night. There were far more parents of A-level students than C-level students, and there were more parents of freshmen than of upperclassmen. The short, passionless sessions gave the parents a chance to put faces on the names of their children's teachers, but there was little time to discuss very much of substance. One parent, the mother of a C-level junior, complained that the C classes were given to the "worst teachers in the school." I felt defensive, and I invited her to come in, observe my teaching, and help me out in as many classes as she cared to. "Of course, I wasn't referring to you," she said.

Another parent wanted to know why there were no books for his son to take home. I told him that, frankly, I did not know, and perhaps he should call one of the members of the board of education. One woman told me that she had the highest respect for teachers. "I don't know how you do it. It's a wonder that you can put up with all of these kids, day after day. . . . Teachers and nurses are just marvelous people."

There were at least forty people in each of the freshmen classes. I was depressed by how young the parents looked. For most of them, this was their first back-to-school night in the high school, and they asked probing questions. "What was the focus of the course?" "What skills were being developed?" "How much writing was required?" "How much reading is expected each night?" "Were there computer applications for the social studies program?"

I answered their questions as best I could. I told them how much

I liked teaching their children, and they seemed to appreciate it. Several of the parents stopped by at the end of each class. A few said nice things, that their son or daughter enjoyed my class.

One parent came into my room after the last class. "Hi, I'm Kris Cahill's mother. She wanted me to stop by and say hello to you."

"It's a pleasure to meet you," I told her. "Kris is a very bright kid and she is interesting to have in class."

"Interesting! Thanks. We know that she can be a pain in the rear, but I'm glad you two get along, and I just wanted to say thanks."

It had been a long day; I left the school at 10 P.M., and I would return in eight hours. I had enjoyed meeting the parents, and it helped me to understand my students better. This would be the last time that I saw most of the parents for the rest of the year, and the only time I would see or hear from any of them under favorable circumstances.

5

TEACHERS AND STUDENTS

What is the best thing about teaching at Oldham High School? "The kids." "It's the students." "Academically oriented students." "Cooperative students, who for the most part, are academically interested." "Good kids. I need not threaten, force, or cajole in order to teach." "Lack of 'problem' kids."

In response to a survey, over 80 percent of the teachers indicated that working with the students was the most satisfying part of teaching at the high school, and no teacher suggested that the students were among those aspects of the job which were unpleasant. The teachers complained that the students could be abrasive, arrogant, and a constant reminder of aging, but these were more than compensated for by their life, enthusiasm, and creative energy. The Oldham students had good academic skills; they were middle class; and they planned to attend college. The students also knew what it took to please teachers and succeed in school. Larry Silverman often said, "This school is paradise. There is no better place to teach."

"The students have learned that it is good to be competitive with each other, and deferential and polite to their teachers," said one of the guidance counselors. He said that there was a great deal of parental pressure on the students to conform and do well in school. "These kids come mainly from corporate environments. Their parents—their fathers, really, let's be honest—work for some of the larger corporations in the country. The kids know about promotions and moving up the corporate ladder. They really believe that to get ahead, you have to play by the rules, and it doesn't matter at all if you believe in them."

The population of the school and the community did not reflect the state or the nation. There were only a half-dozen black students in the school. The 1980 census of the Oldham-Webster area indicated there were 76 blacks and 112 people of Spanish origin in a population of over 16,000. There were no black students on the boys' varsity basketball team not because of racial exclusion, but because there were only three black males in the school, and none over 5'8." The only student who had a problem with the English language was an exchange student from Madrid.

Many of the students did not fully recognize the homogeneity of the student body until they left the Oldham-Webster area. A student who had been president of his senior class at Oldham told me that he had not known how sheltered he had been at the high school. "I knew that there were only two black kids in our graduating class, but we are all born and bred Republicans," he said. "I had no idea how narrow our focus was until I got to college. One day, in class, I was expressing a view about welfare that I said a million times in high school, and some guy yells out, 'Yeah that's easy for you to say—a little, rich, white kid from the country!' I never thought about it."

The students assumed that everyone believed as they did. Race was rarely mentioned in school, but there was a seldom-voiced agreement that Oldham was better off because there were few blacks. In class, when we discussed busing as a means to achieve racial integration in schools, one student protested. She said: "My parents worked very hard to make enough money to move out here and get away from the blacks in [our old town], and it wouldn't be fair to bus them to this school." The majority of the students in the class agreed with her.

If the Oldham students possessed a racism born of insularity and family prejudice, few of the teachers held it against them. Only a handful of the teachers expressed a belief that either the school or the quality of education would be enhanced by the inclusion of more minority and poor students, and several said that such a mix would be to the detriment of Oldham. One of the teachers had taught in city schools, and he enjoyed regaling anyone who would listen with the horrors of teaching the "Mau Maus," and "jungle bunnies" who traded in drugs, violence, and teacher abuse. While most of the teachers may not have shared his prejudices, they appreciated working in the calm of Oldham.

The Oldham students came to school with the attitudes that guaranteed the school would work. They typically admired their parents' success, and the students knew that in order to replicate their parents' life style they had to attend the better colleges. Their parents prized academic achievement, pushed their children, and monitored their progress. The administrators and faculty often took parental support for granted. Larry Silverman, exasperated by the cutting and poor classroom behavior of a senior boy, angrily told him that unless he mended his ways, they would have to bring the boy's mother into school. "Good," the student responded. "You find the bitch, you bring her in. We haven't seen her in two months!"

This was an anomaly. Oldham parents were generally eager to come in for a conference with teachers, and in many cases a report card grade of less than B would guarantee a phone call from the child's parent inquiring about the grade and asking for a meeting with the teacher. After the first ten-week marking period, I was besieged with requests for parent conferences. The conferences were scheduled for me at either 7:00 or 7:15 A.M. A note in my mailbox would inform me how much sleep I would need to give up. I asked one of the guidance counselors if the two conferences I was averaging per week were typical for the school. "I don't know what you're complaining about," he said, facetiously. "You're the one who gave too many Cs. If you don't want conferences, give better grades next marking period. I could use the extra sleep myself."

Every quarter the supervisors were told to report the grade distributions to the members of their department. Teachers who gave too many high grades were teased for their lack of standards; teachers who gave too many low grades were said to be courting disaster. I asked Troy why he gave the grade distributions to us.

"I don't know for certain," he said, with a smile. "Dr. Mokowski [the assistant superintendent] just says to give them out, but I'm sure there is a message here."

After the second marking period my grades were somewhat higher than the departmental mean. Several teachers complimented my rapid rate of socialization. I told them that I had become a much better teacher since coming to the high school, and the higher student grades simply reflected my new-found skills.

DISCIPLINE

Oldham was a very pleasant, relaxed, and informal school. There was some tension among various student groups, and there was evidence of adolescent jealousy, hostility, and cruelty, but it was usually psychological, not physical warfare. There were very few confrontations between students during the school year, and the palpable tension and anger that characterize many urban schools were not part of the Oldham climate. There were no guards in the halls, no need for an elaborate pass system, and very few locked doors. According to Don Brandt,

the assistant principal in charge of discipline, there were only a handful of "volatile kids," and he said he was able to keep an eye on them.
The students were discreet: They did not smoke cigarettes in the
building. They did not often drink alcohol during the day; and teachers rarely came upon marijuana smokers. Compliant students made
discipline easy. As one of the teachers said, "The kids here are like silly
putty."

Even in the most tranquil schools, students have to be supervised,
watched, and regulated. Although the goal of the school was to imbue
students with an internal sense of discipline, while they were in school
discipline was exercised externally by the administrators and teachers.
Teachers disliked "playing cop," as they termed their role in the en-
forcement of school rules. Typical of public high schools, there was no
shortage of rules to be enforced at Oldham. Students were not permitted to leave the school grounds without parental permission; the
school regulated when and where they could eat and smoke, and when
they could use the lavs. The faculty were outnumbered by a ratio of
20:1, and without a compliant student body it would have been impossible to enforce the rules. School duties such as library/lobby duty,
cafeteria duty, and the other discipline maintenance tasks were tolera-
ble only because they were easy, but they always had the potential for
turning students and teachers into antagonists.

During one particularly hot fall afternoon, I was assigned to supervise students in the auditorium. The students were attending a required assembly on career choices sponsored by the United States
Army. There were five hundred students in the audience, surrounded
by about fifteen teachers. It was an interesting multimedia presentation narrated by a good-looking young man who drew more than a
few whistles from the girls in the auditorium. The students were
generally well-behaved, and I was able to watch the presentation. As
a classroom teacher with few props at my disposal, I admired the
speaker's microphone, rear-screen projectors, stereo speakers, and
light show. Willa Green was on duty next to me, and toward the end
of the period she whispered, "Get ready! The assembly is going to end
early and the kids will make a break for it. Spread the word."

I began to get tense. I looked at my watch. There were less than
ten minutes left in the school day, but it was obvious that the presentation would draw to a close before the last bell would ring. The rules
said that the school day ended at 2:40 P.M. regardless of when the
assembly ended, and we had to keep the students in the auditorium
until the bell rang.

Willa was right. Just before the lights went on, one student bolted by her and ran out through the side door. Willa made a lunge for the student, but missed her. "Stop! Come back here!" she screamed at the back of the fleeing student. "I don't know your name, but I know your face. I'll be looking for you! Get back here!"

The girl did not return. Willa later told me that she had been bluffing. She would not be able to recognize the girl again, although she looked for her. It bothered Willa that somewhere in the school there was a student who had defied her and had gotten away with it. The lights came up and, reflexively, the students in the auditorium began to stand and head for the exits. Willa shouted, "Get back! Wait for the bell!" I turned to confront the students in front of me.

"I'm sorry," I told them, "but you'll have to keep your seats until the bell rings."

I was uncomfortable, unsure of my ability to control the students; I was apologetic in the hopes that if they did storm out, they would just push me aside and not trample me. The students grimaced, but to my surprise, they took their seats. I felt very powerful, more powerful than I did when I sanctioned the use of the lavatories or told students to raise their hands before asking a question. Several tons of students were controlled by the sound of my quivering voice. One of the teachers told me that most of the Oldham students were so far out of the mainstream of American public education that they did not know high school students were supposed to be rebellious and naturally contemptuous of authority. "One of the nice things about teaching at Oldham," he said, "is that it is really easy to break up a fight here. None of the kids wants to ruin two thousand dollars' worth of orthodontia."

Physical violence was very rare among Oldham students, but there was one fight I knew about after school at the Oldham Village Racquet Club. In the middle of my workout, I noticed that about a dozen junior boys had gathered in the rear of the building. They were crowding around two students who were posing as boxers and pumping themselves up with mild profanity and exchanges of powerful braggadocio. I heard them each vowing to do the other in because of something which had taken place that day in school. I drifted out the back door wondering if I should, or could, do something to stop the fight. By the time I got there, the students had thrown a few punches. Red marks rose on the face of one and on the chest of the other, but no blood was drawn, and no serious physical damage had been done. The fight was over.

"Did I stop the fight?" I whispered to one of the few students I knew in the group—a junior boy from my first period class.

"Nope. That was an Oldham fight. They don't last long. Most of us have known each other all of our lives. We really don't want to hurt each other. We'll give you credit for stopping the fight if you want that tough-guy image. Hey, guys, did you see the way Doc tore into those two. . . ?"

"Thanks anyway," I interrupted, "I don't need to build a reputation I can't back up."

We parted laughing, and I resumed my workout.

Some of the teachers wanted an angrier student body, one that could muster more outrage at social injustice and world problems. Many did not like the conformity or the lack of intellectual curiosity among the students. One teacher who had grown up in the 1960s referred to them as "corporate clones" who all looked alike and thought alike. But all the teachers admired the students' ease, humor, and self-confidence. It was easy to teach them, and they were fun to be around.

TROUBLE IN PARADISE

In my American history course we discussed the role income played in determining social class, and I asked the students what level of income they thought separated the middle class from the upper class. One student suggested $50,000.

"Fifty thousand dollars? No way!" shouted another student. "Fifty thousand is nothing! If my father made only fifty thousand, we'd be broke. We have a big family. It's gotta be a hundred and fifty thousand, at least."

I reminded the student that no one in the school earned fifty thousand dollars a year.

"Yeah, but you're only teachers. No offense, Doc."

On one hand, it was wonderful to have students who were well behaved and easy to teach. On the other hand, it was difficult to be regularly reminded of your comparative disadvantage. Many of the Oldham students had money to spend on things which their parents believed had some educational value. Some of the more enterprising teachers planned trips to foreign countries, enlisted twenty or more students, and had their own trips paid for. While it was unquestionably a great deal of work to plan, organize, and chaperone school trips, it was the only way in which some of the teachers could afford to travel. In the course of the year, Paul De Faro and Mike Werge organized a trip to the Soviet Union. Willa Green and another English teacher took students to England, and there were also trips to Mexico and France led by members of the language department.

"I really enjoyed the trip to the Soviet Union," Mike Werge told me. "I love to travel; I've always wanted to go to Leningrad and Moscow, and I got to know the students better. It was really a good trip in every regard, and this might seem silly," he added, "but I also felt like a mature, responsible adult. Paul and I planned the itinerary. We recruited the students. We arranged for the visas, and negotiated for the best price with the travel agencies. We were in charge of a pretty sophisticated enterprise which we organized from scratch in our spare time. It was completely unlike my work as a teacher: I felt that I had responsibility and that I had accomplished something."

While planning the trip to the Soviet Union, Paul and Mike had to meet with the students and their parents several times to discuss the trip, protocol, and the constraints on the students' behavior. During a meeting held in the home of one of the parents, Paul and Mike showed videotapes of their previous foreign travels to assure the parents they were experienced in these matters. Mike later told me about the evening:

"We were in an incredibly lovely home—Oriental rugs, expensive antiques, all elegantly arranged. I was showing a videotape, and one of the mothers yells out, 'Oh, look at that guy with the Italian tan!' I cringed. One of the shots showed a worker bare to the waist, and you could see tan lines left by his T shirt. I was really glad that Paul was in another room at that time, and I said, 'You're not winning many points with Mr. De Faro.' The woman excused herself, and said that the guy had a 'construction-worker look.' I tried to make light of it. I laughed, and told her that she ought to quit when she was ahead, and that she had insulted Paul twice. She obviously didn't know that Paul worked construction in the summer. What can you do? You wouldn't hear this shit in a working class community, but they wouldn't have the money to travel."

Most of the teachers and all the administrators had grown up in working class homes. They were typically the first generation of college graduates in their families, and many had attended local, inexpensive state colleges attractive to working class students. At Oldham, nearly half of the college-bound students could be expected to enroll in private colleges, and over two-thirds of the students enrolled in out-of-state colleges.

"It doesn't bother me to see the honors kids go to Yale or Stanford," one of the teachers told me. "What pisses me off is to have some arrogant little bastard from one of my slower classes get into a private school and then look down his nose at me because I went to a state teachers' college. We were poor; I didn't have the money to go anywhere else."

Some of the teachers resented the opportunities available to the students, and one claimed that they were the "victims of their parents' wealth."

"These kids have it too good," said one of the teachers who had grown up in a nearby community. "They're spoiled. My [athletic] teams don't work hard; they expect everything to be handed to them. They don't need to win. They don't like to sweat."

Other teachers were envious.

"In some ways it's hard for me to teach in this school," a foreign language teacher told me. "I hear the kids talk about their private riding lessons and their private tennis lessons, and I'd like to give those things to my own kids, but I can't afford it. I have to do landscaping in the summer just to make ends meet."

Part-time and summer jobs were a way of life for teachers. Many of the teachers claimed that their salary was so low they could not afford to travel or go to graduate school full-time during the summers. They laughed at the idea of year-round twelve-month schools. "It will never happen," said the head of the language department. "It will be too expensive for the districts, and besides that, who will paint all the houses and mow all the lawns if teachers have to teach in the summers?"

Most of the teachers claimed they could not afford to live in either Webster or Oldham, and many of them considered the schools their children attended to be inferior to Oldham's schools. "I feel like a servant in a rich man's house," said a math teacher. "I take very good care of the rich man's children, but my own children do not get the same care."

The students knew of the teachers' envy and resentment. "You think we're all loaded, don't you?" asked a senior boy, angrily. "All the teachers think we're rolling in money. You can't even look at us without seeing our money! If you knew you were going to be so uptight about money, why did you go into teaching?"

"My father works ten or twelve hour days," said another student. "You guys have the summers off! What more do you want?"

Many of the students were wealthy, but many more came from families that worked hard and budgeted carefully to get by; some came from families that were struggling. About 25 percent of my juniors and seniors held down part-time jobs. They worked as waitresses, bus boys, and dishwashers in restaurants, as stock boys in supermarkets, and as garage mechanics. Few made more than the minimum wage; most claimed that working was more than a luxury, and all the students who worked laughed at the notion that they were spoiled rich kids. "I know it! I know it! All the teachers think that we sit around in our Jacuzzis and clip coupons," said one student. "That's a joke! Yeah, we have a nice house, but my parents are divorced, my mom has to work, and we're scuffling. I wouldn't work six nights a week waitressing if I didn't have to."

Another student claimed that one of his coaches blamed every team loss on the students' soft middle class life style, telling them, "Go home to your Cadillacs."

"He would yell at us on the team bus after a loss, calling us a bunch of 'Oldham asses.' That was his favorite expression when he was mad at us. It meant that we didn't work hard, we didn't put out, and we didn't try. It just got the team mad."

It was rumored that the coach's verbal attacks were a contributing factor in the dismissal of this nontenured teacher.

The Oldham students could not understand why some of the younger teachers spent hours on the phone trying to get tickets for an upcoming concert by the rock and roll hero of the working class, Bruce Springsteen. "Why would anyone want to go to listen to him?" asked one of my junior boys. "He sings about looking for work, and hating your job, and running away. *De*pressing!"

"Yeah," agreed another. "He sings about being in a union. How could anybody be in a union? I would never take a job that I had to join a union for."

"Me neither," agreed the first student. "Someone told me that Springsteen comes from a part of New Jersey that's real congested. You know, where the houses are close to each other with only a driveway and a little land between them."

The students with dirt under their nails from garage work and those with red eyes from late nights in the kitchen said nothing. Even when I asked them to comment on anti-union and anti-worker sentiments, they would just shrug their shoulders. More often than not, these were the students from Webster, the students some of the Oldham residents referred to as the "Websterricans."

The administration and the head of the pupil personnel department denied it, and some of the supervisors said that it did not exist, but most of the counselors and teachers knew that there was a constant low-keyed antagonism between the Oldham students and the Webster students. The Oldham students came from the wealthier parts of the district. They were more preppy in their dress, and they were more compliant students. The Webster students had a harder edge. They were less willing to give unquestioned respect to their teachers, and less willing to play the school game. But the Webster students represented the only area in the district that was experiencing a population increase, and the teachers worried openly about the change in the school this would create. "This school is changing for the worse," lamented Willa Green. "There is more crime, less respect. There are fewer good kids now. I hate to say it, but I think it's because of the Webster kids."

The rivalry between the two groups could affect teaching. In one of my American history classes, there was a vocal group of Oldham girls and an equally vocal group of Webster girls. Whenever there was a class discussion, the two groups would invariably take opposing sides based on personal antagonisms more than disagreements over the issue. One of the Oldham girls, a cheerleader, approached me after class.

"Doc, you have to stop making us talk in class. Just give notes, okay? Every time I say something that little bitch jumps down my throat. Sorry, Doc, but she is a bitch."

I told her that I would think about it. Later in the day, one of the Webster girls stopped me in the hall and asked me about my conversation with the cheerleader.

"What was she saying about us? I know she was complaining again. I'd like to scratch her eyes out."

I told her that the two groups were making it hard for me to teach. I could not hold a discussion or a debate, or play a simulation game in class, I explained, because of the hostility among the students.

"Look, Doc, it's them. The Oldham preppy-fags think that we are a bunch of burn-outs and dope fiends. I hate being in class with them. They look down at us and they rag on us all the time. I'd like to tear her tongue out."

It was well over ninety degrees in the school. The Webster student was wearing jeans, a tube top, and a denim jacket, and she was perspiring and flushed.

"Why don't you take your jacket off? You look uncomfortable," I told her.

"You wanna know why? Because I got a tattoo last night, and if those Oldham bitches see it, they'll bust on me the whole period. They won't say boo to my face, but I can hear them cackle to themselves. Wanna see my tattoo?"

I nodded, and the student showed me a burn mark on her shoulder that would eventually turn into a multicolored butterfly. I admired the tattoo and made a mental note to lecture in class on the following day instead of trying to get active class participation.

One of the guidance counselors told me that Oldham High School was very "cliqueish." It was a hard place for new kids to fit in, he said. In some ways the Webster students were outsiders. They came from a part of the district that had been sending students to Oldham High for only three or four years. The high school was located in Oldham Borough, and the Oldham students felt it was their school. The Oldham kids all knew each other from Little League and soccer and other community activities, and many of them were cold to the Webster students.

"The grovers are the exception," the counselor told me. "They'll take in anybody. All you have to do is smoke cigarettes and wear jeans, and you can share your dislike of the school. They're the most disaffected kids in the school, and there's good reason for their disaffection. There is a lot of snobbery here. It's easy to be a grover; it's harder to be accepted by the preps. I'm surprised there aren't more grovers."

GUIDANCE

One of the guidance counselors told me: "It was easy for the teachers to forget that the students were individuals. When you deal with hundreds of them a day," he said, "you forget that they have a wide array of problems that get in the way of their learning anything." In addition to the Oldham–Webster antipathies, he cited problems of sex, drugs, alcohol, family relationships, and self-image. "A lot of these kids are sensitive, and they are easily hurt," he added.

On occasion I found myself inadvertently trampling on a student's feelings. Sometimes the student would tell me about it later; sometimes the student's friend would tell me; occasionally, I would hear through the official line of communication. Late on a Friday night, there was a message on my telephone answering machine to call Larry Silverman, the assistant principal. In public schools, a call from a building administrator rarely augured well for teachers, especially if the call came on a weekend. Teachers claimed that if you did not hear anything, everything was going well. Any news, they said, had to be bad news.

I returned Larry's call the following morning.

"Hey, sorry to bother you at home," he said, "but we got a problem. Did you send a progress report home on Bobby Daria?"

Progress reports were sent out midway through the ten-week marking period to indicate an academic, attendance, or attitude problem. The parents of all students who were doing less than satisfactory work were to be notified by mail. I told Larry that I remembered filling out something about Bobby, but I could not recall what I had written. I asked him what the trouble was.

"Did you write this? Listen. 'Bobby is more interested in booze, broads, and parties [his words] than school. If it were not for the fact that his father has a good deal of money, Bobby would not have been able to buy his way into a third-rate college, and he probably would be a lot happier.'"

"Uh oh!" I told Larry that I did write that, but it was part of a confidential memo I had sent to Daria's guidance counselor indicating that he should talk to Bobby about some problems he was having in my class. It was not supposed to be mailed home. Bobby Daria was no one's favorite student. He was an eighteen-year-old senior in a C-level history class. He had trouble reading, he disliked writing, and he rarely paid attention in class. He cheated on tests, and he was so clumsy at it that all his teachers knew he cheated. During one test, I looked up and found Bobby pretending to be stretching while searching desperately for answers on another paper.

"I was just loosening up, Doc."

I moved his seat and he did not protest. When I again caught him looking for help from another student, I asked him to move his desk into the hall. He meekly argued, "How can I concentrate on the test with all these interruptions?"

A few minutes later one of the math teachers brought him into the room, and explained that Bobby had been asking people in the hall for answers to the test questions.

"Who does that scumbag think he is?" asked an infuriated Bobby Daria after the teacher had left. "This is social studies. I wasn't cheating on a math test. I'll remember that guy."

It was not difficult to find reasons to fail Bobby, but he was not an unlikable kid. For all his bombast, he was gentle and sensitive, and he would have been hurt if he had read the memo that had been sent home. "We gotta do something," Larry told me on the phone. "I gotta live in this town. Bobby's father drove over here when he came home from work on Friday night, and he was here until eight o'clock. He was furious, and I told him I would look into it. I think I calmed him down."

I told Larry that I would call Bobby's guidance counselor, and that we would straighten it out. I also told Larry that everything I had written was true. One of his former teachers had described Bobby as being "as dumb as a box of rocks," and I was sure that I could get all his present teachers to agree. This did not make Larry feel any better.

Bobby's guidance counselor was one of the more respected counselors in the school; both the students and the teachers trusted him. He had a reputation for being especially sympathetic to the more troubled kids. "I guess I'm a crusader," he told me. "I was a social studies teacher for three years, but I was worried about becoming stagnant, you know, whipping out the same old tests year after year. I got a master's degree in guidance from [the state university], and I went into the field basically so I could help people."

He told me that as a classroom teacher he did not have the time to work with students as people. The demands of teaching academic content kept him away from the personal side of teaching too much. Now as a guidance counselor he did not teach at all, but he had over three hundred students to counsel, advise, and get into college. Much of his time was spent buried in paperwork in a department he described as "chaotic" and "inefficient."

"This place is a zoo," he said. "The secretaries schedule kids to see me every fifteen minutes. There are always calls from parents, college applications to fill out, special projects to do, and the learning community to look in on."

I began to understand how a memo could be sent home by mistake. I later learned that the incident distressed no one in the guidance office. They were surprised, they told me, that it had not happened before. The guidance office had been operating with a very small clerical staff, and it was under unusual strain trying to master a new data processing system. The director of pupil personnel and one secretary spent most of their time learning to operate the new system and getting the bugs out of it.

"I really didn't read all of what you wrote," admitted the counselor. "I just gave it to the secretary, and she mailed it home instead of filing it, thinking that it was a progress report. The problem is that we use the same forms for progress reports and confidential memos."

We agreed that I would call Mr. Daria and tell him the truth. I called him Sunday afternoon. As someone who worked for a large corporation, we hoped he would understand the nature of bureaucratic foul-ups. He did, but he was angry. He kept me on the phone for a long time, forcing me to restate and rephrase my apologies. I understood the reasons for his anger, and I felt responsible. I told him that

I was sorry for writing the memo, sorry the school had mailed it out, and sorry for any implied attack on his position and wealth.

Bobby's guidance counselor called him at work on Monday morning and apologized for the problems created by his department. I saw the counselor later in the day. "I think everything is going to be smoothed over," he said. "I told Mr. Daria that it was a mistake, etcetera, etcetera."

"Good," I said, "I'm glad that's over."

"Well, it's not completely over yet. There is one more thing. Mr. Daria would like a formal letter of apology from you on school stationery."

"Screw him. I have exhausted my contrition. If I write anything I will apologize for his son being as dumb as a box of rocks. . . ."

"I thought you would feel that way," empathized the counselor. "I think he's going too far, but I'll write a letter and formally apologize for both of us. Again."

The teachers were not surprised there had been a problem, and some were privately glad that guidance had "messed up." The teachers tended to view guidance as easy work, and one of the few avenues of escape from the classroom. Guidance counselors had no classes for which to prepare, no papers to grade, no content to cover, and they were not trapped by the bell schedule. Their salary was 5 percent higher than that of a teacher with similar experience and degrees. They had their own offices and their own phones, and more important, they had the chance to work with students and function as student advocates more than anyone else in the school.

The teachers advised me not to be too candid, and not to put anything in writing that could cause trouble. "Yeah, all that stuff you wrote was true," said Gus Poulus, "but see what happens when you write it. They throw it back in your face. Never write anything. This way you can deny saying something, and they have no proof. Everything you write that is critical of the school or the administration is put in your file, and they will use it against you."

"You know what bothers me the most about this whole thing?" said Paul De Faro. "When parents have a problem, they never contact the teacher directly. The first thing they do is go over his head to the principal, or the superintendent, or one of their friends on the board of education. Why don't they call us first? Didn't they ever hear of a chain of command?"

The other teachers agreed. Parents rarely contacted teachers directly when there was a problem. Teachers ordinarily could not be contacted by phone. There were no phones in classrooms, and teachers did not have offices or secretaries. When parents called and asked to speak to their child's teacher, they were directed to the child's guidance counselor or the teacher's department supervisor. Teachers resented this line of communication, which denied them the opportunity to solve their own problems and which always put them in jeopardy. "If we had our own phones," argued one teacher, "they would lose some of their control."

The pattern of communication triggered by parental complaints was predictable. At the beginning of the second marking period, the head of pupil personnel services stopped me in the main office before school. "You should check with Chris Buckley's guidance counselor. The CST classified him NI, and the parents say that you're not adhering to his IEP."

"Did he try penicillin?" I asked, not knowing what he was talking about.

The head of guidance smiled, and it was obvious that he was not upset. There had been a complaint from one of the parents, but the counselor had been in guidance for over twenty years, and he was accustomed to parental complaints. He knew that I had no idea what all these initials meant, and he just wanted me to contact one of the guidance counselors to placate the parents. I learned that Chris had been classified "neurologically impaired" (NI) by the "child study team" (CST), but I, and most of his other teachers, had disregarded his "individualized educational plan" (IEP), and his parents were threatening to sue the teachers, the counselor, and the school.

By state law, every school district had to have at least one CST composed of the school psychologist, a school social worker, and a learning disabilities teacher-consultant. The state guaranteed that all educationally handicapped students would be given appropriate education. Students like Chris, who had been referred to the team because of some suspected learning disorder, were evaluated, classified, and given a special program of instruction. Their teachers were informed of their specific learning problem, and a list of specialized instructional strategies was devised to help the teachers address the students' problems. At the beginning of the school year, all teachers met with the CST to review IEPs for those students in their classes who had been classified as learning disabled. The teachers held the CST in very low esteem. CST members were generally considered to be unhelpful in remediating learning problems, and they added to the teachers' paperwork.

"What do I think of the CST?" one teacher asked. "It's an example of early retirement. Those guys do so little they should be embarrassed when they cash their paychecks. I have a student who they described as 'suffering from dyslexia.' They recommend that I use nonprint materials in my teaching as much as possible. How do I do that and teach literature?"

I had four students who were classified NI and three classified as PI (perceptually impaired). I asked the learning consultant to explain the differences between these classifications. One teacher mumbled, "Spelling." I noticed some of the other teachers in the room shift position uncomfortably in their chairs. The learning consultant said, "There really isn't a whole lot of difference between NI and PI. We have a great deal of freedom in classifying students. In Oldham and Webster a kid is classified NI or PI. If he lived in a city, he would be classified MR (mentally retarded) or SM (socially maladjusted). The parents here find it easier to accept that their child is perceptually impaired or neurologically impaired than mentally retarded. It doesn't sound so horrible when they tell their friends about it at cocktail parties."

I looked over the strategies suggested by the IEPs and noted few variations, despite differences in classifications. It was recommended that some students be given extra time with their writing assignments and other students needed to see things as well as hear them. A few needed additional help from one of the three special education teachers. Chris Buckley's IEP indicated that because Chris had trouble writing and reading, his essay tests and writing assignments should be administered in another form. I had not done this; Chris failed the first marking period. His parents claimed the school was in violation of a contract and state law, and that we had caused Chris to suffer unnecessarily. Chris's guidance counselor had to assure the parents that I, and the other teachers, would follow the IEP; and he had to encourage us to do so.

"Well, Chris," I said to him after psychology class, "you have a cassette tape recorder, right? How would it be if you talked into the recorder rather than write your papers and tests?"

Chris was an open and agreeable kid. "Sure, Doc," he said. "That's fine." Chris giggled, and added, "I have a VCR at home. Would you prefer a video?"

I assured him that hearing him would be more than enough for me. I had a cassette player in the car and I listened to Chris on my way home from school. It took me longer to return his "papers" and tests, but Chris did not seem to mind. He passed the course with a grade of C, and entered a small private college in New England that had a special program for students with learning disabilities. I was glad to help Chris out, but I had no idea what I would have done if I had had twenty students with Chris's problem.

GIFTED AND TALENTED

While the teachers believed that the students were the best part of the job, many said that their most satisfying experiences with students took place outside the classroom. One teacher wrote: "The problem with teaching is that you have to force the kids to do things which neither of you think are important. I enjoy the kids best when I'm coaching or leading a field trip." A math teacher said: "We're all in this business because we like kids, but some of the kids get shortchanged. Unless you work with the students outside the class, many of them get very little from the school. The classroom really serves only the smart kids, but they get shortchanged too. It's cruel, but it's true."

I thought it would be fun to work with students outside the classroom, and I volunteered to become an adviser to the gifted and talented program. The G&T program would allow me to work with small groups of four or five students in weekly meetings. Each student was expected to complete an individual research project; there would be group trips to the Metropolitan Opera and to another high school; and there would be a series of guest speakers. According to the curriculum guide:

> The gifted and talented program is a program for students who have been identified as possessing exceptional intellectual ability. . . . The program is designed to provide these students with special individual, small group, and counseling opportunities, on a regularly-scheduled basis under the supervision of a staff advisor. . . .

An English teacher glanced over my shoulder as I read the announcement calling for volunteers to work with the G&T program. "You're going to be a 'Gin and Tonic' adviser, huh! Well, that's terrific. Have a nice time, coach. Let me know what you think of it." I asked him what he thought of the program, but he simply smiled and said, "You'll find out for yourself."

G&T advisers received a $400 stipend, and they had to give up one free period a week. The students in my group had all scored well on a group intelligence test, the sole selection criterion, but they seemed not very different from many other students in the school. The faculty advisers had decided that the G&T program would explore music and economics. As part of the music unit, students were invited to a series of conversations with professional musicians. There was a jazz musician, an opera singer, a fiddler who played bluegrass and country music, and the impresario of wedding bands. The musicians talked about their work, their art, and their life styles. We studied the libretto from Mozart's opera *Don Giovanni* and went into New York for the live performance. I sat next to Willa Green, an opera buff, whose enthusiasm I did not find infectious. It was hot, our seats were far from the stage, and I dozed off a couple of times.

One of my advisees caught me napping, and during the intermission he pulled me aside and lectured me. "You'll never make it as a G&T adviser," he said. "We were as bored as you were, but we're high school kids, and we know how to fake interest."

Another student told me that he would never again listen to adult criticisms of rock and roll. "My parents say they can't understand rock lyrics. I listened to the whole opera and didn't understand one word!"

Some students said they enjoyed the opera, but they were not sure why this was part of a gifted and talented program. Nor was I. During our weekly session, the students told me not to be concerned about it. "We're here to make our high school records look better. We show up once a week, go on a few trips, and fake-out a few colleges. It's no big deal," he advised me, "don't get too hung up about it."

None of my students completed their individual projects, nor did most of them ever intend to. Some of the students had been in the program for two years, and they said my experience was not atypical. "Not much goes on," admitted one student. "Last year our adviser sat and talked about things we didn't understand. This is better. At least *you* don't pretend to be doing something intellectual and important."

Several of the other G&T advisers shared my discomfort. "I don't feel like I'm doing anything," confided a math teacher who sat on the board of education of another district, "but you just can't have a suburban high school that doesn't have a G&T program."

There was little general agreement among the teachers concerning the goals of the gifted and talented program. Typical of most issues in the curriculum, each teacher had his or her own idea based largely on past personal experiences and a gut feeling about what should be done to improve education. The teachers who had planned the G&T program had their own agenda. They recognized that many of the Oldham–Webster students lacked contact with other than white, middle class people, and as part of the economics unit, the Oldham Gifted and Talented Program initiated an exchange of visits with a predominantly black inner-city school. The city school was receiving a good deal of positive media attention. A new principal was being credited for instilling pride, stronger discipline, and higher expectations among the students.

A trip to the city school had gone well; the city school was pleased to have the Oldham students visit, and the Oldham students offered an invitation to come to their school in return. Several months later, the students from an academic honors program in the city school visited Oldham High, and the G&T students served as hosts. It was easy to tell the students apart. All the Oldham students were white; all the city students were black or Hispanic. As an opening activity, the students were divided into pairs, one student from each school, and they were asked to interview each other using a set of questions written by the teachers from both schools. The students seemed a little shy at first, and after some initial hesitance they mixed politely if not easily. Fifteen minutes later, the students formed a large circle and introduced the student they had been interviewing to the rest of the group. One of the questions on the interview sheet concerned future plans: "What do you plan to do after high school?"

There was a great similarity in the responses. Students from both schools planned to go to college, and career choices of computer scientist, engineer, and doctor rolled off their lips with equal ease and frequency. There the similarities ended. All the city students had used computers in school, but the Oldham students who planned to study engineering or computer science owned their own computers. Some Oldham students had more than one computer at home, many had gone to computer camps in the summer, and several had access to the mainframe computers of their parents' employers. When the city students introduced the Oldham students to the group, their shock was apparent. One of the students pointed to his partner and said, "This guy has an IBM XT and an Apple 2C, and he is building a robot with the money he made writing programs! Can you believe that!"

I met with some of the Oldham students after the session, and they too were surprised by some of the things they learned.

"Do you know that the salutatorian of their graduating class is pregnant with her second child, and she's not married!" one student told me.

Another said, "Did you see the way they ate in the cafeteria? I think they took extra food just because it was free."

"One girl told me she didn't think she could come today because there was no one to take care of her baby, but she left it with a neighbor at the last minute. I can't imagine doing that," said a very shocked freshman girl.

SOME LONERS

Not all of the brightest students were in the G&T program. A few found no place to satisfy their academic curiosity; many were just hanging out, waiting for high school to finish and hoping that college would be better. The school served most of the students reasonably well, but those on the fringes had difficulty. The very bright, the creative, the athletic who did not like team sports, the alienated, the loners, and the rebellious students had trouble in a school where there was great pressure to adapt and conform, and too few opportunities for individual attention.

During the first full-period test I gave in American history, a girl sitting by the door grabbed her stomach and doubled up, apparently in pain. I took her out into the hall, and we talked as I looked into the classroom through the small rectangular window in the door.

"Are you okay? Do you want to go to the nurse?"

"I'll be okay. I'm just upset," she said, and she started to cry.

"I hope you're not worried about the test. You know you can take it over as many times as you need to until you pass. . . ."

"I know," she interrupted. "I'm not worried about the test. I'll be okay."

"Is there something else?"

"It's got nothing to do with school. I hate this fuckin' place. It sucks. Life sucks."

After a few moments, she composed herself and became more specific. She said, "My sister's pregnant, and she's afraid to tell my parents. We're Catholic. My father will just flip out. I hate it when he gets mad. He wants me to go to college. I don't want to go to college. I just want to run away to California with my boyfriend. I'm thinking of quitting school."

We talked in the empty hallway while the other students completed the test. The student trusted me enough to share her feelings, and I felt some responsibility to try to help. We talked a few more times during a three-week period. We did not have a common free period; the student attended a vocational program in another school during the afternoons, but we managed to get together for a few minutes before school. She was able to resolve some of her problems well enough to stay in school and graduate, but she slipped through the school without creating much of a ripple. She gave the barest in effort, attendance, and attention, and she asked for little help from the teachers and staff.

School was not pleasant for her. She rarely received grades higher than C; most of her teachers gave her no special attention or help; she had few friends in school, and she was just marking time until she graduated. Somebody else would get the lead part in the school play; others would be team captains, and voted most popular and most likely to succeed; she just hung out and got high in the grove. I did not know if any of the teachers had her in mind when they responded "The students were the best part of Oldham High School," but she would have been surprised if they had. A few of the teachers told me to refer the student to her guidance counselor and not to get involved. One teacher seemed more interested in the gossip than in the student, and he asked me for the student's name. "Her?" he asked. "I know her sister. I can't imagine anyone knocking her up."

The student was too alienated from the school to use its support services. She had nothing against her guidance counselor, she said, but she would not go to talk with him. She knew about the adolescent drop-in clinic run by a local mental health agency, and she knew which days the school psychologist was in the building, but she would not go to either of them. "This place is a prison," she told me. "If you want to help me, just listen to me bitch every once in a while. You don't have to say anything, just listen. I need to get some stuff off my chest."

The school psychologist told me that many of the students found themselves trapped by a school which was unresponsive to them. He said most of the students who came to see him were there to escape from the restraints imposed by the institution, and he claimed that it was a highly controlled school, regardless of what the administration contended. Oldham High School was a tough place to be comfortable as a student unless you succeeded in narrow areas of success defined by the school. Unless a student participated in athletics or did well academically, there was little chance for status or recognition. Most of the students would go unrecognized.[1]

The teachers understood that all the students needed help from time to time. Troy Thayer, my department supervisor, claimed that this was one of the more important, although unofficial, functions of a teacher. Every teacher I spoke to could recall several students he or she had counseled over the years. Students sought out teachers with whom they felt some rapport, or whom they perceived as a source of

---

[1]In another ethnographic study, I attended classes with high school students. The brighter students and the athletes had far more interactions with their teachers than the other students. Among the students I observed was a junior girl who followed a vocational business program. In the more than twenty classes we attended together, she never volunteered an answer, and no teacher called on her, joked with her, or teased her. For her, there was very little pleasure to be derived from school or her interactions with teachers (Palonsky, 1975).

help. Some teachers said they reached out for students who were "outsiders," or "troubled," or perhaps a reminder of the problems they themselves had experienced as adolescents. Every teacher identified with different students. Some liked the rebellious, others the disaffected, or the terribly shy. Paul De Faro liked those students who were having trouble adjusting to Oldham. "I like the kids with real problems. I relate better to the screwed up kids. It's really hard on a lot of the kids who don't fit the Oldham model of a college-bound preppy. I can identify with their alienation."

Formally, teachers had no role as counselors. They had little or no training in adolescent psychology or counseling, and none in therapy. There was no time in the school day set aside for teachers to meet with students, and it was not part of their job description. The teachers were not evaluated on the basis of their work as counselors, but teachers regularly reached out for students they thought they could help. If you do not like the students, the teachers said, you should not be a teacher.

"I like to work with kids," said Mike Werge. "It's one of the reasons I went into teaching. I think that this is what the job is all about. Helping a kid keep his head screwed on right is certainly a lot more important than teaching about American history. What else is there? You can't pretend you are a high school teacher for the academics. You don't come to school for the quality of food in the cafeteria. It's the kids. If you do not like the students, you can't stay in teaching. There is nothing else. It takes a lot of time, and there are insufficient rewards, but someone has to do it."

There was little money in teaching. It was not a glamorous or exciting job. The single source of both teachers' frustration and job satisfaction was the students. Most of the teachers did not question a student who asked for help, whether it was an academic or a personal problem. This, they said, is what the job was all about. I could not help but try. When students came to talk about problems, I listened. If they needed encouragement, I tried to encourage them. If they needed counseling, I tried to counsel them. When I thought they needed therapy, I had to tell their parents.

I told the mother of one student that I thought her son was having some serious problems. School had become a very unpleasant place for him. He seemed to have no friends, and many of the students picked on him unmercifully in class. He was teased and verbally attacked by boys and girls alike, and he was the butt of classroom jokes and ridicule. Although he was very bright, he rarely completed homework assignments or papers. He failed tests, and he was in jeopardy of failing for the year. He was absent from school nearly half the time, and there was little evidence of somatic illness. He was overweight and self-conscious about it. He told me that he always wore long sleeve shirts to cover what he considered excessively fat arms, and he said that he tried to wear dark colors to make himself look thinner. The student often sought me out during my lobby duty. "Do you think I'm screwed up because I worry so much about my appearance?" he asked me.

I told him that it sounded typical of teenagers. I admitted when I was in high school I wore long sleeve shirts because I was embarrassed by my skinny arms, and I wore sweaters to look heavier. I suggested to him that perhaps he should see his guidance counselor about some of these things, and that he knew where to find me if he wanted to talk.

I went to see his counselor. She agreed that while the student suffered from a self-consciousness not unusual among adolescents, his difficulty in developing relationships with other students was troublesome, and she thought he could use psychotherapy. The guidance counselor had several years of experience in other schools, and she was not enamored of this high school.

"You should see this place after the bell rings," she said conspiratorially, knowing that the school did not like new staff members to be critical. "It's like a morgue. All the kids in class, quiet, deserted halls, no signs of life anywhere. It's very spooky. The administration thinks these are signs of a good school, but there are no signs of joy or spontaneity. There is a lot of pressure on kids here, but we pretend they have no problems because they have middle class comforts."

The counselor arranged for a conference with the student's mother. His parents were divorced and his father lived in another state. Larry Silverman sat in on the conference to represent the administration. If necessary, he would indicate the extent of the student's troubles with the school: excessive absenteeism and poor academic performance. He would withhold the threat of failing the student for the year unless the parent refused to consider therapy for her son.

It was a difficult conference. Initially, the parent denied there was a problem. We did not understand her son; we did not appreciate him; we did not see him as she saw him, she told us. I told her that I did not know what was wrong with her son, but I said he was very unhappy, friendless, and failing in school. I thought he needed some professional psychological help.

It was the most difficult thing I had to tell a parent. The woman did not know me, and I did not have much time to develop trust. This was a forty-two-minute period, and I had to make my pitch in behalf of her son and get to my next class. The counselor was gentle with the parent and supportive of my argument, and Larry did not have to make his threats. The parent agreed to have her son see a clinical psychologist in the area who specialized in the problems of adolescents. Several times during the remainder of the year the student stopped by my room before school to thank me, and to assure me that things were going well, and that he would be "cured" in a matter of weeks. Late in the year, he walked up to me in the lobby to show me his new short sleeve beige shirt.

THE REAL KID BEHIND THE ALLIGATOR SHIRT

The students seemed to understand the narrowness of scope and the strained artificiality in their classroom encounters with teachers. The way in which we speak in schools—the topics discussed, the language used, and the constant evaluation of student responses—makes it unlikely that discussions are ever more than academic exercises. Most classroom discussions appear to be more scripted than spontaneous. Teachers typically ask questions to which they already know the answer, and students often have to guess what the teacher has in mind. After what I thought was a very open series of exchanges with most of the members in one freshman class, one student later qualified it by saying, "That was a good discussion—for school."

The students seemed to be more interested in the personal side of their teachers than the subject being taught. They inquired about my marital status, living arrangements, and age with greater curiosity than they asked about history or economics. "You live on the sixteenth floor? Did you ever spit off the balcony?" "What's it like when people visit you?" "What kind of music do you listen to?" "You don't talk about history, do you?"

Most of the students seemed eager to talk about themselves; they wanted me to know there was a lot more to them than just the narrow part I got to see in class. One of my students advised me that if I wanted to become a good teacher, I should get to know "the real kid behind the alligator shirt." Some of the students invited me to join them for after-school tennis, racquetball, and weightlifting at the Oldham Village Racquet Club. The club, which offered discount membership rates to the teachers, was one of the few places where students and teachers could get together outside of school.

My best relationships with students were developed at the club. We had the time to talk informally about academic subjects, personal problems, and career plans free of the bell schedule and other restraints of the institution. While I was still a teacher, and had the responsibilities of a teacher, I could give students more and better attention than I could in the classroom, where I had academic, clerical, and disciplinary tasks to attend to. On the tennis and racquetball courts, we competed as equals without the roles of teacher and student. In the weights room, the typical roles of teacher and student were reversed. Most of the students were football players who trained seriously, and they were stronger and more experienced than I. They taught me training techniques, encouraged my efforts, complimented my progress, and compared my performance to other teachers.

The teachers who worked out at the club got to know their students better, and it probably helped them in school. It did not seem to matter that Willa Green was a terrible racquetball player. The students respected her because she tried hard and was concerned about being in shape. They enjoyed seeing another side of an academically demanding chemistry teacher who played a form of volleyball with his students in one of the racquetball courts. The students knew that Mike Werge, Paul De Faro, and I were not hired by Oldham for our Olympic potential, but they enjoyed seeing us pursue things at which we were not better or more knowledgeable than they.

I was able to form stronger relationships with those students with whom I played racquetball or lifted weights. When I had trouble in school with students who did not do their work or who failed tests, they did not let it carry over to our shared after-school workouts. I had to tell one student that he was failing my American history class. Another teacher had turned his name in for cutting that day, and he knew his parents would be furious. He was upset and sulked the whole class period, but when the bell rang, he asked me the same question he asked every Monday, Wednesday, and Friday: "Hey, Doc, ya liftin' today?"

On the day of final exams, as I left the school with a bundle of unread test papers, two students I knew from the club jumped out of a car and forced me to the ground with their combined weight and a series of gentle punches. I protested that I was carrying official documents and was protected by state law, but they were undeterred. "We just wanted to say, it was nice getting to know you, Doc. Come back and lift with us next year, okay."

* * *

For most of the teachers, there was more joy in the personal side of the job than the academic. While it was fun to see students learn, there was a repetitiousness in it that was predictable and ultimately boring. Books had to last from five to ten years, films even longer. Most of the content was based on low-level information, and heavily laden with trivial facts. The academic side of teaching was often as dull for the teachers as it was for the students. The variation in the job came from working with students. "We teach the basics in high school," the head of the foreign language department told me. "We don't read Marcel Proust, we teach verb conjugations, restaurant conversations, and idiomatic expressions. Of course it gets boring. I don't learn anything. I get most of my enjoyment out of the development of my track team."

A teacher of calculus and advanced mathematics courses admitted that only one of his five classes was capable of asking questions which forced him to think. In the others, he said, the students were learning, but he was "just going through the motions."

There were teachers in every department who believed high school was primarily an academic experience, but most of the teachers seemed to agree that the academic rewards of teaching were limited by the nonacademic nature of instruction, the limited resources, and the general nonacademic focus of high schools. The pleasures, they said, were the informal dealings with the kids. The greatest rewards came from helping a student cope with a personal crisis or solve some emotional difficulty. "Anyone can teach subject matter," said one of the math teachers. "The kids will forget who taught them the Pythagorean theorem, but they will always remember a teacher who stood behind them and encouraged them."

6

POWER, POLITICS, AND ATHLETICS

Power, in a general social science sense, is the influence or control exerted by one on the behavior of others. It is sometimes interpreted as the ability of a person to direct his or her own life. In a work setting, power implies being in charge of one's job, being able to make or influence decisions, and being rewarded and recognized for one's skills, knowledge, and achievements. Outside their classroom interactions with students, teachers had very little power. They had control of few aspects of their working lives. They did not make policy, curricular or personnel decisions, and they had no formal influence on those who did. Teaching seemed to be controlled by nonteachers. Classroom teachers were observed and evaluated by their department supervisors; they were monitored and managed by the building principals and the superintendents; and they were subject to the decisions of a lay board of education. The librarian could, but never did, make it difficult to bring classes into the library. The audiovisual coordinator could, and occasionally did, punish teachers who treated him badly by intentionally failing to deliver a piece of equipment, or retrieving it unexpectedly in the middle of the day.

CLASSROOM OBSERVATIONS OF TEACHERS

Most of my teaching was unobserved by other adults. The daily patterns of my work were not seen or evaluated, and little was done to improve my skills or morale. Although parents, administrators, supervisors, board members, and colleagues could come into my class, few ever did. Of the 900 classes I taught, 8 were observed. Troy observed 4 of my classes; Cal Bullinger, Larry Silverman, Krystyna Mokowski,

139

and two members of the board of education observed 1 class each. Most of the observations were unannounced.

Two members of the board dropped in one period while we were watching a documentary entitled "Bataan—the Forgotten Hell." The tape and the VCR belonged to Mike Werge, and they were part of our patched-together unit on World War II. The materials were not approved by the board, nor were they part of the curriculum, but the board members did not ask about them.[1]

I introduced the board members to the class. We watched the videotape together, and I stopped it every few minutes to clarify information and allow the class to develop some generalizations about war. At the end of the period, one board member told me that she "loved history," and that her husband had been a history major in college. She told me it was too bad we did not have a videotape of the television production of Herman Wouk's *Winds of War*. It was "great history," she said. No, she had not read the book, she said, but she planned to get to it when she had the time. The board members told me they had enjoyed the class discussion, and thanked me for letting them sit in. Later, at a board meeting, one of the women claimed I had embarrassed her by mispronouncing her name in front of the students. The administrator who told me about it shrugged his shoulders, stared at the floor, and said, "What are you going to do? In this state to be on a board of education you have only to meet a residency requirement and prove that you can read and write."

Teachers claimed they disliked being observed because the observations were conducted as evaluations rather than as a means to improve teaching. They believed observations always placed them in jeopardy. "No one comes in to help us," said one teacher. "They just find fault."

The assistant principal, Don Brandt, sympathized with the teachers. "Sometimes teachers can go for weeks, or even months, without hearing a positive word," he said. "Sometimes I think I should just go around and sit in, and tell teachers the things that they are doing right. You can't have good teaching unless teachers feel good about what they are doing. I know they need it, but there just isn't time to do it."

By district policy, all nontenured teachers were to be observed four times, and all tenured teachers were to be observed twice. At the end of the year, an annual performance review was written based on these

---

[1]One of the board members who observed me was later elected president of the Oldham–Webster Board of Education. During an interview after my field work was completed, she admitted she did not know that there was no written curriculum in the social studies department. At that time, she had been a member of the board of education for seven years.

observations. The district used a three-part evaluation which described what was observed; listed commendations; and concluded
with recommendations for change. The form infuriated one of the
French teachers. He wrote: "There *must* always be recommendations
for change. The implication is that we *never* teach a satisfactory lesson.
Something *must* be wrong each time we are observed. That's frustrating and demoralizing. We are *always* less than good! Don't they ever
find a class in which no change is warranted?"

"They always find something wrong with my teaching," claimed
another foreign language teacher. "Sometimes I ask too many questions, sometimes not enough, but never once has my department supervisor invited me in to observe how he, the master teacher, does it."

Troy Thayer, the supervisor of the social studies department,
claimed that Dr. Mokowski, the assistant superintendent for curriculum and instruction, forced the supervisors and teachers into adver-
sarial positions. "She wants us to be very critical," he said. "If our
reports aren't critical enough, she lets us know about it. Sometime in
the last few years, for example, they changed the name of the form
we use when observing teachers. It used to be called the 'observation
form,' now it's called the 'evaluation form.' Same form, different
name. It's a subtle change, but there definitely has been a change of
emphasis."

Troy did not invite teachers to observe him, and he may have been
self-conscious about his own teaching and command of the subject,
but he was a sensitive classroom observer who understood the nature
of social studies instruction as well as any supervisor I had met in the
state. He encouraged teachers to use varied strategies to increase student involvement and participation. He liked simulation games and
group work, and he supported innovative teaching. Troy was, however, timid about some content. When my classes discussed whether
government officials should be dismissed because they were homosex-
uals, he warned me that I might be upsetting some of my students.
When we viewed a videotape that mentioned, in passing, a president's
extramarital affairs, he asked if this was the best film we had. He did
not include these concerns in his written evaluation, but the message
was clear: Be careful about what you do and say in class. Troy believed
that he was being protective of his faculty. The social studies teachers
felt that Troy privately disapproved of discussing controversial issues
in class.

The teachers also complained that Troy was too reserved in his
commendations. They said they needed more positive feedback about
the things they were doing well. "After twelve years in the classroom,
I know what I'm doing wrong," claimed Mike Werge. "I don't need

to be told about all of the negative things. Every once in a while I just want unreserved praise for the good things."

"I need my strokes, too," said Paul De Faro. "Sometimes I would like to hear that I'm doing a good job or that I taught a good class. There is a constant flow of criticism and only a trickle of praise coming down to us. It's a lonely job. Why don't they understand that?"

Three of Troy's annual observations were general evaluations. He checked lesson plans, objectives, discipline, presentation skills, and the neatness of the room. The other observation was designed to be a "clinical" observation in which the teacher identified one aspect of teaching on which he or she would like to concentrate, such as encouraging greater student involvement or asking more sophisticated questions. Troy's evaluation would ignore other dimensions of instruction, and he would focus only on those parts of the teaching process identified by the teacher. It was an opportunity for the teacher to improve his or her teaching, and while this was a generally recommended supervisory approach,[2] it was not district policy. Troy pursued this on his own, but it was not always appreciated by the teachers.

"Troy is good at finding fault," observed Gus Poulos, the psychology teacher, "but he doesn't help you. I need help. I know I need help. We all need help. My teaching could be improved by showing me new approaches or new ideas, not by telling me that the blinds are out of whack, or asking me to focus on something that I already do! I have not gotten any help from Troy or the administration since I've been here. I don't understand what he's talking about. I know Troy is not happy with the way I teach, but he can't make concrete suggestions about what I should do. First of all, he doesn't know anything about psychology. Then he stumbles, and fumbles, and mumbles about this, and that, and the other thing, and after one of our post-observation conferences, the only thing I know for sure is that he doesn't like the stuff I have on the wall. His most concrete suggestion to me has been to change my bulletin boards and posters."

Another nontenured teacher agreed that Troy's suggestions were confusing. "It was frustrating to be observed my first year," he said. "After our post-observation conferences, I didn't know where to go. If it were not for Paul De Faro pulling me aside and helping me on his own time, I would never have made it. . . . Next year I'm team teaching

[2]For example, Keith A. Acheson and Meredith D. Gall, *Techniques in the Clinical Supervision of Teachers* (New York: Longman, 1980); Morris L. Cogan, *Clinical Supervision* (Boston: Houghton Mifflin, 1973); Robert Goldhammer et al., *Clinical Supervision: Special Methods for the Supervision of Teachers*, 2nd ed. (New York: Holt, Rinehart and Winston, 1980).

with Mike Werge, and I'm really looking forward to it. I know he'll be able to help me."

The results of a survey indicated that teachers felt largely unsupported in their teaching. They considered the building principals to be less helpful than their department supervisors, and the central administration to be the least helpful. At the same time, the teachers believed that the greatest threat to their job security came from central administration, in the form of Krystyna Mokowski. Dr. Mokowski had a reputation as a knowledgeable, hardworking administrator whose many skills were shrouded by her inability to get along with teachers and building principals. At the building level, she was considered arrogant and insensitive, and her classroom observations were the stuff of faculty lore. Dr. Mokowski tried to observe me on two separate occasions. It was her job to evaluate every nontenured teacher. "I must make between twenty-five and thirty observations a year," she said, "and unfortunately, they have to be more critical and evaluative than supportive. I don't have time to give teachers support (although I know they need it)."

She came to observe me for the first time on a Friday afternoon during the last period of the day. We were in the middle of a simulation that involved all of the students in an "international relations game." Every student had been assigned a role as a head of state, diplomat, or cabinet official. Nearly half of the students were out of class that day because of a special last-minute band rehearsal, and I had to change my plans. We decided to discuss a current events topic. I told Dr. Mokowski about the change, and suggested this might not be a representative class, but that she was certainly welcome to observe it. She decided to come back at another time. The teachers heard about the observation and stopped me at the end of the day.

"Hey, I saw the Dragon Lady heading down to your room," said Gus Poulos. "I would have warned you, but I didn't see her until it was too late. What balls! Observing a teacher on the last period on a Friday!"

Troy was apologetic. "I hear the Polish Princess was in to see you today," he said. "I'm sorry that I did not know in advance. Sometimes she tells me, this time she did not. How did it go?"

When I told him that she did not stay, he cringed. "You'll hear about that. She'll probably be harder on you because you asked her to leave." I explained to Troy that I did not ask her to leave. He said that she would interpret it that way.

Two weeks later, on a Friday, again during the last period of the day, Dr. Mokowski returned. My class was discussing the reasons why they had been subjected to two days of statewide tests of their minimal competencies in math and reading. We read excerpts from the state constitution and the state court cases that had led to the testing program, and the students argued about it in class. Dr. Mokowski told me she would not make a written report of this class observation because the lesson "deviated from the curriculum."

"You do know that you call on one row more than the others," she added, smiling. I looked at her blankly. Did she think that I was unaware of it? Did she want to know why? We talked for about an hour after school, but we did not discuss the observation, and I did not tell her that four of the most talkative students in the class were all in one row, but I wanted to because I felt she had not understood my teaching. We chatted about the shortage of books and teaching materials, and we discussed the absence of a written curriculum. I thought it had been an honest, pleasant conversation, but Dr. Mokowski reported to Dr. Szabo that I needed to be watched: I did not follow the curriculum and I complained about the supplies.

Don Brandt smiled and shook his head recalling the incident several months later. "I don't know if you want to come back here next year, but that could have cost you your chance," he said. Then he whispered, "You can't go around and piss on the Princess's fire hydrant." The teachers were not supposed to mention curricular or book problems, he told me. "It makes you look like a malcontent."

I felt bad after my observation. Gus Poulos tried to console me. "Don't feel like the Lone Ranger," he said. "Everybody feels bad after she observes them. It just adds to the depression of being a teacher. Welcome to the club. It doesn't take long to get that abused, lonely feeling around here."

SUPERVISION OF INSTRUCTION

There were eight subject area supervisors. All were male, and they could be distinguished from other faculty mainly because they always wore ties. All the subject supervisors had been selected by the previous building principal; all had tenure; and all were considered less than adequate. In interviews with the superintendents, principals, and teachers, no one identified them as being either among the best teachers in their department or the academically strongest members of the department, although they had the responsibility to lead in both areas.

"The major problem with this school," admitted Larry Silverman, "rests in middle management. We have very weak department supervisors, but what are you going to do? They are all tenured."

"If I had my way," argued Don Brandt, "I would simply eliminate all the departments and have four assistant principals. This way you get rid of the department supervisors without having to try and fire them."

As department supervisor, Troy did not have an easy job. He taught three classes; he supervised eight teachers and one duty assignment; and he had to contend with what he considered excessive paperwork without secretarial support. He knew the social studies curriculum should be written down more systematically, but he was not given money for summer work or the extra help with which to do it. "They tell you to do things," he said, "but they don't give you any help. Every year there are more things expected of the supervisors and there is no additional support. Mokowski tells me to organize the curriculum, but she does not give me any money or free up the people to do it. Since I have been here, there has not been one serious discussion about curriculum initiated by the central administration."

Troy was caught between the administration and the faculty, and it was unclear if he permitted himself to choose sides. The majority of the teachers in his department questioned his support of them, and he was unappreciated and distrusted. "Troy will sell you out in a minute," claimed an experienced social studies teacher. "Anytime there is a conflict between a teacher and a student, a teacher and an administrator, or a teacher and a parent, Troy will line up against the teacher. He's a nice guy, but he's a wimp. The only way for us to survive around here is CYA, cover your ass."

The supervisors played an important role in the tenure decisions at the high school. It was not easy to win tenure at Oldham, and the social studies department had the greatest faculty turnover rate in the school. When Paul De Faro had been awarded tenure three years earlier, he felt he had been fortunate. He did not coach, and he believed his undergraduate teacher education program had not prepared him sufficiently for the classroom. "I was lucky my first year," Paul said. "There was a guy here who was a terrific teacher, the best teacher I have ever seen. He was creative, intelligent, and extremely effective. Of course, he quit to take a higher-paying job, but he helped me make it. Without him, I would not have understood what teaching was all about. Troy was no help."[3]

Paul also believed he was fortunate the school overlooked his background. "I felt that I didn't fit in here," he said. "An Italian from

[3]In a survey administered to the faculty during my second year in the school, teachers were asked to rate the "extent to which their department supervisor was helpful to their teaching." On a scale of $+3$ (very helpful) to -3 (very unhelpful), Troy received a mean rating score of -1.56, the lowest of any department supervisor. There were four ratings of -3, and only one of $+1$.

[an urban part of the state] in WASPy Oldham." Paul shook his head from side to side. "No matter how well I taught, if they knew that I wore an earring on weekends and had a tattoo on my arm, I would have been fired."

At the end of the year, two social studies teachers were fired. One, the only female in the department, was dismissed after teaching part-time for one year because she had "discipline problems." The students in her C-level class were "eating her up," in the words of a teacher who taught next door to her. She had a hard time getting their attention, maintaining interest, and establishing her authority in the classroom. She was a gentle, thoughtful person who found it impossible to impose her will on students. "They [sophomore C-level students] greeted my honesty with indifference, and they regarded my openness as a weakness," she said. "I guess I'm not cut out to be a teacher."

The teacher had a background in psychology, but was assigned courses in history, and she was ill at ease with the material. Because there was no written curriculum, she was unsure of the content to cover or how long to spend on each unit. Because she was not lucky enough to find a mentor, as had Paul De Faro, she did not develop successful teaching strategies. She worked hard, but she had become discouraged. She did not get enough help, and she did not perform well this one year on her first teaching job.

Another social studies teacher, who coached football and baseball, was denied tenure after three years of teaching at Oldham. Of the three social studies teachers being considered for tenure that year, he was the only one not to get it. Tenure decisions were officially announced in April of the candidate's third year, but the coach had been notified in January that he was "on probation." He was in his early thirties, married, with a young child. He had a master's degree in education, ten years of experience in several districts, and he had given up tenure at another school to become head baseball coach at Oldham. It was no secret that he taught mainly so he could coach. "I love it," he said, "and I work hard at it, but I'm also a pretty good teacher."

The coach was a large man, nicknamed the Bear, who had played college football and baseball. He often dressed in what was called the Oldham-coach-style: blue nylon windbreaker, V-neck sweater with "Oldham" emblazoned on the front, and plaid polyester pants. Not all the coaches adhered to this fashion, but no one other than coaches ever dressed this way.

Troy claimed that although the coach worked hard, he had a "wooden teaching style," with neither the intellect nor the technique to be a successful teacher. The coach claimed that in the other schools in which he had taught, he had been allowed to coast, and he had learned little about teaching until coming to Oldham. He questioned how he had been permitted to stay for three years if he was as poor a teacher as they said, and why it was that no one tried to help him. During my initial interview for the job, Cal Bullinger had mentioned that one member of the department was "having trouble," and he suggested that part of my responsibility would be to help that person. Nothing more was ever said about it, and the only nonteaching responsibility assigned to me was library/lobby duty. In an interview after the coach had been fired, Krystyna Mokowski blamed Troy for not utilizing me better. Troy thought it was Cal's responsibility, and Cal thought that Krystyna should have made the assignment to help the foundering teacher.

Thayer and Mokowski recommended to Szabo that the coach not be given tenure, and Szabo forwarded their recommendation to the board of education. The board voted to deny tenure with one dissenting vote. The coach was popular with many of the students, and the next day about a hundred students staged a protest rally in the lobby of the high school. Don Brandt broke up the rally after a few minutes, asking the students to return to class, and thanking them on behalf of the coach for their show of sympathy and support. The students went back to class. The coach found another teaching/coaching job elsewhere in the state, and he harbors a good deal of resentment about his treatment at Oldham.

The athletic director had never seen the coach teach. He knew of the problems he was having in the classroom, but he was surprised that the coach was let go. "There's a place for [him] in the high school. There's a need for intellectual teachers, but there is a place for him, too. He may not have been the greatest teacher, but guys like him can do more things than just teach. They can coach; they can lead the band; they help kids. We need intellectuals to help the smart kids, and teachers like [the coach] to help with the nonacademic things. There is a middle group of teachers, and frankly, I don't think they should be kept on. They're the teachers who don't do much for the kids after school, and they don't teach well in school."

There was general agreement among all the building principals, the supervisor, and the assistant superintendent that the coach should be fired, but most of the teachers and the coach singled out Troy as the principal culprit. Some said he should have helped him more as a teacher; others said he should have supported his tenure candidacy more forcefully. Whenever there was a problem in the school, the most likely people to be blamed were the department supervisors.

The teachers in the school who were sympathetic to their department supervisors saw them as convenient whipping boys for both the administration and the teachers. Mike Flynn, an English teacher and coordinator of student activities, claimed that his supervisor was a flak catcher. "Everyone blames him for the problems of the department," Mike said, "but he really has no control over the department. Most of the teachers are tenured, and they do as they please. The supervisors are in the middle. Teachers blame them for inadequate supplies, and for the lack of control over the curriculum, but they have no power over these matters. The administration blames them for weak teachers, but how many tenured teachers are ever fired in the whole state?"

One part of a survey I conducted asked the teachers to list the characteristics of a "good supervisor." Most teachers indicated that a supervisor should be a "scholar," and an "instructional leader," who was "honest" and "open." They also said that because the supervisors at Oldham did not possess these qualities, the best thing the supervisors could do was to "protect the department," and "not interfere with teaching."

"Our supervisor," one science teacher wrote," is smart enough to leave us alone, and we do pretty well without him." Another science teacher said that the supervisor "was among the least academically able people in the department, but he absorbs a lot of the paperwork." A foreign language teacher told me that Troy was the only supervisor who required teachers to turn in weekly lesson plans. "Our supervisor," she said, "trusts us." An English teacher claimed that she liked her department supervisor because, "After every classroom observation, he never failed to ask, 'What do you want me to write?' and he usually wrote what we told him to." The supervisor of mathematics was in his final year before retirement. The math teachers said that he left them alone, and they thought it was the most helpful thing he could do.

Many teachers wanted supervisors who had influence with the superintendent and the board of education, and could protect the department. An English teacher told of a board member who called the department supervisor and demanded that a new teacher be fired because "he lectured all the time, and the kids were not learning anything." The supervisor confirmed the story, and said that he told the board member it was not true. The teacher did not lecture in every class, and the evidence showed that the kids were learning from the teacher, though they may not have liked him.

THE PRINCIPALSHIP

Other than inservice days, the Oldham High School teachers met as a group only during the monthly faculty meetings. The meetings were not run by rules of parliamentary procedure. There were no debates to win, no issues to discuss, and no votes to cast. There were no standing committees and very few special committees. These were primarily informational meetings in which the administrators announced new procedures or clarified existing policies. The meetings typically began ten minutes after the last class was dismissed on the second Monday of the month. Don Brandt took attendance; Cal Bullinger spoke; most teachers fidgeted, watched the clock, or graded papers. Faculty meetings were in many ways analogous to the classroom, but the role of the teachers was now that of the student. The teachers did not plan the meetings, introduce agenda items, or do much more than receive information. They were as passive in the faculty meetings as students were in the classroom, and like the students, they often did not enjoy their role. The teachers talked during the meetings, made wisecracks, and occasionally attempted to distract the speaker. Like the students, they had the power to be disruptive.

During the first faculty meeting of the year, a male teacher held up an Oldham wrestling T shirt and called for everyone's attention. The shirt showed two wrestlers both on their knees in the down position. One wrestler had his right arm around the back and waist of the other in the traditional ready position of high school wrestlers. The teacher bellowed, "Look at this! This is obscene!" He continued, "This appears to me to be a blatant example of homosexuality. Do you mean to tell me, Mr. Bullinger, that the school condones this sort of activity?"

Cal Bullinger flushed slightly, but he seemed more annoyed than embarrassed. Most teachers said nothing. A few teachers thought it was very funny, and no one suggested that it was inappropriate or out of order. Faculty meetings were the place for irreverent comments. There were no students there, and the normally pristine standards of language and subject could be relaxed. The teachers were careful not to waste too much time because there was an agenda to cover before the meeting could be adjourned, and no one wanted to stay later than necessary. It was not unreasonable to expect to have a good laugh at most faculty meetings. During the March meeting, for example, Cal asked us to redouble our efforts in enforcing the school rules.

"Willa Green has brought to my attention," he announced, "that the lobby and the halls have become the scenes of excessive amorous behavior on the part of the students. Willa—and it certainly isn't just Willa who has complained about this—but, she is absolutely right. Willa says that the teachers are not doing their job. Some of you—and I know this to be true—simply walk right by and do nothing when you come across these individuals. If only one teacher enforces the rules, it makes them look like a bad guy. We all must enforce the rules.

"Just today, on my way here, I walked around the corner of the lobby, and there were two guys. . . ." Bawdy laughter from some of the male teachers interrupted Cal. He blushed deeply, and his voice trailed off, but he continued: "All right, you guys. What I meant to say was that there were two guys with two girls on their lap. That is . . . each guy had one girl each on their . . . I mean . . . his lap. Well . . . you know what I mean."

"Draw us a picture, Cal," yelled one male teacher.

"All I had to do was look at them," Cal continued, "and they knew that they were doing something wrong, and the girls got up and took their own seat."

"Did you check the guys' pants?" mumbled another male teacher, and the people seated around him giggled.

"The point is," Cal concluded, "if we all work together on this, it will not be much of a problem."

"He probably believes in coitus interruptus," said the English teacher seated next to me. He stopped grading papers long enough to add, "I bet he wants us to carry buckets of water to throw on the dogs copulating in the parking lot. It would make our jobs a lot easier if they just put some chemical in the kids' food. Make a motion, coach. Get the science department on this right away."

I asked the English teacher if he broke up couples in the hall. "I used to," he said. "I used to try to embarrass them a little. I'd say something like, 'Can I have a hug, too?' That used to work. The kids would be embarrassed and stop. But kids are different today. Now they look at me as if I'm a dirty old man. One kid said that I was just jealous. Maybe he was right. I don't say anything to them anymore as long as they have their clothes on."

I asked if Cal's speech would change the way he acted. "No, of course not. You were in the army, weren't you, coach? When they ask you to do something, say, 'yes sir.' Then do whatever you please. Hey, would you like to grade some papers?"

The atmosphere was more subdued during the April faculty meeting. The teachers knew that Cal Bullinger had an important announcement to make. In a small school which thrived on gossip and rumors, everyone knew there would be less levity during the April meeting.

Cal announced he had resigned effective June 30. His resignation, he admitted, had been submitted because the board had not offered him a new contract. The board's action did not come as a complete surprise to Cal. He had been formally notified that he had been placed "on probation" in September. Cal had a short speech prepared. He thanked the teachers for their support during his two years at the high school. He also made some sexually suggestive remarks about the relationship between Drs. Mokowski and Szabo that drew only polite laughter. Ordinarily, this sort of attack on superiors would have been appreciated, but it was out of character for Cal. One of the teachers later told me that he had expected better from the director of a church choir and the son-in-law of a Protestant minister.

Cal was clearly hurt by the board's decision. He had only two and a half years to work before he was eligible for a pension under the state's retirement system. He had one son in college, other children at home, and a wife who, he claimed, now regarded him as a failure and was threatening to leave him. When the students found out about Cal's announcement the next day, there were no protests or demonstrations. Cal was not as popular as the coach who had been denied tenure. The teachers were relieved, and they looked forward to a new principal. Cal told me that I was the only teacher to telephone him and offer condolences.

Teachers offered several explanations for Cal's failure as principal. Some said it was because he was a weak leader who had succeeded a very strong principal. One of the secretaries told me that the former principal claimed he had been "hired to be a prick," and that's what he was. He enjoyed political battles with the board and the faculty, and he did not mind taking firm stands. According to Larry Silverman and several of the teachers, the former principal had surrounded himself with weak department supervisors and made all the decisions in the building by himself. He did not support textbook requests, and he had little interest in curriculum or improving teachers' skills. Cal Bullinger, they said, inherited the resentments created under the administration of his predecessor, and he was too weak to quell them. According to Mike Flynn, the humanities teacher, the former principal had an open door policy. "Teachers," Flynn said, "could go into his office anytime, and say anything they wanted to. He would sit back in his chair, fold his hands in his lap, close his eyes and tilt his head slightly toward the ceiling. You never knew if he was listening to you or taking a nap. It was a very effective administrative technique; after a while, I stopped going to see him."

Cal was viewed as a weak and frightened principal. He seemed uncomfortable talking with students, and the few students who dealt with him did not like him. The senior class president described him as a "wet noodle" who could not stand up to authority. One of the editors of the underground newspaper said that he was an "incompetent." "They [the board of education] wanted a wimp," he said, "and they got one."

The teachers, ordinarily a tranquil, nonpolitical group, had sent a letter to the board of education complaining about conditions in the school. It was a strongly worded letter which spoke of the "threats to our school" unless something was done to remedy the "administrative problems." Some of the board members were known to be upset by the teachers' actions. They did not believe this was appropriate behavior; the principalship, they said, was a board concern, not a teacher concern. One board member referred to the letter of complaint as being "unprofessional."

"Unprofessional! Unprofessional!" fumed Willa Green, one of the authors of the letter. "I'd like to kick him in the balls!" she said, referring to her critic.

The teachers were uncomfortable with a weak leader. One of the math teachers said: "You go in and talk to Cal; he agrees with you, but nothing happens. He doesn't do anything. We need someone in the principal's office who can make some decisions." An English teacher asked me how I liked serving on a "rudderless ship." Even the department supervisors, who bore a collective reputation for timidity, met with Dr. Szabo to complain about conditions in the school.

Bullinger knew he was in trouble. Formally, he had been notified by the board that he had not fulfilled their expectations as building principal; the annual performance review of the first year of his principalship was negative. Informally, he felt the social ostracism of the faculty and the other building administrators. The only experienced principal, Don Brandt, was resentful because he had been passed over for the job. Larry Silverman was publicly contemptuous of Cal. The director of pupil personnel services, who had a good deal of influence in the daily operation of the school, had little respect for Cal. As a former music teacher, Cal could have expected support from the music department, but while the two music teachers were publicly polite and friendly toward him, they disparaged his musical talents and knowledge behind his back.

Cal felt the isolation. He ate lunch alone in the nonsmoking section of the faculty room. Few people ever joined him, even if it meant that they had to crowd uncomfortably at one of the other three tables. It was as though the teachers wanted to physically dissociate themselves from him. Cal thought his efforts were unappreciated. He claimed that he worked hard, but change takes place slowly in public schools. He wondered why his superiors were judging him so harshly and so soon.

Cal Bullinger said he enjoyed reading and discussing literature and history, but he complained that his long days and long commutes did not allow him the time to read very much. Although he regularly disavowed any pretense at scholarship, he was probably the best read of the three administrators, and he had the most sophisticated understanding of education research. Bullinger appeared to know more about testing, teaching, assessment, evaluation, and curriculum than either Brandt or Silverman, and his knowledge of the current education literature was more complete. "There are some real problems here," Cal confided, after his resignation. "I have to review all of the final exams, and it amazed me how little some of the teachers know about testing. Some of the finals are filled with trivia and minutiae, but the supervisors must think they're okay because they just pass them on to me."

He also complained about the quality of teaching, the poorly written curricula, the communication problems in the district, and the lack of support from the central administration. "Mokowski is desk-bound. She doesn't get out here enough to know what's going on," he said, "and Szabo only criticizes. There are only two schools in this district, but Szabo is here, at most, once a week. To my knowledge, he has never observed a teacher here. He doesn't know what's going on, but he hears a lot of complaining."

The teachers had been complaining since Cal was hired, but they did not do so in a collective or organized manner. The teacher militancy and union activism of the 1970s seemed not to have touched Oldham. Most teachers in the state had a comprehensive contract, which meant that every aspect of a teacher's day was subject to collective negotiations. There were contractual agreements regulating the number and length of faculty meetings; the time period between the observation of a teacher and the filing of a written evaluation of that teacher; and the length of the school day. In the Oldham–Webster district, there was only a salary agreement between the teachers and the board of education. Teachers negotiated for salaries, typically on a two-year basis, and everything else was left to the board's discretion. The teachers may not have been content, but they did not think collective negotiations would solve their problems.

Willa Green was the vice-president of the teachers' association and the senior association officer in the building. Association meetings were held before school in the faculty cafeteria. The meetings were brief and poorly attended. While most of the teachers were members of the association, only a few took an active part in it. Willa complained that she found it hard to get teachers to join the association, attend meetings, and run for office. "This is our only voice," she said. "I can't understand why the teachers won't get involved."

Several weeks after Cal announced his resignation, Willa burst into the faculty room, asked for everyone's attention, and pleaded for volunteers to run for association offices. "This is a perfect time," she said, referring to the newly vacated principalship, "to assert our strength as a faculty and get the kind of person who will turn this place around."

Willa got no response, and it was not clear if the problem was with the message or the messenger. Willa approached a table of coaches and the director of athletics. "How about you guys taking a lead in this?" she asked.

"Who has time for this freakin' union?" asked the athletic director. "I don't have time for this stuff. I'm around here until ten o'clock every night walking the freakin' fields, checking on teams, paying officials. You can't expect the coaches to do any more than they do!" he yelled at Willa. After she left, he said that "Willa couldn't give away life vests on a sinking ship." The coaches laughed and returned to their conversation.

Some of the teachers were vigorously anti-union. One English teacher vowed he would resign if the teachers voted to have a union represent them. "I refuse to have anyone tell me how to teach, or regulate my hours." Referring to a picket line established during a strike at a nearby business, he said: "If teachers struck and formed a picket line, I would certainly not hesitate to run them over with my truck."

"I wouldn't want to cross a picket line," said the wood shop teacher, "but I hope things never get bad enough that people start to think that a union would help us. Cal's the wrong man for the job, but we don't have to strike to get rid of him."

The president of the board of education claimed the board knew Cal Bullinger was the wrong man for the job "right away." She complained: "He had good references and good letters of recommendation, but we could see that he just did not take over."

The board president claimed that despite Cal's good recommendations, his former employers had found him to be less than strong. She said: "I was surprised when I met the superintendent from his former district, and he told me that Cal's lack of leadership ability and decisiveness had been a problem there too." The problem was, she said, his letters of recommendation had not alluded to his leadership problems. When Cal left Oldham, the Webster–Oldham Board of Education wrote a letter for him lauding his personal qualities and suggesting his work at the high school was not necessarily negative, only that it was not the right district for him.

If the new principal was to be an "insider," as the betting odds favored, the choices would have to be narrowed to the two assistant principals, Don Brandt and Larry Silverman. They were an unmatched pair. Silverman was a large bundle of energy who wore loud handmade ties, and permed his short red hair. Brandt was about fourteen years older than Silverman. He was short and balding, and he tended toward conservative sports jackets and three-piece suits. He was quiet, private, and frugal, while Silverman was exuberant and expansive. One former teacher in the school described them as St. Francis and Rasputin.

Brandt's office was wood-paneled, windowless, and dark. He sat with his back toward the door. The office was tidy and organized, and his desk was always neat. Don was an amateur photographer, and there were several examples of his work on the walls of his office. One picture showed a kitten peering out of a paned glass window. "That's a little like me," he said. "People may not know this about me, but I'm a loner."

The teachers knew it. He had no close friends on the faculty, and it was hard for him to relax with the teachers. He teased and joked, but he did not seem to enjoy himself at parties or social events. Brandt had been a physical education teacher. He was graduated from a state college in his home town, and he had gained notoriety as an innovative department supervisor of physical education. He developed a program in which students could elect various physical education electives throughout the year instead of being required to follow one class activity. Several activities were scheduled at the same time; some were competitive, some cooperative, and students were free to choose among them. There were team sports as well as dance and fitness activities. It was more work for the teachers, but it was designed to serve the students better. For his work in physical education, he was honored by being enshrined in his alma mater's "hall of fame." When asked why he went into administration, he said he needed more challenges. "I did all I could do in physical education, and I wanted to do more." He also said he "just couldn't handle the noise of the gym any longer."

"I am the same person as assistant principal as I was when I was a coach," Brandt told me. "When I coached basketball, we had a rule that every kid had to have his ankles taped, and I remember this one kid, a good ballplayer, but he was a little lax about following the rules. Well, one day, he goes down on the court grabbing his ankle, and I told him to take off his sneaker so I could take a look at it. 'No, coach,' he says, 'I don't need to. I'm okay.' Well, I knew by the way he went down that his ankle wasn't taped, and the kid knew that I knew. It was a rule. He broke it, and he knew that he couldn't play for me unless he played by my rules. I did not need to say another word."

Brandt described himself as a student advocate who believed in helping students develop an internal sense of discipline. "I think of myself as being a fair person," he said. "If a kid is reasonable and honest with me, he will have very few problems in this school." Veteran teachers claimed that Brandt was not always calm, reasonable, and rule governed. "The 'old Brandt,'" claimed Mike Flynn, was a madman who threw temper tantrums all the time. "He was really a wild guy with a quick temper. When he learned that he had a heart problem, he changed. What you see now is the 'new Brandt,' mellow and reasonable. You have to be careful, the old one could still be lurking around."

Another teacher who had been in the school since it opened agreed. "Yeah, the old Brandt was a tyrant. He was forever running around enforcing every niggling rule and regulation. . . . Now he's Mr. Humanism, and speaks as though Abraham Maslow were sitting on his shoulder, guiding his every memo."

A few of the teachers would have been happier with an assistant principal who was a "head knocker," a disciplinarian who enforced the school rules with speed and severity, but most of the faculty was more than happy with the "new Brandt." Several teachers said the only problem with Don was that he had been an assistant principal for too long. As assistant principal, his job was mainly discipline, scheduling, and attendance. It was hardly a substantive or creative set of responsibilities, but assistant principals are supposed to be in transit through this purgatory, on the way to becoming building principals where they can make loftier decisions and leave their mark on the school.

Don Brandt, however, had been passed over for the principalship once. When the school's first principal had retired two years earlier, Don had applied for the job but had lost out to Cal Bullinger, an outsider. It was rumored that Don was too much of an apologist for the students to admit to problems at Oldham, and that the superintendent and several of the board members did not think he would be a good leader. Brandt feared he would never become principal as long as Dr. Szabo was superintendent, arguing that he was not sufficiently deferential to ingratiate himself with superiors. "I tell him the truth," Brandt said, "and he doesn't like that. But, I've got to live with myself."

"I'm looking forward to retirement," said the fifty-two-year-old. "I was really disappointed when they hired Bullinger, and I'll apply for the principalship again, but I don't expect to get it. If I can't get a principalship in another district, I'll stay here and retire early."

Some members of the board of education felt that Brandt had undermined Cal Bullinger's authority in a petty and spiteful way. Brandt explained that someone had to make decisions, and he was the only one around who had experience with scheduling classes, observing teachers, and running a school. "There were times when we had to force Bullinger to act, and now it comes back to me that I was usurping his authority. That really hurts me. We were just trying to keep the ship afloat. Two assistant principals and the head of pupil personnel services were doing their jobs and his, and now the board claims that I was undermining his authority. It's absurd."

Mike Flynn had some personal disagreements with Brandt, but argued that he would not have been uncomfortable with him as principal. "He's consistent and honest, and you always know where he's coming from." He added: "The thing which makes Oldham a good school is people like Don Brandt. He was passed over for the principalship, and he is unappreciated for the work he does, but he still gives it everything he has."

No one doubted Larry Silverman's enthusiasm or dedication, either. Silverman was in love with teaching. He had been the chief salary negotiator for the teachers' association. He was active in the state association of mathematics teachers, and as assistant principal he still taught two math courses. As a new administrator, his duties were restricted to enforcing the school's attendance rules and observing teachers, and he did not especially like either of them. "Hey," he said, "if this is all there is to the job, they can have it. Unless I get to be principal, I will have to seriously consider going back to being a math teacher."

There were aspects of the job he seemed to enjoy. "I've been in this building since it opened," he said, "but I never saw anyone but math teachers in class. Some of the people I thought were good teachers are terrible. I can't believe how they get by on their reputations. They have everybody fooled. We gotta try to help these people. I was bored out of my mind after forty-two minutes. How can the kids stand it for a whole year?"

Some of the teachers were less than enthusiastic about the help Silverman could give them in the classroom. He observed Paul De Faro's Western civilization elective. The students were role playing a

fictionalized sixteenth-century debate. All the students had been assigned the roles of historic characters, and had spent several days in
the library researching their parts. "The next day," Paul said, "Silverman told me he really liked the class. He said that the students who
played Henry VIII and the popes did a good job, but that Martin
Luther King seemed 'not to be involved.' I told him that it was four
hundred years before Martin Luther King's birth. I didn't want his
observation report to come back and embarrass him. He's my friend,
but I can't see how he's going to help me in the classroom."

The teachers liked Silverman. He was one of them, even if he now
wore a jacket and tie every day, as Szabo had requested. He had a
reputation as a good math teacher, and although he was not known
as a scholar or someone with a great understanding of curriculum, he
was hardworking and one of the school's major boosters. Most of the
teachers thought he could be trusted not to change the school too
much, and that he understood the problems of teaching. The teachers
also knew he had friends on the board of education. As the board
president of Webster's K–8 district, Silverman knew all the members
of the Oldham–Webster Regional High School District. They shared
common problems and attended the same conventions. At the previous national convention of school boards held in San Francisco, Silverman had dinner with several members of the Oldham board.
Silverman and the president of the board denied they had discussed
the principalship, but Dr. Szabo, the superintendent, was suspicious.

Szabo believed that Silverman would eventually become a good
principal, but that he would make a great many mistakes due to his
lack of administrative experience. Szabo favored an outsider as his first
choice, and only reluctantly endorsed Silverman when his candidate
refused the job, reportedly because the salary was not high enough.

The teachers did not formally line up behind either of the two
assistant principals. Each had his supporters, and there were those
teachers, though a minority, who favored bringing in someone with
fresh ideas from outside the district. The teachers demanded to be part
of the selection process. Paul De Faro and Mike Flynn circulated a
petition that was signed by three-fourths of the teachers and sent to
Dr. Szabo. The petition asked for active teacher involvement in the
recruitment and selection of candidates, but Szabo promised only to
allow the teachers to interview the candidates after the field had been
narrowed to three finalists. Teachers would not be given an opportunity to establish a job description, conduct initial screenings of candidates, or contact the candidates' employers or the teachers who
worked under them.

"That's great!" said Paul De Faro sarcastically. "After they've culled all of those with good ideas, we can choose between Tweedledum and Tweedledee!"

The selection of a new principal would not take place until fall. Dr. Szabo would officially serve as acting principal during the summer months while the decision was being made. During that time, Silverman was recovering from a heart attack and coronary bypass surgery. Brandt was still on the job, and unhappy. "They wouldn't even give me the courtesy of serving as acting principal," he said, obviously hurt by the snub.

While most of the teachers supported the appointment of Silverman, they had largely been excluded from decision making in the district, and they were frustrated by it. They did not have official contact with the board, and they felt that the superintendents were not adequately representing their views to board members. Some people in the school thought this was not an accident. One of the social studies teachers who had a master's degree in political science and served as the elected mayor of a nearby town said: "It's difficult to give the teachers a chance to be heard and then disregard what they say. That's tricky. It's hard to disregard people after you've heard them. It's easier to give them no voice."[4]

COACHING

Jim Donegan, the newly appointed director of athletics (AD), had an office, a telephone with outside lines, and student assistants to help him with his paperwork. Jim taught two classes a day, one fewer than the supervisor of his department, and two fewer than the coordinator of student activities.[5] On Jim's note stationery was a two-inch-high likeness of a male athlete dressed in shorts. The athlete held aloft a torch and a laurel wreath, and he was standing on an open book under which was inscribed the motto "To Excel in Both Body and Mind."

---

[4]Dr. Szabo developed a faculty liaison committee to discuss districtwide problems. Teachers had no legislative authority, and they used the meetings largely to complain. For example, they wanted to know why "bus number six is always late; why kids are loitering in the halls; why there is no help from the psychiatric social worker."

At the building level, the Oldham teachers served on one permanent committee which was advisory to the principal, the Daily Operations Committee, abbreviated DOA. "DOA is a good name for it," complained one physical education teacher, "dead on arrival. Nothing much goes on there." During the year the committee dealt with the problem of the flies in the faculty room, the shortage of salt and pepper in the faculty room, and they complained that the yellow chalk was messier than the white chalk.

[5]After two years on the job, Jim Donegan claimed that board members had suggested to him that if he wanted to, he could be relieved of all teaching assignments.

Donegan claimed, "Athletics are incredibly important to a high school. If you asked every kid who ever graduated from this high school to name the ten teachers who they identify with the school, I bet 90 percent of them would name the football coach. Look what happens every Thanksgiving: The graduates come back and crowd around the coaches. The coaches are very important people in a high school kid's life. Sports are one of the few things that the teachers and the kids can participate in together. You can't underestimate the importance of sports in public schools."

I first met Jim Donegan in the board office while I was waiting to be interviewed by Dr. Szabo. Jim was Oldham's varsity basketball coach. He had just been appointed the new AD, and he was pleased and in an expansive mood. Jim had been teaching at Oldham for six years, and at thirty-one he was younger than the head football coach, the soccer coach, and his assistant basketball coach. Jim had played basketball in high school and college, and despite a few additional pounds, he still played in evening leagues and regularly scrimmaged against his players. He was graduated from Susquehanna University, and he had recently completed a master's degree in education at Bucknell University.

Donegan viewed the position of athletic director as a super coach over all the interscholastic activities of the school. It was a visible position, and Jim's name appeared on the school's letterhead. The athletic director had major budgetary responsibility; it was his job to approve requests for new uniforms, travel, and equipment; he had to deal with vendors, bus companies, sporting goods dealers, other athletic directors, and coaches. The athletic director had a more varied job than any teacher in the school, and he was less regulated by the bell schedule.

"I've been on school time all my life," he said. "I got tired of eating at exactly 11:57. Now, I can do my work and eat when I'm hungry. This job gave me the opportunity to break out of the routines of teaching, and to deal more with adults. I was lucky to get out of the classroom before I got tired of it."

Jim enjoyed the students, but like most of the teachers, he admitted that he did not like spending his entire day in the students' world. As AD, Jim found a way to be relieved of classroom assignments, interact more with adults, and gain new experiences. He claimed that the job was more "business oriented" than other teaching positions, and like most other young teachers in the building, Jim Donegan mentally entertained a career change that would allow him to exit from public school teaching. He saw the work he did as athletic director as helping to prepare him for a job in athletic administration at the college level.

According to Donegan, when the position of athletic director opened up, several board members had suggested that he apply. The former AD, who was also the head wrestling coach, had left the district to take another public school job. There were no other inside candidates, and according to Jim, only one person from outside the district had applied. Unlike every other position in public schools, no state certificate was needed to be athletic director or coach.

"I looked at the job as a challenge," Jim said, "but there were other reasons that I applied for it. I was worried about losing some of the freedom I enjoyed as a coach. For example, I could come in here during the summer and open up the gym for my players, and we could workout. I was afraid that if a new AD came in, I could lose some of that freedom.

"It's a very important position in the school. The coaches and the kids know that I can help them. I can get things done for them. I get to see the kids in a nonclassroom setting for long periods of time, and we get to know each other. Being the AD is very different than being the coach. As the coach, I am intent on winning and competing. As the AD, I am in a more helping role. I help the coaches. I help the kids. The ADs that I have met are more understanding people than coaches. It's really a nice job and a nice role to play."

Jim was considered to be ideal for the job of AD by the administrators and coaches. He had been an athlete; he knew what it was like to be competitive; he had paid his dues, they said. Jim was also a straight arrow. A married man, he did not smoke and rarely drank. He said he had never experimented with drugs, although he had attended an in-state urban high school where drugs were not uncommon. Jim often repeated a story about his first encounter with marijuana in high school: He was in one of the boys' lavatories and he noticed strange-smelling smoke coming from one of the stalls. He looked inside, and found two students smoking marijuana. They offered him some, but he said that he was shocked and offended, and he ran out. "My whole life was sports. I couldn't see messing it up by fooling around with drugs. It just wasn't for me."

It was left to the athletic director to select coaches. By school policy, all coaching positions were considered open at the beginning of every year. Teachers were asked to apply for any coaching position for which they felt qualified. Although I had not applied for the varsity wrestling position, I believed the promise I had made to Dr. Szabo during my job interview still obligated me. Donegan too thought the job was mine. During the first social studies department meeting of the year, he told me that if I wanted to, I could start working out with the wrestlers after school. I protested that it was only late September, and wrestling season did not begin until November.

"You're right," he said. "This isn't really practice. Officially, practice can't begin until November first. These are workouts, informal workouts. The basketball teams work out now, but we can share the gym with you, if you want to."

I told Jim that I could wait until the official start of the season. I was not interested in starting early, although it was common practice for high school athletic teams to begin before the official start of the season. Sometimes they were called "workouts" in which all students were invited to participate under the direction of a coach. Sometimes they were called "captains' practices" in which the elected team captains led the practice without the coaches. It was a violation of the state athletic rules, but it was considered a very minor infraction by most school athletic directors, and thought to be necessary for conditioning and team morale.

Jim knew by my response that I lacked the enthusiasm he wanted in a coach. Despite the deal I had made with Dr. Szabo, coaching was never mentioned to me again. If I did not want to coach and promise to do it with commitment and energy, Jim Donegan did not want me on his staff. If I had known it was that easy to get out of coaching, I would have told him earlier about my lack of interest. Jim Donegan was a direct person with subordinates. He told me that he did not want anyone coaching who did not have a very strong desire to coach, but he did not resent me for it, and we were able to develop an easy working relationship as teachers.

Jim approached Gus Poulos and asked him to apply for the head coaching spot in wrestling. Gus had been one of the assistant coaches during the past two years. He knew how to coach, and he felt that he needed the job because he was being considered for tenure, and coaching could make him look more valuable to the district. "I was told when I first got here, 'Don't quit coaching until you get tenure,'" Gus said. "It's not enough that you teach all day. The board wants to know what else you can do. Believe me, the fifteen hundred dollars I get doesn't begin to compensate me for my time.[6] I don't have the enthusiasm for it, but I need the job."

---

[6]According to the coaches' salary guide, the athletic director's salary ranged from $2,500 to $3,500. The head football coach's salary ranged from $1,700 to $2,700, and the boy's basketball coach, the girl's basketball coach, and the head wrestling coach could earn between $1,100 and $2,200 a year. Less money was earned by the coaches in baseball, soccer, field hockey, softball, gymnastics, lacrosse, track, cross county, tennis, and golf.

There were aspects of coaching Gus enjoyed. "It's challenging," he said. "I like to compete, and I like to have my teams compete against bigger and supposedly tougher schools. I also like to compete against other adults, and coaching gives you the opportunity to match yourself against other coaches. You plan; you scheme; you practice; and at the end of a match, you know if you've won or lost. In teaching you never know what you've accomplished."

There were poor practice facilities for the wrestling team. A winter sport, wrestling traditionally had to share space with the basketball teams, and since the inclusion of women's teams in the athletic constellation, few high schools had enough room in the gymnasium to give to wrestlers. As it was, practices for the basketball teams had to be coordinated sequentially to accommodate the three boys' teams and the two girls' teams. The wrestlers were forced to practice in a double classroom on the social studies wing. Every evening after school, all the desks had to be removed, the sliding partition between the rooms had to be opened, and the wrestling mats had to be dragged in. After practice, the process was reversed, and every morning traces of sweat and oil of wintergreen still hung in the air.

Gus had a sense of theatrics about his coaching. On the evening of a tough home match against a local rival, Gus arranged a prematch show. He had the gymnasium lights dimmed, and his wrestlers ran into the darkened gym with the hoods up on their warmup jackets. They formed a circle, and a spotlight focused on a senior boy, the team manager, who was formally dressed in black tie and tails. He solemnly walked to the center of the circle of wrestlers, and to the delight of the Oldham fans, he gave his best effort at the national anthem. It was a very spectacular opening, but Gus was not able to choreograph the rest of the evening as effectively, and the Oldham High School wrestling team lost badly. Oldham had a few good wrestlers, and it was obvious from watching them that Gus and his assistant, Sal, the physics teacher, had taught sound wrestling principles. But wrestling requires an aggressiveness and a physical combativeness that were uncommon among Oldham students. It is not a sport for the polite and well-behaved.

Gus was obviously keyed up for the match. He paced the sidelines encouraging his wrestlers, and he remained intent on every match even after it was mathematically obvious that Oldham could not win. The match ended at 10 P.M. It would be nearly 10:30 before the last wrestler left the locker room and Gus could go home. He did not arrive at the house he rented until eleven, and although he had missed dinner, he could not eat; he said the first bite of food he took felt like a stone in his knotted stomach. Gus had put in a sixteen-hour day. It would be well into the morning before he fell asleep. The next day he had to get up before 6 A.M., teach five classes, console his team, go over the match they lost, and practice for the next one.

Gus Poulos was awarded tenure. The extent to which his coaching affected the tenure decision could not be determined, but Gus knew at the very least it did not hurt. He enjoyed coaching and working with the students, but he said he could no longer put up with the "tension" and the feeling that his work was "unrewarded." He had made up his mind not to coach the following year, but he would not officially announce it until the fall. According to state law he had to teach for three years and a day to be tenured, and he did not want his chances hurt by a premature announcement.

Coaching was a tough job, and several of the coaches complained about the pressures they were under. Jim Donegan said that many of the parents had very high expectations for their children, and they often made unrealistic assessments of the children's athletic talents. He complained of phone calls from parents asking why their son or daughter was not playing. He said: "There are three things that the parents in this community want for their children: academic success, athletic success, and social acceptance."

Donegan said the parents were more than willing to intercede with the school or the coaches to secure these things for their children. "We get a lot of business people and executives up here who are used to wielding influence. The parents are used to solving problems for their children, and the kids are used to saying 'my mother will call you,' or, 'my father will call you' when they have a problem. It's natural for the parents to call up on behalf of the kid in the areas they feel are important."

Donegan claimed that it would have been a social stigma to ask his parents for help when he was in high school, but he knew it was part of the social system in Oldham. "I was sick for part of one basketball season, and I lost my starting position to a black guy," Jim said. "My father asked me if he should call the coach and explain to him that I was sick, but now I was back and healthy, and maybe I could start again. I said absolutely not. That was not the way that I wanted to get my position back. People wouldn't have thought that it was right to put pressure on a coach like that. Here, it's a way of life," he said, without any apparent resentment.

The jayvee and freshman coaches claimed to experience the least pressure from parents. There was less notoriety, fewer fans, and more pleasure, according to the coaches. "I feel like I really teach these kids sound fundamentals and good sportsmanship," the freshman basketball coach told me. "It's really a pleasure to work with these kids. We work hard; we play hard; but we have a good time. After a game, the kids always come up to me and shake my hand. I enjoy coaching them; they're terrific kids. I enjoy being around them. I drive them to athletic events all over the place, and I really enjoy their company. I've been lucky. I've had a lot of good athletes and a lot of really nice kids. I have no desire to coach basketball at a higher level."

The girls' softball coach, the field hockey coach, and the freshman football coach seemed to enjoy themselves more than the boys' varsity coaches. Watching the girls' varsity softball team play a game on the day of the Oldham junior prom, I noticed that the shortstop had her hair in rollers, and I teased the coach and asked him if one of his players was "out of uniform." He dismissed my question with a smile and a wave of the hand. "This is terrific," he said. "I used to coach wrestling and football, but it got to be too intense after a while. This is fun, the way it should be. I teach some fundamentals; we laugh and clown around; we have a good time."[7]

Jim Donegan believed the school asked more from coaches than it did from teachers. "First of all," he said, "coaches and ADs are not tenured. They can be fired after any period of service. There is absolutely no security in these positions." He also noted that coaches perform in front of hundreds of spectators, including many adults, and he said: "Teachers would be terrified to teach in such a situation, to have all their teaching scrutinized and second guessed by adults. It's unbelievable the amount of criticism coaches are subjected to. Teachers are insulated in their classrooms; coaching is done in the open."

Basketball and football were the two most popular sports in the school. Jim Donegan's basketball team typically did well in the conference, and they usually won a game or two in the state tournament at the end of the season before losing to larger urban schools. There were disclaimers attached to the teams' successes and Donegan's coaching: Some people said that the teams won primarily because Oldham was the largest school in the conference and therefore had the largest pool of players from which to select. Others said that Donegan was a good coach at this level, in this league, but he would have to stay at a place like Oldham and could never move up to college coaching because he had no history of coaching black players. Despite the criticisms, the team and the coach seemed satisfied, and the school and the community were more than satisfied with them.

The same could not be said of the football team. The football coach

---

[7]In 1985 the girls' softball team won the state championship, and the coach was named softball "coach of the year" by the state's major newspaper.

was in his late thirties and had coached for sixteen years, but he was not doing well in the conference. His offense had trouble scoring points, and parents and fans claimed his play selection was so pedestrian and predictable that they were able to call nearly every play from the stands. To make matters worse, three sons of school board members were on the team, and the board members were known to be very critical of the coach.

"Yeah, I was under a lot of pressure," he admitted. "They said that they knew my offense, and this and that. They don't realize what kind of talent I'm dealing with. You have to keep the offense simple so that the kids can execute."

Some of his former players admitted that his play calling was simplistic, and his game strategies were not very elaborate, but they were universally enthusiastic about him. He was considered to be a great coach for whom to play. He loved the game, and he loved the kids. He scrimmaged with them in practice, and he made tackles without pads. He encouraged them, teased them, wrestled with them and played with them. If he was less than a great tactician, the players forgave him and worked hard for him. The parents and some of the board members were not as forgiving. Cal Bullinger was asked to speak to the coach. "It was the most ridiculous thing in the world," the coach said. "Here's this tall, skinny gawk who played in the band asking me why I called this play on third down. I asked him if he understood the veer offense we were running. He says, 'No.' I ask him what play he would have called, and he says, 'That's not the point.' I walked out of his office."

The football coach was certain that the board members had put Cal up to it, and Cal admitted that "perhaps there was excessive board concern about athletics." The problem was ameliorated by a winning season. Open criticisms of the coach subsided, and there was less talk about him losing his job. He appeared to relax. It had been a tough time for him, and it was not until well after the season had ended that I could ask him about it.

Other coaches reported that several members of the board of education were consumed by athletics. "They certainly seem to be more interested in athletics than academics," said one of the coaches. "One guy on the board calls every once in a while and complains about different things, who's playing, who's not, that sort of thing. One time he kept me on the phone for over an hour complaining about another [Oldham] coach. Some of them are frustrated jocks who have never wanted to give up their involvement with sports."

Another coach likened them to George Steinbrenner, the principal owner of the New York Yankees. "They think that they own the teams," he said. "They call me up, question what I do. I'm sure that, at times, they'd fire me on the spot if they could."

All the coaches and the athletic director agreed that if a head coach was fired, it would be personally devastating. They said perhaps the person would stay on as a teacher, but most likely he would try to find another coaching spot and resign, even if it meant giving up tenure. Some of the coaches admitted they taught so they could coach.

Coaching provided many things the classroom could not. There were challenges, victories, and control over what you were doing and how you were doing it. Coaches were not as regulated by the bell schedule, and they had a powerful and intimate relationship with students. "When there's two minutes to go in a close ball game," said Jim Donegan, "and I call a time out, I'm the most important person in the kids' lives. It's a tremendous feeling that you just can't get as a classroom teacher."

Donegan believed that in some ways his coaching was an extension of his teaching. He claimed that you get a chance to do the things you would like to do as a teacher: spend more time with kids, work individually with kids, gear instruction toward the needs of the kids, and share real emotions with them. He said he would like his players to evaluate him as they would a teacher. "At the end of four years in high school, I would like someone to ask my players 'Who was the best teacher you had in high school?' and I want some of them to say it was my basketball coach. That's how I would judge my success as a coach. I really believe that."

One of the football coaches passed around an article written by a professional athlete which credited the athlete's high school coach with being one of the most influential people in his life. "Look at this," the coach said. "This guy says that his coach kept him away from drugs, and crime . . . and made him what he is today. Can you do that in your social studies class?"

While the impact of coaches on students was arguable, their influence in the community was not. They were clearly the most recognized teachers in the school. The head coaches were quoted in the local newspapers and interviewed on the radio. They had fame and notoriety that engendered a great deal of jealousy among teachers whose major accomplishments and successes were known only to them and their students. When the head baseball coach was denied tenure as a classroom teacher it was not reported in the main section of the local paper, but the sports section contained a story and his photograph under the caption, "Oldham Coach Fired."

"Can you imagine that?" asked Paul De Faro, glancing at the headline. "It's as though his work as a teacher was not important. It looks as though we fired a popular coach for no reason. I wonder what kind of dumb jock they'll hire to replace him. What do we need? A baseball coach? A track coach?"

The social studies department was home to more coaches than any other department in the school. There were nine full-time faculty members in the department, and among them they coached eight sports. Jim Donegan was a member of the department, as were the varsity baseball coach, who also coached football; the varsity wrestling coach; the coach for the freshman basketball and baseball teams; and an assistant track coach. When Troy volunteered to coach the girls' soccer team, he confused the members of the department. Troy had participated in high school sports, but claimed that he did not like the hostile competition they engendered. He also believed, and expressed openly, that the social studies department had been saddled with too many jocks. "Dr. Szabo thinks that social studies is a dumping ground for coaches," Troy told me. "Every year I recommend certain individuals to him for a teaching position, and often they are rejected because we need a line coach or a weight coach for the track team. There aren't many highly qualified individuals out there, and it makes it very difficult when we have to find a good social studies teacher who can coach too."

Paul De Faro was the only member of the department who had never coached, and he claimed that he never intended to. "They have to stop looking at this department as second class. If they need new coaches, hire more gym teachers."

The teachers agreed that it was very hard to be a good teacher and a good coach. Most teachers believed coaches neglected the classroom during their coaching season, and because 40 percent of the Oldham teachers coached at least one sport, the cumulative neglect of teaching responsibilities may have been considerable.

Jim Donegan disagreed. He said coaching gave teachers new insights into their students which enabled them to be more effective in the long run. Donegan admitted certain subjects (he used chemistry as an example) required an unusual amount of preparation, and that head coaches should come most often from the physical education department, but he allowed that they could also be social studies teachers with little harm to the students. One of the teachers claimed Donegan probably slighted his own students during the basketball season. "I walked into his class one day to get something. There he was at the front of the room, copying notes on the board from some review book. When he saw me, he secreted the book in his top drawer. Now tell me, is that good teaching?"

There was a division among the male teachers between jocks and the nonjocks. The nonjocks thought the jocks were dumb, and the jocks thought the nonjocks were pretentious. "The coaches have to be the dumbest people in the school," claimed a teacher who did not coach. "One of the football coaches just came up to me and asked, 'Hey, that guy the kids read in English class, J. D. Salinger. Wasn't he in Kennedy's cabinet?' And this guy is a teacher on the same pay scale that I am!"

The male and female teachers who did not coach resented the privileged status and recognition afforded the coaches. "It is just as hard to direct the plays as it is to coach football," claimed one of the teachers, "but there is only a fraction of the salary and recognition given to nonathletic activities. The band has to raise money to help pay for their uniforms. Could you imagine the football team being forced to do the same thing?"

"If the board of education were as interested in academics and innovation as they are in athletics, maybe this school would be a more interesting place to work," added an English teacher who did not coach.

While some of the teachers believed the school was placing too much emphasis on sports, Jim Donegan did not. "There's no overemphasis on athletics in this school," he argued. "We're doing what the society wants us to," he said. "You can argue that there is an overemphasis on athletics in the society, but the schools only reflect the society, and the society values athletics more than it does academics. More people can appreciate athletics. The schools will never emphasize academics until the society does. . . ."

Donegan also believed that those who did not coach were jealous of the coaches' celebrity and popularity with the students. "The nonjocks are envious of our recognition and the enjoyment we get from coaching," claimed Donegan. "Everyone wants to be one of the guys, and coaching makes you one of the guys. I personally enjoy the camaraderie of the coaches. We relax and enjoy each other's company. It's being a regular guy, and most people just want to be a regular guy."

The split between the jocks and the nonjocks was one of the defining characteristics of the school. Sports were among the few things ever discussed in a serious manner, especially by the male teachers. Regardless of their subject field, the men spoke with more knowledge and enthusiasm about sports than any other topic. Teaching was rarely discussed. New books were seldom mentioned, and conversations about content areas were infrequent, but every day there were discussions and arguments about sports. If you did not keep up with the current athletic season, you could not participate in much of the daily interactions of the majority of the male teachers. Teachers listened to radio talk shows about sports, they read sports magazines and the *Sporting News,* and they kept up with local, regional, and national teams. The faculty room was typically littered with newspapers. There were local papers, *The New York Times*, a state paper, and several of New York City's more lurid tabloids. It was not uncommon to find most of the papers left open to the sports section. It was the strongest link among the male teachers in a school in which the males clearly dominated.

Coaching could make teachers into celebrities. Mike Werge was a very good teacher, but his greatest notoriety came as an assistant track coach. Mike was not a track athlete in high school or college, but he had read a few books and talked with a few knowledgeable track people, and he believed he knew as much about the sport as most high school coaches. "Track is a very easy sport to coach," he said. "At the high school level there really isn't that much to it."

Mike became embroiled in an argument with a rival coach about some alleged unethical tricks the coach had used during a meet. One of Oldham's better track athletes ran the 800 meter event. The rival coach used a "rabbit" to lure the Oldham runner into a detrimentally rapid pace. The rabbit began the race with a sprinter's speed, and the Oldham runner panicked and tried to keep up. The rabbit eventually dropped out after 400 meters, and the exhausted Oldham runner was easily passed by another runner from the other school. Oldham went on to lose the meet, and the other team later won a state title. Mike had become angry at the track meet and confronted the coach. The usually calm, mild-mannered teacher had gotten into a heated argument. Most of the male teachers wanted Mike to tell the story and explain his point of view. His presence in the faculty room was greeted with a greater interest and curiosity than he had ever received as a teacher. He downplayed his notoriety. "It's just the end of the year. Teachers need something new to talk about," he said.

In some ways the incident bothered Mike. He knew that no matter how well he taught, he would never be interviewed by the local newspapers. He would not get on the local radio shows, and he would not be the talk of the faculty room. Board members would not call him to discuss his classroom teaching strategies. Coaching could offer faculty those things that were denied them in the classroom: control, a sense of accomplishment, competition, camaraderie, and recognition.

7

SUMMARY AND CONCLUSIONS

It seemed as if one day we were teaching classes, preparing tests and marking papers, and the next day, without warning, the students were gone, the halls were empty, and there were suddenly no more papers to grade. In reality, the end had not been that abrupt or unheralded. The school year wound down gradually. The beginning of the end came when seniors received their acceptance letters from colleges in the early spring; it was hastened by the warm weather, class picnics, proms, and celebrations. In May, a senior boy draped a banner along the side of his car that read, "Let's Party!"

The seniors' attitudes quickly infected the whole school. Every sunny day, my students begged me to hold class on the lawn. They were less willing to do any work. The pace of the classroom had slowed down, and less material was covered. Most classes offered only a suggestion of the academic demands that had been placed on students in the fall. By June, the temperature in the school was often above eighty degrees. We all wore shorts, perspired, and looked forward to the summer. Up and down the corridors, teachers were issuing their final threats: "Listen up, people. According to my calendar, we still have two weeks of school left! I know it's hot, but this stuff is important, and it's going to be on the final. If you don't pay attention. . . ."

Many of the teachers capitulated to the students' end-of-year attitudes. "You have to work them like hell for the first three marking periods," a math teacher told me. "After that, it's all downhill. You're better off to go with the flow and enjoy it."

Willa Green would have none of that. She had heard that the seniors were planning to take a day off from school, pile into cars, and head for the Jersey shore. Willa headed off the illegal event by announcing that her final exam would be given in class on senior "cut day," and she vowed to change the date of the final to coincide with any future rescheduling. Willa taught A-level seniors, and they did not want to jeopardize graduating by failing English. They cursed and moaned, but they did not cut. Willa told us that no one had been absent on the day of her final, and she urged the rest of us to "uphold academic standards."

The school had to depend on the voluntary compliance of the students more than ever. Although they could threaten to fail an underclassman for the year or withhold a senior's diploma, or bar a student from graduation, administrators were understandably reluctant to make good on these threats, and they were left with little power to control behavior. "We're hanging on by our fingernails in June," said Larry Silverman. "You just hold your breath and hope that nothing happens."

Nothing happened. The school year ended gently if not spectacularly. Discipline was good; attendance was not bad. Although the photocopying machine broke down several times, it was quickly repaired each time, and we were all able to duplicate copies of our final exams. Willa Green complained to Troy Thayer that I did not include an essay on my freshman final. Troy told me that I should always include an essay question, even if I did not read the answers carefully. We said goodby to students and wished graduating seniors well. We cleaned up the rooms; emptied the desks; and took the decorations down from the walls. Before we could pick up our final paychecks, the faculty had to have a checkout sheet signed by the librarian, the audiovisual coordinator, and three secretaries. Teachers submitted grade books to their department supervisors. The supervisors made sure they conformed to school policy, and held onto them in case a parent questioned a grade during the summer. There was a polite faculty party at the end of the year. We wished each other a pleasant summer, and went our separate ways.

In June 1984, I was an invited speaker at the Oldham High School commencement. In my address I praised good teachers, and I encouraged the graduating seniors to consider teaching as a career. I told them that as recently as 1970, nearly 25 percent of college freshmen were enrolled in a course of studies that would lead them to certification as teachers. By 1980, I said, fewer than 5 percent were enrolled in such programs, and many of those who had dropped out of the pool of potential teachers were the bright, talented people needed to make schools work. Despite my invitation for others to become public school teachers, I had decided to return to the university. Two years at Oldham had been enough to remind me of both the pleasures of teaching high school students and the difficulty of doing it well.

By the end of my second year of teaching at the high school I was no longer an outsider; I had become part of the school. Formal and informal signals from the faculty and administrators indicated that my behavior as a teacher was within the limits of acceptability. The Oldham–Webster Board of Education had offered me a new contract with no stipulations about coaching. The administration had asked me to conduct inservice workshops and school surveys. My department supervisor had asked me to help with curriculum revision and curriculum articulation with the elementary and middle schools. Teachers invited me to parties, asked for my opinion, argued with me, and shared both personal and professional problems with me. I felt that I was part of the organization, and I had been afforded the protection of the informal systems of the school. For example, on the day I had been observed by two members of the board of education, I was given ten minutes' advance notice by a colleague who had seen them in the main office and had heard an administrator loudly announce their purpose.

I was an insider, one of the teachers. I learned the joys, problems, and secrets of working in a public high school. I experienced the routines, pressures, and the the occasional emergencies that characterized the job, and I found out from the other teachers how to interpret them and contend with them. I learned at firsthand how teachers view their work and what importance they gave to it. I grew to understand the nature of teaching as the teachers understood it, and I defined teaching as the teachers defined it.

A DIFFICULT, DEMANDING JOB

The Oldham teachers worked a seven and a half hour day; they were always busy in school, and typically they had to take work home every night and on weekends. It was not uncommon for English and social studies teachers to read, evaluate, correct, and grade three or four hundred pages of student writing a week. While I spent hours on student papers every day, I read less during that year than any year of my adult life. Few teachers seemed to have the time to read much during the school year, and most admitted that they were able to "catch up" with current fiction only in the summer. Fewer seemed to delight in the literature of their subject or feel the necessity to keep current.

There never seemed to be enough time to prepare for classes. I was responsible for instruction in four subject areas. Many of my classes were hastily put together, and I often wondered how many content errors I made every day. I was always rushing around looking up information, searching for books and articles to photocopy. I had to preview films, videotapes, and simulation games. Tests had to be typed, collated, and graded, and there was no time to check their validity or reliability. I had to keep track of the academic progress of 125 students, and the psychological health of as many of them as I could.

Teachers taught five classes, supervised students during their two duty assignments, and had either twenty-one or forty-two minutes to eat lunch. The four minutes between classes provided barely enough time to catch my breath, and none to plan, work, or talk with colleagues. Every forty-two minutes a new group of students came spilling into the room, filling up the seats and the silence, and I was on again.

Nagging clerical chores consumed my free period and lunch period: There were attendance forms to complete, cut slips to check, discipline follow-ups, makeup tests, lesson plans, and photocopying. There were college recommendations to write, progress reports to fill out, report card grades to enter, and there always seemed to be a new form to complete for the school, the district, or the state. There were no faculty workrooms, no file cabinets, and no office space. The one typewriter to which I had access was shared by the language department and the social studies department, and each of the seventeen teachers had to do his or her own typing.

I learned that it was not possible for teachers to assign as much work as they thought necessary because there was not enough time to read papers, grade tests, provide extra help, or assist individual students. The brightest students admitted they were not working very hard, and the slower students felt they were being cheated. Teachers were unable to give all but the most insistent students the attention they needed, and both guidance counselors and teachers admitted that a few students received a disproportionate share of their time.

Most teachers seemed to encourage passive behavior in the classroom. Despite the efforts of some administrators and supervisors, lecture and discussion were the primary modes of classroom teaching, and student learning was limited by how fast the teachers could talk and how much the students could remember. Perhaps it was the only way in which adults were able to accommodate the greater numbers and higher energy level of adolescents. Observing teachers and students, one could not help but conclude that Oldham High subscribed to the notion that learning meant quietly sitting in class and listening to teachers.

While teachers worked hard, they were rarely sure of their accomplishments. Measures of student content attainment, where they existed, were of questionable validity. Teachers could not be sure of the extent to which they met their content, skill, or attitude objectives. They could not demonstrate that the time and attention given to the academic side of teaching were well spent, and it served as another frustration for the teachers. Too often, at the end of the school year they were left only with a vague sense of having done something worthwhile and a few thank yous from their students.

Teachers and administrators believed the school was serving its students, and that the graduates had profited from their school experience, but these assumptions were untested. The efforts of the pupil personnel department in gathering follow-up data on the graduates were not very productive. The head of the department told me that surveys were sent to graduates one year after they had been graduated and again four years later. The response rate was very low (12 to 20 percent), and the data were not of much use. Some recent graduates complained that they had not received the surveys; others said the questions asked had not tapped their reservoir of comments and criticisms, and they chose not to respond.

FEELING UNSUPPORTED AND VULNERABLE

The school lacked an academic focus. No one occupied a position of responsibility for academic instruction analagous to the director of athletics or the coordinator of student activities. The teachers did not regard the administrators as either academic or instructional leaders, and the school lacked cohesive curricula or an agreed-upon plan of instruction. The teachers concluded that the school was unconcerned about the quality of instruction, and they felt they were on their own.

The loneliness of teaching is one of its most widely recognized characteristics (see Boyer, 1983; Lortie, 1975; Sizer, 1984). Teachers spent most of their working lives away from colleagues, supervisors, administrators or other adults. Of the 900 classes they taught each year, fewer than 1 percent were observed, and most of those observations were designed as critical evaluations.

Teachers at Oldham, other than those teamed in the learning communities, rarely discussed teaching.[1] The teachers had no mechanisms to resolve conflicts over curriculum or teaching styles, so they avoided them. Conversations about sports, new homes, television programs, automobile maintenance, and other practical matters were the social glue that held the faculty together. Teachers could not determine policy or select the new principal; they could not tinker with the schedule or the teaching day, so they complained. Their conversations were typical of those who were without power in large organizations: irreverent, sometimes crude, and filled with gossip and rumors.

Left to their own devices, teachers defined the job independent of the goals of the school, and they associated only with those people who could share their interpretation of the job. Teaching was a highly personal enterprise, and teachers invested a great deal of themselves in their classes. The ways in which their rooms were decorated, the arrangement of the desks, and their instructional styles were statements about the teachers' personal beliefs about education. Some teachers did an extraordinary job of charging their classes with life, enthusiasm for the subject, and respect for the students. There were truly exceptional teachers in every department. There were also those who confused teaching with entertaining, academic rigor with pedantry, and discipline with Draconianism.

The heterogeneity of the faculty was not due to a conscious effort to assemble a diverse group of teacher-scholars, an academic buffet for students to sample. It was due to the insularity of the teachers, and to the nature of the field of education, which is sufficiently ambiguous to allow everyone in and out of it to define what constitutes good teaching and worthwhile learning. The diversity of the faculty was reinforced by the varied hiring practices of succeeding administrations. One superintendent may have favored one type of teacher; his successor may have favored another, and there had been three district superintendents in the twelve-year history of the school. Every year new teachers were dumped into the faculty mixture and they had to find some place to fit. The result was a faculty that was less than a unified group working toward common goals and the solution of common problems than sixty-six individuals each defining the job personally, often united by little more than a common bell schedule.

---

[1]In an ethnographic study of elementary school teachers, McPherson (1972) found that teachers rarely discussed teaching. Teachers were not expected to boast about their successes in the classroom because this implied that other teachers were less successful. Teachers were not expected to complain about classroom problems because this was seen as a sign of vulnerability. McPherson also noted that the enthusiasm of new teachers was greeted with indifference or sarcasm. They were told that "innovative ideas" would not work, and that they were better off sticking to the "old methods."

The bells defined the teachers' working day: One bell signaled when you began a class, another when you ended it. Bells told you when to eat lunch; when you could have coffee; and when you could go to the lavatory. Administrators and supervisors said that good teaching was bell-to-bell teaching. Meet the students at the door; make sure they get to class on time; start teaching when the bell rings; don't stop teaching until you hear another bell; never, never dismiss the students before the bell.

The school existed as a minor academic island isolated from colleges and universities and other high schools. There were no formal ties to private or state colleges or the state university. The only university faculty with whom the teachers had contact were those who came in either for entrepreneurial ventures contracted with the board of education, or those who were conducting personal research from which the teachers could see no direct benefit. Unless teachers pursued graduate courses on their own time, they had only chance encounters with their academic discipline and the field of education.

The structure of the school further served to isolate the teachers by establishing the subject supervisors as intermediaries between the teachers and the administrators. The supervisors, who were appointed without faculty consultation, were charged with an impossible task: In addition to teaching three classes and supervising a school duty, they had to supervise as many as ten teachers in their departments. They had to be subject-matter specialists who were also aware of the latest teaching strategies, curriculum designs, and personnel management techniques. The administration expected them to be critical evaluators of teachers; teachers wanted them to be sympathetic colleagues who helped them to improve as practitioners and scholars. It was inevitable that both teachers and administrators would find the supervisors wanting. That the supervisors were tenured, and thereby locked into their positions, further exacerbated the frustrations of the teachers and the administrators.

Administrators seemed as concerned with order as they were with instruction. It was hard to determine if the students were learning anything; it was easier to tell if they had their feet on the library tables or if they were cutting, smoking, or running in the halls. There was, even in this calm, tranquil school, an administrative preoccupation with "keeping the lid on." The emphasis on discipline maintenance procedures was based on the implicit assumption that if administrators and teachers were not vigilant, the barely controlled energy of adolescents would explode. Students had to be watched, checked, and reminded of appropriate school behavior, dress, and language. Students were not given very much free time; they were kept busy and moving in the hope that this would keep them out of trouble.

The administrators may have been locked into their roles as apologists for the school, and they were forced to ignore substantive school problems because they had to project the image that the school was functioning safely, efficiently, and without conflict or dissent (see Cusick, 1983). When the search was underway to find a successor to Cal Bullinger, one of the teachers said, "We need a principal who can shake this place up and deal with some of the problems, but we'll probably get another Dr. Pangloss who pretends that Oldham is the best of all possible worlds."

Teachers believed that the school treated them poorly. There was, in the working lives of teachers, a pattern of rudeness and minor insults that contributed to their sense of being undervalued. Classes were routinely interrupted; conferences with parents were scheduled without consultation; teaching was recognized only when it was unsatisfactory; the faculty room was dirty; and teachers could not on their own leave the building during the school day. "It's hard to feel like a professional," one teacher told me, "when you have to ask the principal for permission to leave the school in order to deposit a paycheck so your mortgage payment won't bounce."

There were so many interactions with so many students in the course of every school day that it was inevitable teachers would say something or do something that could get them into trouble. My physical confrontation with Jeff, and the memo that was sent inadvertently to the parents of Bobby Daria, were errors of judgment. My failure to preview the videotape of *Johnny Got His Gun* was an omission of teaching responsibility. But these actions were by no means rare or unusual. After each of these incidents, teachers came forward with similar stories about themselves and other members of the faculty. The teachers complained about their vulnerability, and their inability to resolve problems without administrative intervention. They advised me to avoid controversy and to cover myself at all times. When you teach 900 classes of adolescents a year, they said, there are bound to be problems.

THE POLITICS OF CURRICULUM

There is a body of literature which suggests that everything that goes on in schools is political, and the school curriculum is far more than the sum of the academic content (Apple, 1979; Giroux and Penna,

1979; Giroux, 1983; Young, 1971). Critical theorists[2] argue that schools are forces of social control which ensure that the dominant culture is prized, legitimated, and passed on through the social reality constructed by teachers. Schools are viewed as more than agencies which pass on academic knowledge and which socialize students toward the adoption of acceptable adult roles. Schools are seen as agencies of ideological control designed to reproduce and preserve the inequities of society (Apple, 1979; Giroux, 1983). Schools, it is argued, teach students to accept the social order as correct, and force students to blame themselves for any inability to succeed or advance.

Since Plato, there has been an acknowledged link between the ideal state, the ideal citizen, and the type of schooling that is to produce citizens for the state. The new literature suggests that schools produce an aquiescence toward the dominant culture by creating a social reality of covert control. Through the school's approaches to learning, course offerings, and tracking system, some students learn that they are "dumb," "stupid," or unworthy (Henry, 1963; Rosenbaum, 1976), and they are grouped in vocational or manual skills tracks where they are programmed for a future that will be less socially honored than those in the academic tracks. There is also evidence of an inherent class bias in the verbal interactions of teachers and students (Bernstein, 1971; Labov, 1972) in which the sons and daughters of the middle class receive an education which is different in substance and promise from that given the children of the working classes (Anyon, 1981). The need for overt control of the society is obviated by schools which pass on an unquestioned view that society is functioning as it should (Apple, 1979; Giroux, 1983).

The establishment of ideological hegemony, the notion that the current order is working for everyone's best interest, is not found in the formal curriculum or in a process of scientific inquiry after truth, but in those things that are omitted (Bowers, 1984; Giroux, 1983), the ways in which teachers speak to students (Anyon, 1981; Bernstein, 1971; Labov, 1972), and the "hidden curriculum" of legitimation and class bias (Giroux and Penna, 1979).

This new literature typically focuses on the unequal treatment given social classes and racial groups within schools. Although Old-

[2]The argument that knowledge is not neutral but serves a political purpose which is constructed in part by the language and interactions of teachers and students has been advanced by a number of curriculum theorists in the United States (Apple, 1979; Giroux, 1983; Karabel and Halsey, 1977), and by the "new" sociologists of education in Great Britain (Young, 1971; Young and Whitty, 1977). Critical reviews of the "new sociology" can be found in Demaine (1981), Bernbaum (1977), and Hickox (1982). See Tanner and Tanner (1979) and Jackson (1980) for critical commentary on the American curriculum theorists.

ham was primarily a homogeneous, white, middle class community, the school did afford different treatment to different categories of students. Typical of secondary schools, success at Oldham was defined narrowly and restrictively. Success in physics and calculus was prized more than success in auto shop or home economics. There was not only a hierarchy of honored courses, but ability groupings within the courses further separated students. Nearly half of the students were in C or E-level courses, and the school believed the percentage should be higher. The administrators, supervisors, guidance counselors, and teachers claimed there were too many students in A-level courses who should not be there.

There was different status ascribed to students who had been assigned to the various ability groups, and their labels followed them everywhere. The A and H-level students were prized, and most of the teachers admitted that they liked these students better than other students. Many of the teachers viewed the assignment to teach C and E-level students as punishment. For poor teaching, a teacher could be given lower-level students; for good teaching, a teacher could be given honors classes to teach. Many of the teachers resented the C-level students. The A and H-level students were the major concern of the teachers, and although they constituted only 53 percent of the student body, they received more than that share of faculty attention and praise. Teachers and administrators liked C students who were rule-governed, docile, polite, and deferential. Commonly heard in teachers' conversations were the expressions, "He is a C student, but a very nice kid." "She does the work and doesn't cause any problems." Although the content given the students in C classes may not have been appropriate for them, the teachers expected these marginally academic students to accept it without complaint. The school's curricular emphasis was on the A-level students. No one agreed on how C-level students should be taught or what content they should consider. Typically, C-level courses were watered-down versions of the A-level courses with shorter assignments, less provocative reading material, and lower expectations of the students. Less content was covered in these courses, and across disciplines, the tests, with few exceptions, seemed to emphasize the memory of low-level factual information.

On my first day as a teacher, the social studies department supervisor told me that the C students were a problem, but it was a problem few teachers discussed and few administrators tried to remedy. The C and E-level students knew that the school was not serving them. There was a stigma attached to being among those the school judged as less deserving, and it resulted in the same tensions and group formations that Willis (1977) found in English secondary schools. The "lads" described by Willis were working class students who found school boring, alienating, and offering only limited opportunities. As a way of coping with the school, they rejected its narrow achievement ideology and chose, as a rebellion, a career of manual labor. At Oldham, those students who hung out in the grove were middle class, but they rejected the school's definition of success, and they were as disaffected and alienated as the lads. Smoking, cutting, coming to class late, and constant flirtation with school trouble were the ways in which they could safely reject the school's culture and maintain a sense of dignity.

TEACHING AS A CAREER

A new teacher is assigned to a rectangular cement block room, given a textbook, and asked to teach five classes a day of twenty-five or more students. One of the problems of teaching is that thirty-five years later, the teacher may be using a revised edition of the same book, and teaching the same material, in the same room, in much the same way, with no additional responsibilities. After my first month in the school, Mike Flynn asked me how I liked the job. I told him the truth: I was enjoying my return to high school teaching. "Can you see yourself doing this for the rest of your life?" he asked, with a smile. "It's okay in the beginning, but a lot of people get bored with it after a few years."

Mike told me he liked teaching. He said that he did not want to get out of education, and he did not seriously entertain notions of becoming a full-time administrator, but he was not entirely comfortable with his decision to remain in the classroom. "I hope my sons won't be disappointed in me because I'm *only a teacher*," he said.

Mike Flynn's reservations about career choice were not uncommon among the teachers. In response to a survey, 63 percent of the Oldham teachers answered "yes" to a question that asked, "If you had it to do again, would you become a teacher?" The other 37 percent answered "no" or were undecided. This statistic is similar to national polls of teachers, despite an absence of many of the problems experienced by teachers in the national sample (see Boyer, 1983: 159; Goodlad, 1984: 172).

In 1984, the Gallup organization published a report of teacher attitudes toward public education. One of the survey questions asked

teachers to identify the three main reasons why teachers leave the
field. The most frequently cited responses of the high school teachers
included:

1. Low salary	89%
2. Discipline problems	41
3. Low standing of teaching	38
4. Unmotivated, uninterested students	41
5. Lack of financial support	28
6. Lack of parental support	16
7. Outstanding teachers unrewarded	25
8. Difficulties of advancement	19
9. Uninterested parents	11

(Numbers to the right indicate the percentage of teachers who included that issue among the top three reasons why they believed
teachers were leaving the field. Figures add to more than 100 percent
because of multiple answers) (A. Gallup, 1984: 102).

Discipline, uninterested students, and the lack of parental involvement were not among the problems experienced by the teachers at
Oldham High. The Oldham teachers believed they were underpaid,
but in response to a survey of attitudes toward the field, they suggested additional reasons for their dissatisfactions with teaching. They
complained about the boredom, routine, and the frustrations in their
daily work, such as poor supervision, pressures from the community,
and paperwork. They also complained about their estrangement from
the authority structure of the school and their lack of ownership of the
curriculum.

The Oldham teachers believed they had a better understanding of
school problems than did administrators. The school, however, was
run from the top down; policies, curriculum improvement, and change
were mandated by the central administration. The teachers did not
make schoolwide decisions about curriculum or instruction, and they
had no formal influence on those who did. Their control was restricted
to the classroom, and with little ability to influence the school beyond
the walls of their room, the classroom (or shop or lab) had become the
unit of the teachers' emotional and intellectual involvement. Lortie
refers to it as the "teachers' cathexis of classrooms" (1975: 169). The
main pleasure of the job, and often its only pleasure, was to be found
in the classroom. Here the teachers had a sense of autonomy and
influence found nowhere else in their working lives, and they were
protective of their power in the classroom and reluctant to change their

classroom routines. They referred to the school with the definite article, "the school," but the possessive pronoun was used for the classroom and the students, "my room," "my kids."

One of the truisms of teaching is that if you don't like kids, you
can't be a teacher; there is little else sustaining about the job. The
students certainly were the best part of the job at Oldham. They were
animated, open, and interesting. The school was working mainly because of the quality of the students. College-bound, middle class,
compliant students were easy to teach. They had good skills, a positive
attitude toward school, and parents who were concerned about education. But students alone were not enough to nourish a career. It was
unfair to ask students to furnish the sense of achievement, advancement, and accomplishment an adult needs to feel worthy in work. The
students were just passing through en route to college and jobs, and
the teacher was often stuck in the classroom. Students openly asked
teachers questions that are not typically asked of other working adults:
"Why are you a teacher?" "Do you like it?" "How much longer do you
plan to be a teacher?" At Thanksgiving, many students returning from
college visit their former schools and teachers. The students ask: "Are
you still teaching in the same room?" "Are you still teaching the same
courses?" By implication they are saying: "Are you still a teacher?
Look at me, I have moved up, and you are still here, in high school."

Paul De Faro fretted about not being able to match achievements
with returning students who asked him, "What's new?" "So far," he
said, "I've always been able to say something positive. I built a cabin
upstate; I'm working on a graduate degree in history; I bought a computer; I'm teaching myself Latin; I got married; I went mountain climbing; I've been to Europe twice, and I learned how to sail."

Just being a very good teacher was not enough. If teachers wanted
a sense of accomplishment, they had to get it outside the job. There
was little room for career advancement in the school or the district.
Good teaching was inadequately recognized. There were no senior
teachers, or master teachers, or levels of teachers as there are levels of
professors at universities. Teachers belong to the category of workers
about whom common sense tells us there exists a great variation in
ability, but for whom remuneration is tied to other things. Teachers'
salaries were determined solely by total number of graduate credits
and years of experience. Individual effort could make teachers feel
better and earn the respect of the students, but it would not get them
a raise.

It frustrated some teachers to work hard and not be rewarded differentially. It angered some teachers to see the board of education withhold one teacher's annual raise for poor teaching,[3] but not reward others for excellent teaching. The teachers had no solution. The state teachers' association opposed merit pay, and the teachers knew of no fair method of measuring teaching success. They felt trapped in an inequitable system that offered them little recognition or opportunity for advancement.

For those in the classroom, there was little job mobility. Switching jobs and moving from one school to another was difficult. Districts were reluctant to hire teachers with many years of experience and advanced degrees because they had to pay them more money than a new teacher fresh out of college. Guidance, administration, and supervision were the only routes that could get teachers out of the classroom. While counselors, principals, and department supervisors suffered many of the frustrations of teachers, and they openly complained about their jobs, none told me that he or she would be willing to go back to full-time teaching, nor did most indicate that they missed their days in the classroom. They knew that teaching was harder and less financially rewarding than what they were then doing, and once they were out of the classroom they would never return voluntarily.

In 1984, Dr. Szabo, the superintendent of schools, resigned to become superintendent in a nearby district. It was a district that had elementary and middle schools as well as a large high school, and there was a larger staff and more buildings to oversee. His new position was considered to be more demanding and more prestigious, and it commanded a higher salary. A few months after his appointment, he convinced his new district to create a position for Dr. Mokowski. She too would assume a position with a greater salary.

While the building administrators and teachers were envious of the mobility of superintendents, few reported any sense of academic or personal loss, and only a handful attended the cash-bar cocktail party held in Dr. Szabo's honor. It was difficult for teachers or ad-

---

[3]The quality of teaching was ill defined by the school. Teaching success was not measured by student achievement in courses, student performance levels measured against national or state norms, or other quantitative measures. Teachers from other schools or universities did not evaluate teachers at Oldham. Good teaching was an unwritten social reality defined by the department supervisors, the building principals, and the assistant superintendent for curriculum. Poor teaching often had little to do with academic competence or the nature of academic instruction. One teacher was dismissed because he missed too many days of school. Another teacher was dismissed because she had problems with student discipline. The one teacher who was denied a salary increment was considered able but burned out, lacking interest and enthusiasm. Officially, the school claimed that his increment was withheld because he did not turn in written lesson plans. There was no school or district policy for dealing with the teacher's problems in any other way.

ministrators to cite the accomplishments of their superintendents, and they felt there was no justice in the ability of administrators to take credit for all the good that went on in their classrooms. The teachers felt the central administration had little effect on their teaching, but because of good teaching administrators could get better jobs. "We do all the work, and they get all the glory," complained Paul De Faro. "Tell me, what did they ever do for me as a teacher?"[4]

The routine of teaching was tiring and monotonous, and much of what we taught was often dull. A few teachers taught the same subject five times a day, and one of my former university colleagues questioned how anyone could be enthusiastic even once about the Webster-Ashburton Treaty. The job was so specialized that teachers did little else but repeatedly teach their narrow academic field, with the blandest of books and resources, in the absence of other adults. "I sometimes feel like an assembly line worker in Detroit," said one English teacher. "I add one part to the vehicle five times a day, 180 days a year. I have no idea what the finished product is supposed to look like; I never get together with the other workers, and I doubt if there ever was an engineer who designed all of this . . . I'm in this business for the vacations."

Factory metaphors were not uncommon in a job in which one day was much like another, characterized by fixed routines and repetitious work (see Sarason, 1982). On occasion teachers wondered aloud how they could make teaching interesting and alive for students when they were too dulled by the job to show much enthusiasm. "I bored myself today," said one English teacher, in a rare admission of classroom problems. "I let one kid go to the nurse and two others to the lav; I wish I could have gone with them."

A math teacher, with degrees in engineering and a background in computers, told me that every time he taught a new math course he became reinvigorated in his teaching. He said that initially it was a challenge to make complex mathematical concepts understandable and enjoyable for high school students. He confided that after several years of teaching, he had taught all the math courses a high school math department offers and he did not know what else he could do to maintain his interest.

The Oldham teachers harbored a fear they would not be able to

---

[4]In an interview, Dr. Szabo cited his contributions to the district: Program assessment; the development of a writing style manual written by the English teachers; the passage of a $2 million building referendum; establishing articulation committees with the elementary schools; hiring experienced teachers; developing a family life curriculum; and the focus on writing skills as a district goal.

sustain their enthusiasm for teaching for many years. They pointed to the older teachers in the school, many of whom, they claimed, had once demonstrated vitality in the classroom, but who were now just going through the motions, making fewer academic demands on students, and giving less and less of themselves every year. These were not teachers at the end of their careers, but people in their late thirties and early forties who had twenty years or more to work before retirement. The younger teachers feared they would suffer the same fate if they did not get out of the classroom in time.

In a study of human service agencies that included secondary school teachers, Cherniss (1980) described the phenomenon known as "burnout," negative changes in work behavior brought about by the stress of the job. Cherniss identified the symptoms of burnout as detachment, discouragement, pessimism about work, apathy, negativism, irritability, loss of interest and creativity. These were similar to the symptoms of burnout reported by those Oldham teachers who had experienced the problem. The Oldham teachers added that the school had done little, if anything, to help them cope with it. "It's like everything else in teaching," one teacher wrote. "You have to solve the problem yourself."

Some research suggests that burnout is caused by the isolation of the job and the lack of a psychological sense of community among the teachers, more than the emotional or physical demands of the job (Farber and Miller, 1981). Working alone, with little collegiality and limited sense of efficacy and control, may be the greatest source of teacher dissatisfaction and stress. Those teachers who advised me to close the door of the classroom, enjoy the students, and ignore the problems of the school and the curriculum may have been inviting burnout more than other teachers.

Many teachers considered career changes. Mike Werge ran an academic travel business on the side. Another social studies teacher worked as a scout for a major league baseball team. A music teacher worked weekends and evenings playing at parties and weddings. Several faculty members had real estate licenses; some ran summer camps; many did home repairs and landscaping. These were ways to supplement their income, but they also represented alternate careers. These avocations arguably detracted from the time teachers could give to teaching. They afforded them less time for preparation, reading in their subject field, or keeping current in education, but they were rational responses to a system that took a great deal from teachers and gave back too little in return.

It is not possible to look at teaching from the teachers' perspective and not sense their powerlessness and frustration. On-site studies of high schools are typically sympathetic to the problems faced by teachers (Boyer, 1983; Goodlad, 1984; National Commission, 1983; Sizer, 1984). Analyses of teaching have called for greater teacher involvement in educational decision making, ranging from textbook selection (Boyer, 1983), through the development of technical knowledge about teaching (Lortie, 1975), all the way to a pedagogy of opposition for social emancipation and the creation of a more just society (Giroux, 1983).

Implicit in this focus on teaching is that teachers are not doing, or are not able to do, the job expected of them. Everywhere, researchers find dull, lifeless classes; the absence of an academic focus; bored, unchallenged students; teachers mired in routine and paperwork. There is also a growing recognition, especially among those who teach at universities, that the attitudes toward teaching found in experienced practitioners are markedly more negative than those exhibited by undergraduates about to enter the field. Experienced teachers seem less interested in academic content, less willing to take risks and teach about controversial issues than they were as undergraduates. There is something about the culture of the school that serves to discourage teachers (Palonsky and Nelson, 1980; Sarason, 1982). The job takes its toll on them in many ways; too often, the brightest teachers leave the field, and many of those who remain find difficulty in maintaining their enthusiasm.

The behaviors of teachers, both desirable and undesirable, are developed as a rational set of responses to the demands of the job. The cause of undesirable behavior lies less with the individuals than with the organization that forces teachers to respond as they do. There are those teachers who perform creditably and beyond, as one school critic notes, "in spite of all adverse conditions" (Adler, 1982: 57). While these teachers no doubt exist in every school, they may be anomalies rather than role models. Good teachers, in the context of public secondary schools, may be examples of social deviance: They survive in face of all the forces that work against them.

National studies of teaching support teachers' demands for higher salaries (Boyer, 1983; Goodlad, 1984; National Commission, 1983). More money would no doubt increase a teacher's sense of worth, and eliminate altruism from the list of prerequisite teacher qualities. But higher pay is not enough. It is not reasonable to assume that teacher behavior will change until the culture of the school changes and encourages teachers to play a more central role. If we were able to sweep out all the less than good teachers overnight and replace them with those who demonstrate outstanding potential for teaching, it is un-likely that after a year or two the schools would be very different than they are today. The culture of the school that produced today's teach-ers, left unchanged, will produce similar teachers tomorrow.

There is no quick fix to improve teaching, no simple remedy for school problems. If there had been a quick fix, it would have been found long ago (Carlson, 1984: i). However, the study at Oldham suggests some changes in schools that could help. These proposed changes are based on two assumptions: The first is that teachers are the central actors in the process of schooling, and unless the work of good teachers is encouraged and supported, we cannot have good schools (see Lightfoot, 1983). The second is that we discour-age good teachers by restricting their influence to the classroom, and defining them in all other aspects of school life as voiceless, powerless employees who have little influence on the ways in which schools are run. The culture of the school has to change to allow teachers to play an empowered role in all policy decisions, including staffing, curricu-lum design, instruction, supervision, counseling, and the management of day-to-day operations. Unless teachers feel a greater sense of per-sonal identification with the school and its essential processes, it is unlikely that they will work cooperatively toward the solution of school problems (cf. Roberts and Cawelti, 1984). Allowing teachers to play only a token role in the school's decision-making structure reinforces their sense of political impotence and leads to indiffer-ence.

Oldham High School may have been working as well as it could, given the structure of the school. Replacing the board of education, the superintendents, the principals, or the department supervisors would probably not change the nature of teaching very much. The problem was not that evil people were in positions of authority. Rather, it was that the teachers were excluded from the authority structure of the school. In order to change schools, there must be a sharing of the power to run them.

The title of this book suggests a theatrical metaphor for teaching. Many teachers did see themselves as performers who competed with television, film, and music for the students' attention. While most teachers agreed that one needed a great deal of acting skill to be a good teacher, it is not reasonable to expect teachers to put on five good shows a day, five days a week. Nine hundred shows is more than double the number of performances given a year by any Broadway actor. Few actors would consider working in the same show for thirty-five or forty years, and if they did, I am sure they would demand greater control than is typically afforded teachers. Teachers need greater artistic control over the enterprise and more opportunities to direct change. They need to be not only the actors but the directors, designers, and producers of the show. If we want bright, creative, individuals teaching in our classrooms, we must reconsider teaching in order to make the job more attractive to the most able candidates.

APPENDIX

METHODOLOGY

A few words on the research methodology used in this study and the model on which it rests are in order. The model assumes that individuals and groups develop reasonable responses to the demands of their lives which may not be understood by outsiders, but which become understandable once you get close to the situation or become a part of it (Goffman, 1961; Schutz, 1967). Reality, those social phenomena we recognize as existing apart from our volition or imagination, is socially constructed (Berger and Luckmann, 1966). That is to say, those beliefs about our social world we commonly think of as real are created and sustained or discarded by the ongoing interactions of those who make up that social world. Implicit in this perspective is that social objects and social phenomena have few intrinsic meanings other than those people assign to them. The reality of family life is developed by the family members; the reality of teaching is developed by the teachers. What constitutes a satisfying marriage can only be defined by the marriage partners; what constitutes a satisfying job can only be defined by the workers.

This perspective is referred to as the sociology of knowledge.[1] It considers the construction of reality to be part of the normal activity by which people make sense out of their world and derive a measure of satisfaction from it (Berger and Luckmann, 1966; Schutz and Luckmann, 1973). People are viewed as the makers of their own social world (Berger and Luckmann, 1966; Schiller, 1969; Stehr and Meja, 1984). It is not in the sense of an actual creation of a social world from nothingness. Rather, it is a view which explains the construction of

---

[1]Lewis Coser traces the history of the sociology of knowledge in Europe and the United States and indicates how it has merged with other areas of research. He notes that fields such as the sociology of the professions, the sociology of science, and research on roles and social interaction are in part derived from the sociology of knowledge. He writes: "Many practitioners of what is in fact the sociology of knowledge may at times be rather surprised when it is pointed out that, like Monsieur Jourdain, they have been 'talking prose' all along." (Coser, 1968: 432)

society through the action of human thought and communication (Schutz, 1967). People are considered rational, cooperative beings who seek to understand their lives, and in the process of doing so, they create meanings and myths, and develop institutions and a social order.

The sociology of knowledge perspective draws on such disparate sources as Parsons and Marx (Merton, 1957). Some of its adherents credit its philosophic origins to American pragmatists such as James, Peirce, and Dewey (Durkheim, 1983; Schutz, 1967). Others see influence from Schutz (Mercer and Covey, 1980; Young, 1971), from George Herbert Mead (Mead, 1956), from Mannheim (Apple, 1979), and Scheler and Nietsche (Berger and Luckmann, 1966). Some educational sociologists claim it is related to the symbolic interactionist approach of Blumer (1962) and Shibutani (1967) through a common debt owed to George Herbert Mead (Karabel and Halsey, 1977), but its emphasis remains on the construction of differing realities, while the interactionists focus on the development of consensual agreements and shared meanings.

What these sociologists, social psychologists and philosophers hold in common is a rejection of the behavioral notion that humans are merely plastic objects whose actions and thoughts are created and shaped by their environment. Humans are viewed, by those who subscribe to a socially created world, as dynamic actors in their own lives who give meaning to the world as it acts upon them. In part, they accept the world they have inherited, but they tend not just to react to it; they reconstruct it, or remake it for their own purposes (Durkheim, 1983). According to George Herbert Mead,

> Human society . . . does not merely stamp the pattern of its organized social behavior upon any one of its individual members, so that the pattern becomes likewise the pattern of the individual's self; it also, at the same time, gives him a mind, . . . And his mind enables him in turn to stamp the pattern of his further developing self (further developing through his mental activity) upon the structure or organization of human society, and thus in a degree, to reconstruct and modify in terms of his self the general pattern of social or group behavior in terms of which his self was originally constituted. (Mead, 1956: 251)

Meanings are created in every social environment. On the job, workers interpret their work, define its importance and their involvement with it (Miller, 1981; MacIver, 1964). By their daily interactions and responses to the complex demands of work, teachers at Oldham

High created and maintained a social reality about teaching, a defini-
tional and interpretational set of characteristics about the job and
themselves as teachers which they understood as reality. They constructed attitudes toward work and one another as a response to the
context or environment of their work. They gave meaning to their
work beyond that which could be found in official job descriptions,
but which was readily understood by other teachers.

The sociology of knowledge perspective implies that complex social relationships are best understood from the vantage point of a
co-actor in that situation. If you want to know what it is like to be a
teacher, if you want to know why it is that teachers behave as they
do, you must work as a teacher, subjecting yourself for an extended
period of time to the same routines, rewards, penalties, and problems
to which teachers are subjected (Cicourel et al., 1974).

For a period of two years I was a teacher in Oldham High School.
Most of the events reported here took place during the first year,[2] but
my perspective as a teacher was an ongoing product developed over
the two-year period. My perspective on teaching was not that of the
administrators, guidance counselors, or supervisors, and it may not
have been that of every teacher in the school. It was probably not
shared by some of the women teachers in a school in which, typical
of public high schools, there was a very sharp division between the
forty-six males and the twenty females on the faculty (cf. Lieberman
and Miller, 1984; Lortie, 1975). The segregation by sex was voluntary,
but women interacted mainly with women, and men with men, and
they constructed separate views of each other and the job. My perspective was more heavily influenced by the social studies teachers
with whom I suffered common problems, the faculty with whom I ate
lunch or shared a free period, and those teachers with whom I talked
while we were on duty in the lobby or the library. My view of the job
was reinforced by interviews and surveys, and my perspective was
influenced by most of the teachers in the building. I believe that most
of the teachers would support my description of teaching, if not my
analysis of it.

In order to describe teaching from the perspective of the teacher,
it was necessary to participate in the interactions of the faculty and
become part of the culture of school over the course of an academic
year. It was necessary to collect data that covered the full range of

---

[2]To have certain events introduced for the readers' consideration, I included a few that took place
during the second year of my teaching. These are limited to the incident with Bobby Daria; Paul
De Faro's exchange with the parent concerning a planned trip; Mike Werge's story about a
student from Iran; my involvement with the "gifted and talented program"; and the superintendent's speech praising teachers.

teaching experiences from vacations and snow days to fire drills and unannounced observations. Ethnographic research design provided the methodology by which the world of teachers could be examined in its natural setting. Ethnography is a set of field research procedures that affords researchers access to the cultural setting they are investigating, and that allows them to take part in the group processes in which social realities are constructed and maintained.

In ethnographic research, explanations of behavior are made contextually; the phenonema are viewed not as isolated variables, but as part of complex interrelationships that may be hidden from outsiders, but that are readily understood by insiders. The research methodology[3] is most often associated with anthropology (Goetz and Le Compte, 1984; Pelto and Pelto, 1978; Spindler, 1982). It was developed by nineteenth-century anthropologists who wanted to abandon their armchair speculations in favor of field research and the participant's perspective on a foreign culture. In this vein, Malinowski has been referred to as the first researcher to pitch his tent in a native village, observing and recording what went on in the manner of a participant in the social setting and a scientific observer who tried to describe the native's point of view and "his vision of his world" (Wax, 1971; see Malinowski, 1922).

In the 1920s and 1930s, the Chicago School of sociologists adopted field techniques of data gathering and applied the intellectual tenets of their academic discipline to these data (Goetz and Le Compte, 1984: 16). The anthropologists developed the methodology in order to make the strange familiar. The sociologists amended it and made the familiar sufficiently strange so that commonplace events and institutions could be held apart from our everyday experiences and studied as unique social phenomena. Twentieth-century researchers have adapted the methodology and "pitched their tents" in slums (Whyte, 1943), streetcorner societies (Liebow, 1967), among ethnic minorities (Gans, 1962), and mental patients (Goffman, 1961).

Anthropological research methods have only recently found their way into the field of education. Typically, as Goetz and Le Compte note, education graduate students are trained in psychology, and the research models used in education courses most often reflect the quantitative models favored by experimental psychologists (1984: 1). In the past ten years, researchers in education have demonstrated none of

[3]At this writing, the two most current and helpful sources are Goetz and Le Compte (1984) and Spindler (1982). Goetz and Le Compte offer an excellent text on the methodology with an extensive bibliography. Spindler provides fourteen examples of ethnographic studies, a useful chapter on the methodology, and an introduction by the editor. This appendix draws heavily from both sources.

their previous reluctance to "go native," and ethnographies have pro-
liferated. Ethnographers have studied the major actors in schools, including principals (Wolcott, 1973), teachers (McPherson, 1972), and
high school students (Cusick, 1973). Researchers have also looked at
the overt and covert processes of schooling (Henry, 1963), classroom
life (Mehan, 1979; Smith and Geoffrey, 1968), the hidden curriculum
(Gearing and Epstein, 1982), and classroom questioning (Heath, 1982).

There is so much ethnographic research being done in education
that even those who once urged its use in school settings caution that
its power as a research tool may have been diminished through inappropriate application or design, and they urge more careful adherence
to the principles and limits of the methodology (Spindler, 1982; Goetz
and Le Compte, 1984; Rist, 1980; Wilcox, 1982). Ethnographic designs
in education have been discussed by Bogdan and Biklen (1982), Dobbert (1982), Goetz and Le Compte (1984), and Spindler (1982), among
others. In general, the criteria for good ethnography include:

1. Extensive Field Observations.

It is necessary to spend a great deal of time in the field under a wide
range of circumstances. The social reality reported is that of the participant in that setting, and the social setting must be understood from
the perspective of the participant. Phenomena must be observed repeatedly before they can be considered other than social anomalies.
The knowledge the participants in that setting use to guide their
behavior must be observed in context and under varied circumstances.

2. Hypotheses and Questions to Explore Should Be Developed in the Field.

While there is disagreement whether the methodology is limited
to studies that generate rather than test hypotheses (Geer, 1964: 209),
it is generally agreed that hypotheses developed before entering the
field tempt the researcher to expose himself or herself to the data
nonrandomly, or selectively perceive them in an attempt at verification. Working hypotheses should be developed after initial exposure
in the field. They should spring from the repetitions or incongruities
in the field data, and they should be refined and tested by examining
their explanatory power in light of subsequent data. The researcher
cannot pretend to enter the field *tabula rasa,* but he or she must be
receptive to unanticipated events or negative findings.

3. Data Gathering Should Not Be Limited to Observation.

Ethnography is typically considered to be a multimethod research
design. Participant observation is the principal means by which ethnographers gather data, but researchers are encouraged to use addi-

tional techniques or devices that allow them to gather information and check perceptions. The faith of the researcher in his or her conclusions is increased when they are supported by two or more independent data sources. Ethnographers often use tape recorders, and film and video recorders. Interviews and questionnaire schedules are developed in the field to explore or corroborate observed phenomena, and special interview procedures are used so that the respondents' views of the culture are allowed to emerge without the bias of the interviewer obtruding (Spradley, 1979).

4. Ethnographers Should Work Toward Achieving Social Intimacy with Subjects.

The researchers must take part in the social constructions of reality that guide the subjects' lives. The researchers and subjects must be exposed to the same routines and pressures. Researchers must speak the same language as their subjects, and they must learn to see things as the subjects see them (cf. Bruyn, 1966: 181–183). The researchers must also, on a regular basis, look for confirmation of those things which they observe but which are unverbalized by the subjects. As Spindler notes, "a significant task of the ethnographer is . . . to make explicit what is implicit and tacit . . . (1982: 7).

5. Ethnographers Should Try to Leave the Culture Intact.

The ethnographer tries to become a normal and accepted member of the community under investigation, but he or she does not attempt to change the behavior of its members or their view of themselves. Researchers, whenever possible, should inform the subjects of the nature of their work. The research, hopefully, should be of benefit to someone in addition to the researcher, but at the very least it should be designed to do as little harm as possible.

6. Selection of Appropriate Research Roles.

Participant observation is the principal method of data collection in ethnographic studies (see Bruyn, 1966; Friedrichs and Ludtke, 1975). The researcher must assume a role that allows him or her to become a part of the groups under investigation. There are any number of roles available, ranging from complete observation to complete participation (Gold, 1969: 373–378). In the former role, the researcher is removed from any direct interaction with informants, obviating the need to explain his or her presence. It is the role often assumed by researchers studying classroom interactions involving elementary school students (see Jackson, 1968; Mehan, 1979). Complete participation involves role pretense; the researcher does not inform the informants that he or she is conducting a field investigation. In a study of the social situation of mental patients, Goffman (1961) assumed a series of safe roles (e.g., an assistant to the athletic director) that brought him into direct contact with his informants, although not as one of them.

In 1982 I had decided to spend a year as a high school teacher for the purpose of renewing my experience, honing my classroom skills, and gathering data for an ethnographic study. I had begun casting about for schools in which I could work, and the friend and former student referred to in this reporting as Paul De Faro suggested that I consider Oldham. The Webster–Oldham School District was a young, growing district which every year hired a few social studies teachers. Paul cautioned me that the school was not typical of high schools in the state: It was wealthy, white, and working reasonably well.

The selection of a research site and sample is critical to all research. In quantified research, the sample must be representative of the universe under consideration. The notion of randomness suggests that the procedure for choosing the sample is such that all members of a population are ensured of an equally likely chance of being selected (see Kerlinger, 1973: 118). Oldham High School was not selected randomly from the universe of high schools or from the subset of all suburban New York area high schools. Similar to site selection in other ethnographies, Oldham was chosen for study largely because it was available (cf. Cusick, 1973: 218–219). The absence of random selection procedures invites questions about the generalizability of the findings. Are ethnographies limited to site-specific conclusions? How much of the social reality of the Oldham teachers can be assumed to be that of any other high school teachers? To what extent can the conclusions of this study be applied to other schools and teachers?

Oldham High is not considered representative or typical of all high schools. However, there are essential commonalities among high school teachers that allow them to construct comparable realities from a shared pool of social knowledge, and permits researchers to generalize from nonrandom samples. High school teachers experience a number of similarities, including socioeconomic status, training, education, the structure of the school and the school day, and isolation and powerlessness on the job. A comparison of survey data of national samples of teachers and the Oldham teachers suggests a great similarity in their attitudes and perceptions, despite demographic differences. Although the school was wealthy and tranquil, the attitudes of the Oldham teachers were not discontinuous with those of the general population of teachers.

While working at Oldham, I would have preferred a research role that permitted me to be open with the teachers about my research. While it may have detracted from the genuineness of our initial interactions, it would have been more honest and responsible to tell them that I was observing their behavior and keeping detailed field notes and a record of our conversations. However, my research role was confused by my employment status. The university at which I had been teaching for eight years decided it no longer was in need of me, and I was not only collecting material for an ethnography of Oldham High School, I had to try to fit in well enough to be acceptable as an employee. I planned instruction, prepared tests, and submitted lesson plans as did the other teachers.

After the first year in the school, I wrote a prospectus for the book and submitted it for consideration to Random House publishers. The prospectus contained material that is part of the first chapter and an outline of the remaining chapters. After we signed a contract for the book, I felt both free and obliged to tell the teachers and administrators that I was going to write about the school. In April 1984, at a regularly scheduled faculty meeting, I invited the teachers to talk to me about any of their concerns and to clear up any misconceptions about what I was doing. At that point I sought out members of the faculty to ask for their confirmation about the way in which I had perceived past events, conversations, and disagreements. The faculty and administration were very supportive, although understandably apprehensive.

I administered two surveys to the faculty and conducted a series of formal interviews. I interviewed the president of the board of education; the superintendent of schools; the assistant superintendent for curriculum; the new building principal; the assistant principal; and the head of pupil personnel services. Interviews were also conducted with the director of athletics, the coordinator of student activities, the social studies supervisor, seven teachers, and one guidance counselor. When the manuscript was complete, I asked four teachers in the school to read it and comment on the accuracy of the reported events and conversations.

By late spring, I explained to the students in my classes what I was working on and asked them to help. I gave them several writing assignments that asked them to describe the school, the classroom, the cafeteria, and the lobby. I also asked them to recall their first impressions of the building and their teachers. A composite of these impressions was included in the text in those instances where I wanted to report the students' perspective. In order to gather additional data, I returned to the school several times after I had resumed teaching at the university.

For several reasons, I decided to report mainly those events that took place during my first year in the school. My perceptions were sharper when I first began teaching. I was not yet part of the culture, and I could view it as an outsider. Those bits of social reality that were so vivid in my first year became part of the scenery in the second year. Also, by the second year I developed friendships among the teachers, and I became more of an apologist for the school. This problem in field work is sometimes referred to as an "over-rapport with the natives" that limits the researcher's objectivity and lines of inquiry (Khleif, 1974: 393).

There was a more political reason for focusing on the first year of the field work. I had begun this research without the school's knowledge, and I wanted to be sure that no one would be hurt by my reporting. At the time of publication, tenure decisions will have been made on all the faculty members and administrators mentioned. In some ways, this self-imposed limitation is unfortunate. It does not allow me to discuss the changes that took place after Larry Silverman became principal during the second year, or the very popular appointment of a new supervisor in mathematics who brought a model of academic freshness and a spirit of collegiality to his department.

A third reason for focusing on the first year concerned an unofficial counseling role I assumed during the second year. A student in one of my classes sought me out as a confidant. The student was troubled, possibly self-destructive. I discussed the problem extensively with the guidance department, the school psychologist, and the student's parents. To write about the second year would have necessitated violating too many confidences.

There are other limitations on this study. Khleif claims that every profession has three types of secrets: open, hidden, and dark (1974: 389). Anyone who spends any time with teachers, in or out of school, can easily learn their open secrets: their idealism; their genuine concern for students; their enjoyment of the classroom; their dislike of clerical tasks; their corny humor. The open secrets are readily accessible. The hidden secrets are generally unknowable by outsiders. These are the ways in which the teachers view themselves, their work, the students, and the administrators. The hidden secrets also include the ideology of the job, the patterns of the daily behavior of the teachers, the extent to which they work hard, and the extent to which their job is pleasant, pressured, or petty. The hidden secrets are the basic stuff of everyday life of a teacher, both good and bad. The dark secrets are those the teachers never discuss in public, and rarely in private. These concern their worst fears about themselves, their abilities, and their usefulness, as well as their more basic passions, fantasies, and the patterns of alcohol and substance abuse. These secrets are sometimes muttered to sympathetic colleagues over a drink, or shared with a spouse, or kept to oneself.

This ethnography of teaching is a description and an analysis of the hidden secrets of the faculty as a collective body; it avoids probing into the dark secrets of individual teachers. It is an examination of the inschool behavior of teachers and their interactions with students, administrators, and the curriculum. The purpose of this study was to examine the working environment of teachers and to explain teaching from their point of view. Out-of-school behavior of individual teachers is of concern here only when it was known by members of the school community and/or it affected their teaching.

All research is subjected to questions of adequacy. Is it accurate? Does it measure and describe what it thinks it does? Would independent researchers discover the same things? Can the study be replicated? These questions of validity and reliability are widely discussed in ethnographic literature (Goetz and Le Compte, 1984; Pelto and Pelto, 1978). Ethnography is often self-conscious in face of challenges from numbers-crunching quantitative researchers because field research lacks statistical tests for validity and reliability. Some ethnographers beg the question by stating that their research is not designed to test hypotheses, but to generate them for future verification using mathematically measurable means (see Goetz and Le Compte, 1984: 209; Cusick, 1973: 231). They argue that ethnographic research, at least in part, is designed to find patterns of behavior that can later be examined by experimental manipulations and statistical analyses. However, many ethnographers are less timid, claiming that the results of a good ethnography are as sound as those of any other carefully designed and honestly pursued research, and some even claim that they can be more powerful than the conclusions from tightly controlled laboratory studies (cf. Bronfenbrenner, 1976).

In the absence of statistical manipulations, the ethnographic researcher must provide adequate descriptions and explanations to demonstrate ample exposure to the culture and an understanding of the reality of the respondents. In addition, the researcher must convince the reader that he or she (1) has conducted the research objectively and fairly; (2) was able to develop an intimacy with the respondents and an understanding of their perspective; (3) did not selectively expose himself or herself to the data; (4) did not selectively perceive them; (5) was not suffering from blunted perceptions; (6) was investigating phenomena and respondents that were not atypical or unique; and (7) used a methodology that generated data that could not readily have been obtained by other means.

REFERENCES

Acheson, K. A., and M. D. Gall. 1980. *Techniques in the Clinical Supervision of Teachers.* New York: Longman.

Adler, M. J. 1982. *The Paideia Proposal: An Educational Manifesto.* New York: Macmillan.

Anyon, J. 1979. Ideology and United States history textbooks. *Harvard Educational Review* 49:361–386.

———. 1981. Social class and school knowledge. *Curriculum Inquiry* 11:3–42.

Apple, M. W. 1979. *Ideology and Curriculum.* London: Routledge & Kegan Paul.

———. 1982. *Education and Power.* London: Routledge & Kegan Paul.

Apple, M. W., and L. Weis, eds. 1983. *Ideology and Practice in Schooling.* Philadelphia: Temple University Press.

Beck, J., et al., eds. 1976. *Worlds Apart: Readings for a Sociology of Education.* London: Collier Macmillan.

Berger, P. L., and T. Luckmann. 1966. *The Social Construction of Reality.* Garden City, N.Y.: Doubleday.

Bernbaum, G. 1977. *Knowledge and Ideology in the Sociology of Education.* London: Macmillan.

Bernstein, B. 1971. *Class, Codes and Control.* Vol I. *Theoretical Studies Towards a Sociology of Language.* London: Routledge & Kegan Paul.

Blumer, H. 1962. Society as symbolic interaction. In *Human Behavior and Social Processes.* Edited by A. Rose. Boston: Houghton Mifflin.

———. 1966. Sociological implications of the thought of George Herbert Mead. *American Journal of Sociology* 21:683–690.

Bogdan, R. 1972. *Participant Observation in Organizational Settings.* Syracuse, N.Y.: Syracuse University Press.

Bogdan, R., and S. Biklen. 1982. *Qualitative Research for Education: An Introduction to Theory and Methods.* Boston: Allyn and Bacon.

Bowers, C. A. 1984. *The Promise of Theory: Education and the Politics of Cultural Change.* New York: Longman.

Boyer, E. L. 1983. *High School: A Report on Secondary Education in America.* New York: Harper and Row.

Bronfenbrenner, U. 1976. The experimental ecology of education. *Teachers College Record* 78:157–204.

Bruyn, S. 1966. *The Human Perspective in Sociology: The Methodology of Participant Observation.* Englewood Cliffs, N.J.: Prentice-Hall.

Campbell, D. T., and J. C. Stanley. 1966. *Experimental and Quasi-Experimental Designs for Research.* Chicago: Rand McNally.

Carlson, K. 1984. The enhancement of teaching as a profession. Paper prepared for the conference on public responsibility for educational success, January 21, Rutgers University, New Brunswick, New Jersey.

Cherniss, C. 1980. *Professional Burnout in Human Service Organizations.* New York: Praeger.

Cicourel, A. V., et al. 1974. *Language Use and School Performance.* New York: Academic Press.

Cogan, M. L. 1973. *Clinical Supervision.* Boston: Houghton Mifflin.

Coser, L. A. 1968. Sociology of knowledge. In *International Encyclopedia of the Social Sciences,* vol. 8. Edited by David Sills. New York: Macmillan.

Cronbach, L. J. 1970. *Essentials of Psychological Testing,* 3rd edition. New York: Harper and Row.

Cusick, P. A. 1973. *Inside High School: The Student's World.* New York: Holt, Rinehart and Winston.

————. 1983. *The Egalitarian Ideal and the American High School: Studies of Three Schools.* New York: Longman.

Cusick, P. A., W. Martin, and S. B. Palonsky. 1976. Organizational structure and student behaviour in secondary schools. *Journal of Curriculum Studies* 8:1–10.

Demaine, J. 1981. *Contemporary Theories in the Sociology of Education.* London: Macmillan.

Denzin, N. K., ed. 1969. *Sociological Methods: A Sourcebook.* Chicago: Aldine.

Dobbert, M. 1982. *Ethnographic Research: Theory and Application for Modern Schools and Societies.* New York: Praeger.

Durkheim, E. 1983. *Pragmatism and Sociology.* Translated by J. C. Whitehouse. Edited and introduced by J. A. Allcock. Cambridge, Eng.: Cambridge University Press.

Ebel, R. L. 1972. *Essentials of Educational Measurement.* Englewood Cliffs, N.J.: Prentice-Hall.

Farber, B. A., and J. Miller. 1981. Teacher burnout: A psychoeducational perspective. *Teachers College Record* 83:235–243.

FitzGerald, F. 1979. *America Revisited: History Schoolbooks in the Twentieth Century.* Boston: Little, Brown.

Friedrichs, J., and H. Ludke. 1975. *Participant Observation: Theory and Practice.* Lexington, Mass.: D. C. Heath.

Gallup, A. 1984. The Gallup poll of teachers' attitudes toward the public schools. *Phi Delta Kappan* 66:97–107.

Gallup, G. H. 1984. The 16th annual Gallup poll of the public's attitudes toward the public schools. *Phi Delta Kappan* 66:23–38.

Gans, H. J. 1962. *The Urban Villagers: Groups and Class in the Life of Italian-Americans.* New York: Free Press.

Gearing, F., and P. Epstein. 1982. Learning to wait: An ethnographic probe into the operations of an item of hidden curriculum. In *Doing the Ethnography of Schooling.* Edited by G. Spindler. New York: Holt, Rinehart and Winston.

Geer, B. 1964. First days in the field. In *Sociologists at Work.* Edited by P. E. Hammond. Garden City, N.Y.: Doubleday.

Giroux, H. A. 1983. *Theory and Resistance in Education: A Pedadogy for the Opposition.* South Hadley: Bergin and Garvey.

Giroux, H. A., and A. N. Penna. 1979. Social education in the classroom: The dynamics of the hidden curriculum. *Theory and Research in Social Education* 3:21–42.

Goetz, J. P., and M. D. LeCompte. 1984. *Ethnography and Qualitative Design in Educational Research.* New York: Academic Press.

Goffman, E. 1961. *Asylums.* Garden City, N.Y.: Anchor Books.

Goodlad, John I. 1984. *A Place Called School: Prospects for the Future.* New York: McGraw-Hill.

Gold, R. 1969. Roles in field observation. In *Sociological Methods.* Edited by N. K. Denzin. Chicago: Aldine.

Goldhammer, R., R. H. Anderson, and R. J. Krajewski. 1980. *Clinical Supervision, Special Methods for the Supervision of Teachers,* 2nd edition. New York: Holt, Rinehart and Winston.

Gorton, R. A. 1982. Teacher job satisfaction. In *Encyclopedia of Educational Research,* 5th edition, vol. 4. Edited by H. E. Mitzel. New York: Free Press.

Hammond, P. E. 1964. *Sociologists at Work.* Garden City, N.Y.: Doubleday.

Heath, S. B. 1982. Questioning at home and at school: A comparative study. In *Doing the Ethnography of Schooling.* Edited by G. Spindler. New York: Holt, Rinehart and Winston.

Henry, J. 1963. *Culture Against Man.* New York: Random House.

Hersey, J. R. 1946. *Hiroshima.* New York: Knopf.

Hickox, M. S. H. 1982. The Marxist sociology of education: A critique. *The British Journal of Sociology* 4:563–577.

Jackson, P. W. 1968. *Life in Classrooms.* New York: Holt, Rinehart and Winston.

———. 1980. Curriculum and its discontents. *Curriculum Inquiry* 10:159–172.

Karabel, J., and A. H. Halsey. 1977. *Power and Ideology in Education.* New York: Oxford University Press.

Kerlinger, F. N. 1973. *Foundations of Behavioral Research,* 2nd edition. New York: Holt, Rinehart and Winston.

Khleif, B. 1974. Issues in anthropological fieldwork in schools. In *Education and Cultural Process.* Edited by G. Spindler. New York: Holt, Rinehart and Winston.

Labov, W. 1972. *Sociolinguistic Patterns.* Philadelphia: University of Pennsylvania Press.

LeCompte, M. D., and J. P. Goetz. 1982. The problem of reliability and validity in ethnographic research. *Review of Educational Research* 52:31–60.

Lieberman, A., and L. Miller. 1984. *Teachers, Their World, and Their Work.* Alexandria, Va.: The Association for Supervision and Curriculum Development.

Liebow, E. 1967. *Tally's Corner.* Boston: Little, Brown.

Lightfoot, S. L. 1983. *The Good High School: Portraits of Character and Culture.* New York: Basic Books.

Lortie, D. C. 1975. *Schoolteacher: A Sociological Study.* Chicago: University of Chicago Press.

MacIver, R. M. 1964. *Social Causation.* New York: Harper and Row.

Malinowski, B. 1922. *Argonauts of the Western Pacific: An Account of Native Enterprise and Adventure in the Archipelagoes of Melanesian New Guinea.* New York: Dutton.

Manis, J. G., and B. N. Meltzer, eds. 1957. *Symbolic Interaction.* Boston: Allyn and Bacon.

McGinniss, Joe. 1983. *Fatal Vision.* New York: Putnam.

McPherson, G. 1972. *Small Town Teacher.* Cambridge, Mass.: Harvard University Press.

Mead, G. H. 1956. *On Social Psychology: Selected Papers.* Edited and with an introduction by A. Strauss. Chicago: University of Chicago Press.

Mehan, H. 1979. *Learning Lesson: Social Organization in the Classroom.* Cambridge, Mass.: Harvard University Press.

Mercer, B., and H. C. Covey. 1980. *Theoretical Frameworks in the Sociology of Education.* Cambridge, Mass.: Schenkman.

Merton, R. K. 1957. *Social Structure and Social Theory.* New York: Free Press.

Miller, G. 1981. *It's a Living: Work in Modern Society.* New York: St. Martin's Press.

National Commission on Excellence in Education. 1983. *A Nation at Risk: The Imperative for Educational Reform.* Washington, D.C.: U.S. Department of Education.

Nelson, J. L., and S. B. Palonsky. 1980. Preservice teacher perceptions of social education. *Journal of Social Studies Research* 4:5–12.

Palonsky, S. B. 1975. Hempies and squeaks, truckers and cruisers: A participant observer investigation in a city high school. *Educational Administration Quarterly* 2:86–103.

Palonsky, S. B., and J. L. Nelson. 1980. Political restraint in the socialization of student teachers. *Theory and Research in Social Education* 7:19–34.

Pelto, P. J., and G. H. Pelto. 1978. *Anthropological Research: The Structure of Inquiry,* 2nd edition. Cambridge, Eng.: Cambridge University Press.

Raths, L. E., et al. 1966. *Values and Teaching: Working with Values in the Classroom.* Columbus: C. E. Merrill.

Rist, R. C. 1980. Blitzkrieg ethnography: On the transformation of a method into a movement. *Educational Researcher* 9:8–10.

Roberts, A. D., and G. Cawelti. 1984. *Redefining General Education in the American High School.* Alexandria, Va.: Association for Supervision and Curriculum Development.

Romanish, B. 1983. Modern secondary economics textbooks and ideological bias. *Theory and Research in Social Education* 11:1–24.

Rose, A. M., ed. 1962. *Human Behavior and Social Processes.* Boston: Houghton Mifflin.

Rosenbaum, J. 1976. *Making Inequality: The Hidden Curriculum of High School Tracking.* New York: Wiley.

Sarason, S. B. 1982. *The Culture of the School and the Problem of Change,* 2nd edition. Boston: Allyn and Bacon.

Schiller, F. C. S. 1969. *Studies in Humanism.* Freeport, N.Y.: Books for Libraries Press.

Schutz, A. 1967. *The Phenomenology of the Social World.* Translated by G. Walsh and F. Lenhardt. Evanston, Ill.: Northwestern University Press.

Schutz, A., and T. Luckmann. 1973. *The Structure of the Life-World.* Translated by R. M. Zaner and H. T. Tristram, Jr. Evanston, Ill.: Northwestern University Press.

Shibutani, T. 1967. Reference groups as perspectives. In *Symbolic Interaction.* Edited by J. G. Manis and B. N. Meltzer. Boston: Allyn and Bacon.

Sizer, T. R. 1984. *Horace's Compromise: The Dilemma of the American High School.* Boston: Houghton Mifflin.

Skinner, B. F. 1948. *Walden Two.* New York: Macmillan.

Smith, L. M., and W. Geoffrey. 1968. *The Complexities of the Urban Classroom: An Analysis Towards and General Theory of Teaching.* New York: Holt, Rinehart and Winston.

Spindler, G. D., ed. 1974. *Educational and the Cultural Process: Toward an Anthropology of Education.* New York: Holt, Rinehart and Winston.

———. 1982. *Doing the Ethnography of Schooling: Educational Anthropology in Action.* New York: Holt, Rinehart and Winston.

Spradley, J. P. 1979. *The Ethnographic Interview.* New York: Holt, Rinehart and Winston.

Stehr, N., and V. Meja, eds. 1984. *Society and Knowledge: Contemporary Perspectives in the Sociology of Knowledge.* New Brunswick, N.J.: Transaction Books.

Tanner, D., and L. N. Tanner. 1979. Emancipation from research: the reconceptualist prescription. *Educational Researcher* 8:8–12.

Trumbo, D. 1939. *Johnny Got His Gun.* New York: Lippincott.

Twentieth Century Fund Task Force on Federal Elementary and Secondary Education Policy. 1983. *Making the Grade.* New York: The Twentieth Century Fund.

Wax, R. 1971. *Doing Fieldwork: Warnings and Advice.* Chicago: University of Chicago Press.

Whyte, W. F. 1943. *Streetcorner Society.* Chicago: University of Chicago Press.

Wilcox, K. 1982. Ethnography as a methodology and its application to the study of schooling: A review. In *Doing the Ethnography of Schooling.* Edited by G. Spindler. New York: Holt, Rinehart and Winston.

Willis, P. 1977. *Learning to Labour: How Working Class Kids Get Working Class Jobs.* Lexington, Mass.: D. C. Heath.

Wolcott, H. F. 1973. *The Man in the Principal's Office: An Ethnography.* New York: Holt, Rinehart and Winston.

Wouk, H. 1971. *Winds of War.* Boston: Little, Brown.

Young, M. F. D., ed. 1971. *Knowledge and Control: New Directions for Sociology of Education.* London: Collier-Macmillan.

Young, M. F. D., and G. Whitty, eds. 1977. *Society, State and Schooling.* Brighton: The Falmer Press.

INDEX

ABOUT THE AUTHOR

Stuart B. Palonsky earned degrees in history, social science, and education at the State University of New York and Michigan State University. He taught social studies for six years in the public schools of New York and New Jersey, and has worked in teacher education programs at Michigan State and Rutgers. Professor Palonsky's articles have been published in *The Elementary School Journal,* the *Journal of Curriculum Studies,* and *Theory and Research in Social Education,* among others. He is currently associate professor of education at the University of Missouri at Columbia and teaches courses in social studies education and ethnographic research. This is his first book.